Exploring the Future of Christian Monasticisms

Exploring the Future of Christian Monasticisms

Special Issue Editor

Greg Peters

MDPI • Basel • Beijing • Wuhan • Barcelona • Belgrade

MDPI

Special Issue Editor
Greg Peters
Biola University
USA

Editorial Office
MDPI
St. Alban-Anlage 66
4052 Basel, Switzerland

This is a reprint of articles from the Special Issue published online in the open access journal *Religions* (ISSN 2077-1444) in 2019 (available at: https://www.mdpi.com/journal/religions/special_issues/ Christian_Monasticisms)

For citation purposes, cite each article independently as indicated on the article page online and as indicated below:

LastName, A.A.; LastName, B.B.; LastName, C.C. Article Title. *Journal Name* **Year**, *Article Number*, Page Range.

ISBN 978-3-03928-024-7 (Pbk)
ISBN 978-3-03928-025-4 (PDF)

Contents

About the Special Issue Editor

Greg Peters (Professor of Medieval and Spiritual Theology) teaches in the Torrey Honors Institute of Biola University and is also the Servants of Christ Research Professor of Monastic Studies and Ascetical Theology at Nashotah House Theological Seminary. He is the author of *The Story of Monasticism* and *The Monkhood of All Believers* (both published with Baker Academic).

religions

MDPI

Editorial

Introduction to the Special Issue "Exploring the Future of Christian Monasticisms"

Greg Peters

Torrey Honors Institute, Biola University, La Mirada, CA 90638, USA; greg.peters@biola.edu

Received: 11 November 2019; Accepted: 19 November 2019; Published: 21 November 2019

The origins of Christian monasticism are buried deep in the shadows of Christian history, but without doubt it came to full fruition during the fourth century and continued to grow nearly unabated for the next millennium and a half. By the late 18th century, it was facing its most difficult challenges, in the forms of secularism and Enlightenment thinking, but it rebounded during the 19th and into the 20th centuries. Even Protestant Christian traditions that historically lacked monasticism (e.g., Anglicanism and Lutheranism) saw its (re-)introduction at this time. Now, in the first two decades of the 21st century, there is the emergence of New Monastic communities and other forms of "secular monasticism." It is clear that monasticism in its many forms in the history of the Christian Church has yet to outlive its spiritual utility.

The articles contained in this Special Issue of *Religions*, entitled "Exploring the Future of Christian Monasticisms", look backwards but, more importantly, forward to the future of the institution of monasticism; or, perhaps more appropriately, monasticisms (notice the "s"). That is, of the many forms of monasticism that have emerged historically, which ones still hold promise for the future? Will those communities be comprised of vowed and non-vowed members, of men and women? Will they be contemplative and/or enclosed in a traditional sense or more open to modern culture by living outside the cloister? For those that might retain a more historic form, what kind of apostolates will the future hold? These questions, and many more, are investigated in the excellent papers gathered here. May these essays provide food for thought as they explore the future of Christian monasticisms.

Funding: No external funding was received for the writing of this article.

Conflicts of Interest: The author declares no conflict of interest.

religions

MDPI

Article

Living *toto corde*: Monastic Vows and the Knowledge of God

John Bayer O. Cist.

Cistercian Preparatory School, 3660 Cistercian Road, Irving, TX 75039, USA; Fr-John@cistercian.org

Received: 6 June 2019; Accepted: 6 July 2019; Published: 11 July 2019

Abstract: Monastic vows have been a source of religious controversy at least since the Reformation. Today, new monastic movements recover many elements of the tradition (e.g., community life and prayer, material solidarity and poverty), but vows—understood as a lifelong or binding commitment to obedience, stability and conversion to the monastic way of life—do not appear to capture much enthusiasm. Even the Benedictine tradition in the Catholic Church appears, at least in certain regions, to struggle to attract young men and women to give themselves away through vows. In this context, I ask whether vows should belong to the "future of Christian monasticisms". I will look at Anselm of Canterbury for inspiration regarding their meaning. For him, monastic vows enact the "total" gift of self or the "total" belonging to God. I will suggest, following Anselm, that such vows enable an existential commitment that is in a unique way morally and intellectually enlivening, and that such vows should remain an element in any future monasticism wanting to stand in continuity with the "Christian monasticism" of the past. During my conclusion, I acknowledge that our imagination regarding the concrete forms the total gift could take may develop.

Keywords: Anselm; vows; new monasticism; Proslogion; proof of God's existence

---

1. Introduction

One of the marks of the monastic vocation is its prophetic witness to the reality of God.[1] And so, it is not surprising if the tradition of monastic life struggles today in lands marked by the 'death' of God, or by the Nietzschean desire to usurp God as the measure of all life and meaning. Our sense for the reality of God and our willingness to give ourselves entirely to him are mutually related. When God is not sensed, monastic life withers; and when men and women resist giving themselves to God, their sense for him atrophies. Thus, I am convinced by what one scholar has written about arguments for God's existence:

> Indeed, if theistic arguments no longer make sense to so many of us today, this may be because we no longer find it possible to participate fully in the forms of life in which they were once so firmly embedded. That, I say, rather than the reverse. It is not because they make no sense to us that we no longer participate, but because we do not participate, they no longer make sense. Understanding can often be gained more readily in *doing* than in *thinking*. To recover a taste for these proofs and their earlier uses, therefore, may require not just or not even principally a change of mind. That recovery may require more radically a change of life. [2]

---

[1] Biblical citations in this article are from the Revised Standard Version. Latin citations of Anselm are from the critical edition by F.S. Schmitt, *S. Anselmi Cantuariensis Archiepiscopi Opera Omnia* (Stuttgart-Bad Cannstatt: 1938–1961, 1968), abbreviated here by "S" along with volume, page and line numbers, and from (Schmitt and Southern 1991), abbreviated here by "SS" along with page and line numbers. English citations of the *Proslogion* are from (Walz 2013). Unless otherwise indicated, English citations of Anselm's letters are from (Fröhlich 1990, 3 volumes). Where necessary, I conformed Fröhlich's spelling to American English.

[2] (Clayton 1995).

In this essay, I attempt to confirm this connection between *doing* and *thinking* by elucidating the connection between monastic life and the knowledge of God in Anselm.[3] In other words, I will be arguing with Anselm that there is a speculative advantage to making the practical commitments that are embodied in monastic life.[4] In this way, I hope to make a spiritual case for the importance of vows in the Church.

Monastic vows have been controversial since at least the Reformation.[5] Today, many new monastic movements are recovering elements of the monastic tradition (such as community life and prayer, material simplicity and solidarity), but monastic vows—which I understand in a traditionally Benedictine way as a lifelong or binding commitment to obedience, stability and the monastic way of life, which includes embracing the evangelical counsels[6]—have not captured much enthusiasm. On the contrary, today even traditional forms of monasticism, such as the Benedictine tradition in the Catholic Church, appear to be struggling, at least in many regions, to attract young men and women to give their lives away in this form. In this context, I would like to consider whether monastic vows should even belong to the future of Christian monasticisms at all. The answer I offer here will be determined by what emerges from the connection between life and thought in Anselm.

Therefore, in this essay I will rely chiefly on Anselm for inspiration regarding the meaning of monastic vows. Briefly stated, for him vows enact the total gift of self (total and so lifelong and binding), or the total belonging to God that is the term or end of Christian life. I argue that these vows enact an existential commitment that is in a unique way morally and intellectually enlivening, and I suggest that they should therefore remain a part of any future monasticism that wants to stand in continuity with what has been called 'Christian monasticism' in the past. Vows, presuming they are made authentically, unify the heart and thus allow it to see God and testify to his reality. As an act by which the human being can give herself entirely over to God, they are integral to the Christian dispensation. However, since what is critical is the existential commitment, and not the specific form in which it is enacted, it seems to me we can and should exercise our imagination regarding the concrete forms in which this total gift could be offered. As far as I can see, we need not feel restricted to those forms known in the middle ages, presuming the intention for spiritual totality remains real and ecclesial.

2. Purity and the Search for God

Anselm opens the *Proslogion*, that most famous effort to prove the existence of God, by exhorting himself to relativize all things and so to be free for the discovery of God.

---

[3]   Parts of this essay are adapted from my dissertation, (Bayer 2019).

[4]   In this respect, I am following an insight of R.W. Southern: "In a word, his monastic commitment was total, because he believed that a total commitment was the only acceptable relationship between Man and God. This aspect of Anselm's thought is fundamental to the understanding of his practical life as well as his theology." (Southern 1990, p. 217). Other authors affirm the real connection between monastic life and thought, or the union of the existential and speculative efforts of the human being: (Ogliari 1991; and Palmeri 2016, pp. 191–209). Similarly, Pope Benedict XVI, in an important address in Paris at the Collège des Bernardins on 12 September 2008, argued for a connection between the monastic *quaerere Deum* and the possibility of culture.

[5]   In (Peters 2014), G. Peters relates the views of various Protestant authors on monasticism. He shows that their views are more nuanced than is often assumed. Several authors, in fact, valued spiritual practices (e.g., community life, prayer) and apostolates (e.g., education, healthcare) of the monastic tradition. However, most of those who appreciated this tradition still rejected lifelong vows as somehow contrary to the Gospel. But there are a few exceptions at least in the Anglican (89) and Lutheran traditions (124).

[6]   In *The Rule of St. Benedict* 58, St. Benedict lists the vows made by the new member of a monastic community: "When he is to be received, he comes before the whole community in the oratory and promises stability, fidelity to monastic life [*conversatione morum suorum*], and obedience." (RB 1980: Benedict 1981, pp. 268–69). The phrase "fidelity to the monastic life" includes the evangelical counsels, that is, those exhortations Christ did not oblige upon anyone other than those who have been called, or "those to whom it is given" (Mt 19:11; cf. Mt 19:1–30; 1 Cor 7:7). As I understand these counsels, they are not open invitations extended to everyone; rather, they are personal invitations extended to those whom God chooses. The words of Christ in Mt 19 do not suggest to me that someone can decide for himself to embrace these counsels; they can only be embraced as a response to a personal call, for the embrace is "given" by God. Thus, the difference between a counsel and a commandment concerns the addressee and not only our sense of obligation. In other words, it appears from the words of Christ that God does not call everyone to something like celibacy for the sake of the Kingdom of God. But he does call some, and so it should be pursued within a horizon of vocation.

Quick now, little man, flee a short while your occupations; hide yourself a short time from your tumultuous thoughts. Cast off your burdensome cares now, and put off until later your laborious distresses. Empty a little bit for God [*Vaca aliquantulum deo*], and rest a little bit in him. Enter into the chamber of your mind, close off all things besides God and what may help you in seeking him, and with door closed seek him. Speak now, my whole heart [*totum cor meum*], speak now to God: I seek your countenance; your countenance, O Lord, I seek again. [7]

To search for God, we must first "be free" for him (*vaca deo*). Everything else must be set aside. To find what is absolute, we must first be able to acknowledge that all else is relative. What we cannot lay down holds our hearts hostage and inhibits us from searching for God. It has in fact taken his place. Interior freedom is necessary to find God. Anselm therefore asserts his freedom by temporarily withdrawing from everything except for what leads to God. Our lives are all filled with good and important things; but none of these things is absolute and so there is a moment in which they should all be relativized—not destroyed or ignored but rather simply subordinated to what is alone truly absolute. Only in this way can the heart find the coherence and wholeness (*totum cor meum*) necessary to search for God.

Vacare deo is essential to understanding who God is in the *Proslogion* and therefore what searching for him means to Anselm. In the monastic tradition, we cannot search for God without putting ourselves into question. Thus, the verb *vacare* is "almost always" (*presque toujours*) used in monastic literature to refer to the moment someone chooses the monastic vocation.[8] To set aside all things and search for God with a "pure" (*totum*) heart—this is the only way to search for him. He must be sought as the absolute, as the one who relativizes and so orders everything else in my life. *Vacare deo* is not about making time in a busy schedule for a new study or discipline. It is about discovering the freedom and desire necessary for the purity that bestows in this life the contemplative insight that is the vision of God: "Blessed are the pure in heart, for they shall see God" (Mt 5:8).

3. Pure Love: The Spirituality of Anselm's Letters

If the vision of God is granted to those who are pure in heart, then the search for him is coincident with the search for purity. It is an effort of integrating all our faculties of mind and will, and of training them upon what alone can animate them all and all together. For Anselm, the ultimate and most enlivening target for our intellect and will is the transcendent greatness of God—whom he identifies with the *summa natura* or divine *rectitudo* that in the *Monologion* and *De Veritate* ontologically anchors and spiritually animates all our intellectual and moral striving by incessantly provoking our thoughts and actions to rise to what is greater. Totalizing love for God is therefore what drives all his life and thought; it is the existential commitment that underlies all his willing and reasoning. This gives his spirituality a real tension, since the faith, hope and love that he seeks are constantly being stretched by the greatness of God. We can see this in the spirituality he enjoins upon all Christians in his letters.

In his letters, we see that Anselm understood the spiritual life most essentially as an effort of love. Everything follows from the desire to gather all his affections and understanding into a coherent, undivided love for God. It is the love called for in the Gospel: "You shall love the Lord your God with all your heart, and with all your soul, and with all your strength, and with all your mind; and your neighbor as yourself" (Lk 10:27; cf. Mt 22:37, Mk 12:30 and Dt 6:5). Anselm described this love in his letters, as well as in other places such as the *Proslogion* and in his homily *De beatitudine*.

We can explore Anselm's view of love and its centrality by beginning with an exposition of Ep 112, which he wrote to a hermit named Hugo. Written around 1086, this letter is basically a homily to

---

[7] *Proslogion* 1 (Walz 2013, 21); S I, 97:4–10.
[8] (Leclercq 1961).

incite secular people (*saecularium mentes hominum*) to contempt for the world and to love for heaven.[9] It is perhaps the most extensive consideration of the love of God and its implications for the love of neighbor in his letters. At times, it parallels passages in the *Proslogion* and *De beatitudine*, suggesting that Anselm's theological insights about God are connected to his understanding of happiness and to his spiritual disposition marked by hope for an eternal union of love among all human beings.

Anselm begins his homily in Ep 112 in a way resonate of the Rule of St. Benedict, namely, by directing his reader to the voice of God inviting all human beings to participate in his kingdom: "Dearest brother, God proclaims that he has the kingdom of heaven up for sale."[10] God is offering a kingdom. Although the eye cannot see, nor the ear hear, nor the heart imagine (*cogitare*) the blessedness and glory of this heavenly kingdom, we can nevertheless in a certain way (*aliquo modo*) imagine (*cogitare*) it by examining our own desires: "if anyone deserves to reign there, whatever he wills shall be done in heaven and on earth; whatever he does not will shall be done neither in heaven nor on earth."[11] Whatever we desire will be in heaven; and whatever we do not desire will be absent. To someone jaded by a world in which selfishness so often rules the human heart, such a description could sound more appropriate for hell rather than heaven. Could heaven really be where each gets what he wants? Do our desires not contradict each other? Can they not be evil? How could our desires give us an insight into union with God? What anthropology corresponds to this description of heaven?

It is likely in response to such questions that Anselm adds his understanding of the human heart and therefore the nature of its desires: he believes that what the heart truly desires is love. Human beings want to love—or to be united in will with God—and this most fundamental human desire is fulfilled in heaven. Beatitude unites the wills of all human beings in God and thereby bestows every blessing imaginable:

> For so great shall be the love between God and those who shall be there, and between themselves, that they shall all love each other as they love themselves but all shall love God more than themselves. And because of this, no one there shall will anything but what God wills; and what one wills, all shall will; and what one or all will, this shall God himself will. Wherefore, whatever anyone individually wills, shall come about for himself and for all the others, for the whole of creation, and for God himself. [12]

Anselm believed that the human heart was made for love, and so he had no fear of its authentic desires. His confidence was so great that he thought all creation and even God himself will one day accede to our desires, since each person will love God above everything else, and therefore all wills will be united in the one will of God.[13]

Since they love nothing more than God, the blessed in heaven rule as kings and queens. They are united to each other and to God as a single human being or king.[14] This is, for Anselm, the essence of

---

[9] Ep 112 (Fröhlich, vol. I, 268); S III, 244:3–7.
[10] Ep 112 (Fröhlich, vol. I, 269); S III, 244:21. This is like the opening exhortation in the Rule of St. Benedict: "Seeking his workman in a multitude of people, the Lord calls out to him and lifts his voice again: *Is there anyone here who yearns for life and desires to see good days?*" (RB 1980, Prologue 14–15, cf. Ps 34:13).
[11] Ep 112 (Fröhlich, vol. I, 269); S III, 245:24–26. Elsewhere, Anselm refers to the heart (*cor*) as the place in which we perceive the ineffable joys of love (*sapor dilectionis*). The experienced conscience (*experta conscientia*) testifies that true love between friends cannot be adequately expressed in words; and nevertheless, that it can in some way be perceived in the heart of someone who loves (Ep 59, S III, 174:12–18).
[12] Ep 112 (Fröhlich, vol. I, 269); S III, 245:26–31.
[13] In *De beatitudine*, Anselm says that no one will desire his own good absolutely; rather each person will desire his good in a way proportionate to his identity within the one Body of Christ (*corpus, ecclesia, sponsa Christi*). No one will want to distort the beauty of the whole by wishing to occupy a position disproportionate to his identity (the foot will not wish to replace the hand, for example). Moreover, no one will want to be equal in identity (*in persona*) to another, for that would be to want to annihilate oneself, which is impossible (*namque si hoc vellet, seipsum nihil esse vellet: quod velle nequit*). Each member of the Body of Christ is unique and irreplaceable; and to wish to be someone other than who one is by the will of God (*dispositione beatae civitatis dei*) is to wish to disturb the *concordia* of the whole and to destroy oneself (SS 282–283). This is impossible in heaven.
[14] Ep 112 (Fröhlich, vol. I, 269); S III, 245:32–34.

heaven: to be welded together (*conglutinari*) with God and all his angels and saints through the love experienced in having a single, regal will (*per dilectionem in unam voluntatem*).[15] This is his definition of heaven; and it is this basic description which emerges in all the heavenly blessings he identifies.[16]

4. Undivided Desire

This union in love is the kingdom God offers to human beings, or the goods (*mercem*) that he has for sale (*venalem*).[17] But what does it mean to say that he *sells* his kingdom? At what price could God sell anything, since he in fact already possesses everything? Can we really buy heaven? Anselm clears up any potential confusion resulting from his economic imagery by again pointing to love. We do not purchase the kingdom of God by compensating him with our affection. Looked at from the point of view of an exchange economy, the kingdom is given without cost—it is a gift. But God, Anselm says, chooses to give his gifts only to those who want them: to those who want his kingdom of love. Thus, there is an exchange, but not one by which two parties mutually enrich each other. In the economy between God and man, God gains nothing for himself by bestowing his gifts. But he still demands a "price" (*pretio*) insofar as the human being must actually choose to love in order to enjoy love's delights.

> Yet God does not give so great a gift for nothing, for he does not give it to anyone who does not love. No one gives what he holds dear away to someone to whom it is not dear. Since God does not need your gift, therefore, he is not bound to give such a gift to someone who scorns loving it: he asks for nothing but love; without it he is not bound to give. Give love, therefore, and receive the kingdom; love and possess. [18]

The gift of God is freely given: "love and possess" (*ama et habe*). But this gift implicates the will of the receiver since it is precisely an opportunity to love—that is, to will in concord with all others, the whole of creation and God. If someone refuses to love, then he also refuses the gift; but if someone wills to love, then he receives the gift, for the gift is simply a power to love. God gives his gift only to those who want it: to whom it is *carum*. This is, of course, not a sign of divine stinginess. It is simply a condition belonging to the nature of the gift. The gift cannot be enjoyed by one to whom it is not desirable (*carum*), since the gift itself is a desiring. Love cannot be given to one who refuses to love.

One must desire the gift or he will not enjoy its possession. For this reason, Anselm spends the rest of Ep 112 exhorting the reader to the undivided love that defines the life of the blessed: "love God more than yourself and you will already begin to hold what you want to have there in perfection."[19] The more one unites his will to God now, the more he anticipates the harmony of wills enjoyed in heaven. Anselm exhorts his readers to unify their love according to the pattern provided by those in heaven, where everyone loves God above everything else. The love of the blessed is undivided, and therefore it can no more be enjoyed by those whose love is divided or incoherent than by those who refuse to love at all: "But you shall not be able to possess this perfect love until you have emptied your

---

15   Ep 112 (Fröhlich, vol. I, 269); S III, 245:42–43.

16   In Ep 112, Anselm identifies the heavenly blessing of love or a regal unity of will (*rex, regnare*). But in the *De beatitudine* and in the *Proslogion*, to which he explicitly refers at the end of Ep 112 (S III, 246:76), he extends the list of blessings to include other goods, all contingent upon obedience or union with the will of God. In the *De beatitudine*, there are separate chapters devoted to such goods as beauty, speed, strength, freedom, impassibility, pleasure, eternal life, wisdom, security, joy, friendship, concord, power and honor. In *Proslogion* 23–26, God is the *unum necessarium* in which all goods of body and soul can be found. Here Anselm lists the same goods as in the *De beatitudine*, adding, it seems, only a few others such as satiety, inebriation and melody. Anselm also says that union of will multiplies every delight, since everyone rejoices over the good of another just as much as over his own. The blessed rejoice because they love God with their whole heart, mind and soul. This joy, being God himself, fills and transcends the capacity of every heart, mind and soul (cf. S II, 120:17–20). Anselm gives other lists of heavenly blessings in *De humanis moribus* 48–71 (SS 57–63) and *Dicta Anselmi* 5 (SS 127–41).

17   Ep 112 (Fröhlich, vol. I, 269), S III, 245:34; cf. 244:21.

18   Ep 112 (Fröhlich, vol. I, 269); S III, 245:37–41.

19   Ep 112 (Fröhlich, vol. I, 270); S III, 245:44–45.

heart of all other love."[20] This love is marked by the singularity of its object: God above everything else. Through the love of God, Anselm wants to unify the human heart.[21]

> Indeed with the human heart and this love it is as with the vessel and the oil. The more water, or any other similar liquid, the vessel holds, the less oil it can contain; so, too, to the extent the heart is occupied by any other love, in the same measure it excludes this one. [22]

Anselm is not suggesting that we love no one other than God. On the contrary, he describes heaven as a love that is shared by everyone for everyone. But what he is claiming is that the human heart cannot *divide* its love: that is, it cannot set one love against another. If my love is not coherent and unified, then the various unreconciled loves exist in my heart like water and oil in a glass: the more I have of one the less I have of the other. In other words, "You cannot serve both God and mammon" (Mt 6:24; Lk 16:13).

> Just as opposites cannot exist together at the same time, therefore, so this love cannot reside within a single heart along with any other love. So it is that those who fill their hearts with love of God and their neighbor will nothing but what God wills or another person wills—as long as this is not contrary to God. [23]

The unity and universality of love are connected. Only if there is an absolute—God above all—can the 'all' truly be loved. For without the absolute, there is no principle or reality by which all loves can be harmonized. Love for God unifies the heart around a single desire; and thus God harmonizes the hearts of all those who love him. For Anselm, when all hearts collectively love the origin and end of all things—namely, God the creator—they are *ipso facto* united in love among themselves. Beatitude is the gift of living and thinking in light of the absolute whose will relativizes and thus also reconciles all others.

5. Love and Life

Anselm's spirituality springs from the pursuit of the undivided love enjoyed by the blessed. In the closing lines of Ep 112, he sketches the ethical vision which expresses this pursuit: those striving for an undivided love will enjoy speaking, listening and thinking about the one they love; they will be united in affection (cf. Rom 12:15) with those whom they love as themselves; and they will scorn riches, power, pleasures and honors since those who love such things often fail in love for God and neighbor: "For someone who loves these things often does something contrary to God and his neighbor."[24] Anselm thus captures the whole of Christian life in the love of God and the love of neighbor, recalling that "On these two commandments depend all the law and the prophets" (Mt 22:40).[25] Loving God above all things and her neighbor as herself, the Christian will "not love the world or the things in the world" (1 Jn 2:15). On the contrary, "anyone who wishes to possess perfectly this love with which the kingdom of heaven is purchased should love contempt, poverty, hard work and submission, as do holy men."[26]

---

[20] Ep 112 (Fröhlich, vol. I, 270); S III, 245–46:52–53.
[21] Anselm's goal of unification is also clear from the way he describes sin as a movement toward disintegration. In *De humanis moribus* 9–36, he compares a sinful will to a well with three separate spouts, each pouring out into innumerable streams that crisscross each other. These are pleasure, exaltation and curiosity: three spouts which lead to the disintegration of our corporeal and spiritual desires (SS 41–50). Elsewhere, he says one good is never opposed to another, and thus all goods can be unified; but one vice can oppose another, and thus they divide the soul (*De humanis moribus*, Appendix; SS 94–97). In heaven, there will be perfect *concordia* between body and soul (*De humanis moribus* 63; SS 61).
[22] Ep 112 (Fröhlich, vol. I, 270); S III, 246:54–56.
[23] Ep 112 (Fröhlich, vol. I, 270); S III, 246:57–61.
[24] Ep 112 (Fröhlich, vol. I, 270); S III, 246:67–68. Anselm does not reject riches, power, pleasure or honors as incompatible with the Christian vocation. Nor does he reject pursuing them for just purposes. But he is suspicious of those "who love" (*qui [. . .] amat*) these things, since these "often" (*saepe*) divide our love. The less we love these things, the better. Here I am reminded of the *Litany of Humility* by Cardinal Merry del Val, in which it is the desire for such things that is rejected, not the things themselves.
[25] Ep 112 (Fröhlich, vol. I, 270); S III, 246:62–72. In *De humanis moribus* Anselm links inseparably the love of God and neighbor (Appendix; SS 95:16–24). These two loves are also the first "tool" for good works according to the Rule of St. Benedict (4:1).
[26] Ep 112 (Fröhlich, vol. I, 270–71); S III, 246:69–71.

The highest expression of undivided love involves contempt for whatever divides it. At the core of Anselm's life and thought there is an absolute: love for God which unifies the heart and reconciles all. Everything is ordered in relation to the one to be loved above all things.

As an elderly archbishop, in Ep 420 Anselm encouraged a lay woman (Basilia) to consider profoundly and keep the "Christian intention" (*Christianam intentionem*).[27] He says, "the whole of Holy Scripture" teaches this intention or the way that Christians are to live.[28] Then he offers to her meditation something which, if considered frequently and intensely, would inspire her to the fear of God and to the love of living well: namely, the transitory character of human life. His point is not simply to remind her that no one knows the hour of his own death. His point is to remind her that our "life is a journey" (*vita praesens* via *est*) and therefore that we are always in motion in one direction or another, either ascending toward heaven or descending toward hell.[29] In every thought and action, we are either approaching the undivided love enjoyed by the blessed or departing from it.[30] There simply are no morally or spiritually neutral moments in life, for each moment is defined by its intention or direction: either toward life in heaven with the holy angels or eternity in hell with the lost angels.

> For this reason a Christian man and a Christian woman should consider carefully in each of their desires or actions whether they are ascending or descending; and they should embrace with their whole heart those things in which they see themselves ascending. Those things, however, in which they perceive descent they should flee and abhor just as they would hell. [31]

Anselm exhorts every Christian to consider *toto corde* the dignity of every moment in his or her life, since even the most seemingly insignificant action is a step along a path toward eternity.

The desire to cultivate an undivided love brings Anselm to be concerned about absolutely everything in his letters. All the advice he gives to Christians, no matter whether they live inside or outside the monastery, manifests his incessant desire to unify our every thought and action in undivided love for God. The pursuit of this love is therefore the critical criterion in all matters of discernment. It is also the critical means by which commitments, such as monastic life, are to be evaluated.

6. Monastic Vows

Up to this point, we have been considering the *Christianam intentionem*, or the spirituality that Anselm enjoined upon all Christians. Now it is time to look at what he thought distinguished the monastic commitment, and to see what effect this commitment could have upon our reason, giving rise to a particularly 'monastic' way of thinking.

In Ep 121, Anselm described monastic life as the "commitment" (*propositum*) "than which one cannot have a greater" (*quo maius habere non potest*) and "than which one cannot make a better" (*proponere quo melius non potest*).[32] These phrases sound strikingly like his identification of God in the *Proslogion*, written about ten years earlier, as "that than which a greater cannot be thought" (*id quo*

---

27 Ep 420 (Fröhlich, vol. III, 191); S V, 365:4.
28 *Quamvis ergo tota sacra scriptura vos doceat qualiter vivere debeatis* (Ep 420 [Fröhlich, vol. III, 191]; S V, 365:6–7).
29 *Vita praesens via est. Nam quamdiu vivit homo, non facit nisi ire. Semper enim aut ascendit aut descendit* (Ep 420 [Fröhlich, vol. III, 191–92]; S V, 365–66:13–15).
30 Anselm teaches the same thing in *De humanis moribus* 41 using the image of a mill: there are no neutral moments in life because we are always either milling thoughts for good or for evil: *Hoc itaque molendinum, semper, aliquid molens, cor est humanum, assidue aliquid cogitans* (SS 54:14–15). In this passage, good thoughts are about God purely, about the increase of virtue or about the abandonment of vice. When we are empty of such thoughts, the devil fills our mill with thoughts that soil, corrupt and destroy. Where vice recedes, virtue necessarily increases, and vice versa. *Semper enim homo vel virtutibus est praeditus, vel vitiis subiectus* (*De humanis moribus*, Appendix; SS 96:1, cf. 1–15).
31 Ep 420 (Fröhlich, vol. III, 192); S V, 366:22–26.
32 *Plus namque placet deo, etiam post grave peccatum, cuius propositum est et ante et post quo maius habere non potest, quam ille, qui nec ante nec post simile peccatum vult proponere quo melius non potest.* (Ep 121, S III, 261:38–40). These phrases have an active infinitive (*habere, proponere*) rather than a passive one (*cogitari*) like in the *Proslogion*. They are active because they appear in reference to a hypothetical sinner rather than in a grammatically impersonal context like in the *Proslogion*.

maius cogitari nequit).[33] The parallels suggest an intrinsic connection between life and thought rooted in the apprehension of the transcendent "greater" (*maius*) and "better" (*melius*) that animates all our intellectual and moral striving. Both Ep 121 and the *Proslogion* refer to something transcendent that impinges upon all our concrete thinking and willing by ordering all our intellectual and moral values. The apprehension of what is *maius* or *melius* always pushes us toward a new way of thinking and living. The parallels between these phrases suggest there is a real connection between Anselm's commitment to monastic life and his intellectual search for God in the *Proslogion*.

Anselm unabashedly proclaimed monastic life as superior to any other. But why?[34] What is it essentially? He described monastic life as a response to a personal call from God. It is not a life that someone chooses by his own initiative or for his own purposes, however noble those purposes might be (like virtue, peace, prayer, service). Therefore, when Anselm tried to convince someone to join the monastery, he frequently distinguishes between the will of God and his own desires for the candidate. Thus, he writes to one man (Albert) that he should come to the monastery, "if ever heavenly grace so enkindles" in him "the desire for heavenly bliss".[35] And when he tries to convince another man (Robert) to become a monk, he acknowledges that the call comes from God and is not subject to our own will.[36] Even though he is not afraid to express his hopes for candidates, he consistently appeals to their freedom to respond to the divine initiative.[37] The decision to become a monk is therefore not based on a calculus that compares vocations in the abstract or initiates in oneself; it emerges in the life of the individual conscience as a personal response to the concrete will of God.[38]

What does it mean to accept the call to monastic life? For Anselm, when someone takes monastic vows he gives everything he is to God and expects to receive from him whatever he needs.[39] In short, the monk enters the monastery in response to the promises of Christ. Referring to Mt 19:21–29, in Ep 56 Anselm encourages a candidate to trust Christ and therefore to pursue the "hundredfold" that he promises.[40] In Ep 161, he again refers to Mt 19:21–29, or to where Christ "counsels those striving for perfection"[41] (*consulit ad perfectionem nitentibus*); he says that the church fathers understood this

---

33 In passing, I note that Anselm also echoed the *Proslogion* when describing monastic life in other letters. In Ep 56, he tells a candidate: *ea semper de te desidero quibus meliora non possum* (S III, 171:11–12). In Ep 232, he tells a monk to love his monastic commitment above all things (*monachicum propositum super omnia dilige*) so that he might enjoy the indwelling of the Holy Spirit, which is sweeter and more joyful than anything he can imagine: *Quae res in tantam tibi convertetur delectationem, ut nihil dulcius, nihil umquam existimare possis iucundius* (S IV, 138:11–12; 139:27–29).

34 In passing, I dismiss certain explanations for Anselm's conviction about the superiority of monastic life. He did not defend its superiority by appealing to an immanent eschatology. On the contrary, he often expressed concern for the temporal well-being and prosperity of others (cf. Epp 9, 32, 33, 36, 39, 53, 75, 147, 196, 243 and 446). He was open to being affected by "every worldly adversity" according to its character: *omnis mundana adversitas pro suo modo et ratione tangat animum meum* (Ep 293, S IV, 213:20–21). Moreover, he did not think that life in the world is inherently sinful. Therefore, we must read carefully those letters in which he tries to persuade someone to leave the world to go to the monastery. In these letters, comparisons between secular and monastic life are often wrapped up in concrete questions about which life was right for the specific person he is addressing. For example, in Ep 168 Anselm tells Gunhilda in no uncertain terms that hell awaits her unless she leaves her husband and returns to the monastery. This is because he understood her life in the world as a failure to follow through on her original monastic commitment to love God above all things. We should take him at his word when he says he is not talking about lawful marriage—*non loquor nunc de legitimo coniugio*—but rather about the situation of someone who, in his view, had broken the dynamism of Christian life by choosing against an ever-increasing love of God (Ep 168, S IV, 44:22). For Anselm, life in the world is not intrinsically sinful; but to withdraw a commitment to love God above all things is spiritually perilous.

35 Ep 36 (Fröhlich, vol. I, 132); S III, 144:13–14.

36 *Quod solius dei commisimus consilio, non audeo proprio decernere arbitrio. Licet mihi tamen meum promere desiderium* (Ep 76, S III, 198:4–5).

37 See Epp 56, 76, 81, 95, 101, 115, 117, 120, 121, 133 and 169. Ep 120 is particularly moving, since here Anselm prays to Jesus to convince the candidates to give up everything to follow him.

38 For example, Anselm advised Matilda to wait in patience until it was clear to her that God willed for her to enter the monastery (Ep 325, S V, 257:23–26).

39 *Vos deo vovistis; ab illo, cui totum dedistis quod habuistis, ab illo exspectate totum quo indigetis* (Ep 156, S IV, 22:146–147).

40 *Unde hortor, precor, obsecro, mi dilectissime: crede verum esse quod veritas dixit, et ama quod relinquentibus saeculum propter se promisit. Incipe parare tam magnum quaestum, accelera ad tantum lucrum, ut quae mundi sunt relinquens,* centuplum *accipias, et* vitam aeternam *possideas* (Ep 56, S III, 171:15–19).

41 Ep 161 (Fröhlich, vol. II, 48-49); S IV, 32:21.

counsel to be fulfilled more in the monastic way of life than in any other.[42] Anselm thus understood monastic vows as a more complete (*magis [. . .] impleri*) response to the promises of Christ.

But why, for Anselm, are monastic vows a more complete response? We can discover an answer to this question by looking at Ep 189, where he encourages a monk (William) to pursue the holiness proper to his monastic commitment. During his exhortation, he compares three ways of life—*laici*, *clerici* and *monachi*—as various ways of responding to the call to Christian perfection. He sees different levels (*gradus*) of holiness (*sanctitas*) corresponding to each way of life.[43] All three responses aim at the same term or end of Christian perfection, even if not all three commit to it in the same degree.

> He will judge every member of the faithful good, who strives to attain perfection in his state of life. For although not everyone can reach the height of perfection equally, yet we will not be excluded from the number of the good, for it is written *your eyes have looked on my imperfection, and all will be written in your book* [Ps 138(139):16], if we are willing to go on trying unceasingly and courageously to reach this perfection. Let laymen in their state of life, clerics in theirs, monks in theirs valiantly apply themselves to making continual progress, so that those placed in a superior position should excel their inferiors in humility—for the more a man advances in this virtue the more he is raised on high—and also in the other virtues. [44]

It is important to notice that the difference between each level of holiness is an interior reality: namely, a commitment to Christian perfection (*propositi gradum*).[45] All Christians, no matter the level in which they "were placed" (*propositi sunt*) by God, should strive for perfection by constantly progressing toward greater things.[46] External differences, such as a monastic habit, are only signs of this interior reality or commitment.[47] This means that anyone placed in a higher level cannot be content to live like someone placed in a lower level, even if those in a lower level will not for that reason "be excluded from the number of the good" (*non tamen erimus extra numerum bonorum*). For while the imperfect can enter heaven, no one will enter who does not strive for perfection. Anselm continues,

> Wherefore, dearest son, remember always the degree of that intention to which you vowed to ascend, and do not let the holiness of your life ever satisfy you unless you exceed in holiness those who are of an inferior degree. For just as those whose intention is inferior merit praise when they rise to the virtues of a superior level, so those who intended to pursue greater things are worthy of censure if they descend to the level of those having chosen lesser things. Since you profess to be a monk by your habit, I exhort, I beg, I advise you always to endeavor to be inwardly, in the sight of God, what you appear to be outwardly, in the sight of men. [48]

Again, it is important to see that what makes monastic life superior is the interior commitment to striving for perfection (*propositi gradum*) and not anything merely external. As Anselm says in this citation, those in a lower order can rise to the virtues proper to those in a higher order. Their difference concerns neither their goal nor their external circumstances. Their difference concerns only their conscious, interior commitment to the pursuit of Christian perfection.

---

[42] *Hoc consilium magis in monachico quam in alio vitae proposito impleri sancti patres intellexerunt* (Ep 161, S IV, 32:26–27).

[43] Ep 189, S IV, 75:33–35.

[44] Ep 189 (Fröhlich, vol. II, 112); S IV, 75:24–32. I have modified Fröhlich's translation of the first sentence. The Latin is: *Bonus autem quisque fidelis ab eo iudicatur, qui in suo ordine perfectionem attingere conatur.*

[45] Ep 189, S IV, 75:33.

[46] In the previous sentence, I quoted Anselm's use of two nouns (*propositi gradum*) to refer to the way of life that William has chosen for himself. But before and after his use of this phrase, Anselm uses the passive form of the related verb, suggesting that lay persons, clerics and monks "were placed" (*propositi sunt*) in their ways of life by another, namely God (S IV, 75:30; 75:35–36). Elsewhere, he exhorts each person to serve God in the way God determines (*De humanis moribus* 126, SS 86:33–34).

[47] Anselm insisted that monastic observances (*consuetudines nostri ordinis*) have a deeper meaning: *nulla inutilis est, nulla supervacua* (Ep 335, S IV, 272:23–25). Ultimately, that meaning is charity. He tells Gundulf their monastic "rule" (*regula*) forms charity (Ep 16, S III, 121:9–12). Praying to St. Benedict, he says charity is the way of life that he enjoined upon monks: *Age, advocate monachorum, per caritatem qua sollicitus fuisti quomodo vivere deberemus* (Oratio 15, S III, 64:59–60). He tells Lanzo that progress in monastic life is useless without love (Ep 37, S III, 147:65–66).

[48] Ep 189 (Fröhlich, vol. II, 112–13); S IV, 75:33–40.

But why do monastic vows represent the highest commitment to Christian perfection? In short, because they are total.[49] While all strive for perfection, only the monk binds himself to do so completely. In *De humanis moribus* 82–84, Anselm uses some images to describe "the great difference" (*tanta distantia*) between someone who makes vows and someone who does not.[50] It is essentially a difference in desire to belong totally to God. Someone who does not make vows is like a servant unwilling to promise total fidelity to his master. He refuses to commit himself fully so that he can avoid the punishment proper to a perjurer if he ever fails to be faithful. Having never promised to belong totally to his master, he expects to be judged more leniently. The lay person, according to this image, chooses to retain some independence from God, his master. By contrast, someone who makes vows is like a servant who promises his fidelity precisely in order to belong to his master totally, such that, in the event that he fails to be faithful, his master will still recognize him as his own and heal him: *non me iudices ut alienum, sed emendes ut proprium servum.*[51] While the lay person chooses to stay relatively uncommitted (*liberius*[52]), and thus to avoid the punishment of a perjurer, the monk commits himself totally to his master, even at the risk of incurring a greater punishment.

Anselm says that the lay person and the monk will be treated differently, even if they both commit the same sin and appeal penitently to the mercy of God. For each will be treated in accordance with his commitment. God will not identify himself as closely with the person who did not want to give himself totally to him. In some measure, he will act toward him as toward a stranger (*adversus alienum*[53]), and so seek full satisfaction for the offense. On the other hand, God identifies closely with the one who committed himself totally to him. When he punishes the monk, God will act toward him as toward a part of himself: *Cum ergo voluero de te vindictam accipiam ut de meo.*[54]

Anselm describes monastic vows in the same way using other images in *De humanis moribus* 83–84. The difference between those who make monastic vows and those who do not is consistently explained as a difference in desire to belong to God: the lay person wishes to retain a measure of independence, while the monk wishes to belong to God entirely. This results in a difference in friendship (*familiarius*), love (*diligere*) and belonging (*proprium* and not *alienum*). Making monastic vows, one wills to belong to God in every way. Anselm attributed the highest significance to this vow, so much that he counseled a noble laywoman (Matilda), whose work on behalf of the Church prohibited her from realizing her desire to make this vow, to keep a veil nearby just so that she could use it to give herself "totally" to God before she died: *vos deo omnino reddatis.*[55] For his culture and imagination, monastic profession was understood as the way in which one gives everything to God.

---

[49] Anselm refers to the monastic vow as the way in which someone binds himself in all things to his good intention: *voto se ligare ad faciendum quod bonum est, ut iam non sit liber ad non faciendum* (Ep 101, S IV, 234:68–69; cf. *De humanis moribus* 82–84, SS 71–74). So, while all Christians strive for perfection, only the monk, according to Anselm, binds himself in all things to its pursuit such that he is no longer free to pursue anything else without risk to his spiritual health. In this passage, he justifies this practice by appeal to Ps 75:12. This seems to have been the understanding of monastic profession at Bec. In an anonymous treatise written at Bec around the time of Anselm, the author says that what is unique about the monastic order is that a monk gives himself to God totally (*seipsum totum*) and can no longer withdraw without incurring the penalties of a perjurer, apostate and thief, having taken from God what belongs to him and that for which he deigned to become man and shed his blood (*illam rem pro qua deus dignatus est fieri homo, et pro qua sanguinem suum fu(n)di permisit id est animam et corpus hominis* (G. Constable–B. Smith, Three Treatises from Bec on the Nature of Monastic Life [Toronto: University of Toronto Press, 2008], 42, 46, cf. 42–71). J. Leclercq referred to this idea of monastic life as a total gift of oneself in a way that suggests it is in some sense original to Anselm—*cette idée anselmienne*—and something that his disciples developed ("Une doctrine de la vie monastique au Bec" in Spicilegium Beccense [Paris: Le Bec-Hellouin, 1959], 482, cf. 478–81).

[50] *De humanis moribus* 82, SS 71:40.

[51] *De humanis moribus* 82, SS 72:5–6.

[52] *De humanis moribus* 82, SS 72:12.

[53] *De humanis moribus* 82, SS 72:13.

[54] *De humanis moribus* 82, SS 72:22–23.

[55] Ep 325 (Fröhlich, vol. III, 39); S V, 257:27–28.

7. The Monastic Heart of All the Baptized

It may seem strange to attribute such importance to the monastic vow, and especially to deathbed professions.[56] Is a veil really so important? Is this not simply a sign of some medieval prejudice against the laity? I think Anselm's position is intelligible if we appreciate the centrality of love for him. The veil is only a means by which an interior act is expressed, and it is this act—the act of love—that is important. Moreover, before judging Anselm negatively, we must, I think, be careful to identify our terms. For him, the essential difference between secular and monastic life had little to do with external matters such as outward observances. For him, the essence of monastic life was an interior reality: an act of the will, or the desire to commit oneself to God entirely. If we want to criticize him, we should do so carefully. For he cannot be faulted for giving absolute value to the greatest commandment of Christ: to love God above all things (Mt 22:37; Mk 12:30; Lk 10:27; cf. Dt 6:5). If Anselm failed to appreciate the lay vocation, it is because he could not imagine a way for secular persons—as seculars in the world—to commit themselves entirely to God, and not because he made this commitment the criterion by which to evaluate the spiritual life.

Surely, Anselm could not have been wrong to insist that we enjoy salvation in proportion to our love for God, and that we risk his wrath in the measure that our love for him is divided.[57] But he could be criticized for lacking the imagination through which other vocations can be seen to involve an absolute or monastic commitment to the pursuit of Christian perfection. We share his fault, however, so long as we accept the presupposition that a lay vocation can be defined as one not wholly given to God: in other words, we should accept that the lay vocation is ultimately open to a monastic vocation in the interior or Anselmian sense, and that lifelong or 'totallizing' vows are crucial. We should not deny the superiority of monastic life; but we should insist that one can indeed undertake this commitment in other ways than the ones we identify exteriorly as the monastic life. We should insist someone can commit himself entirely—his days, thoughts, affections, sexuality, possessions and whatever else—to the love of God, and therefore to contempt for the world, without entering into the currently recognized orders. For what is to stop laypeople today from committing themselves to evangelical obedience and poverty in new forms hitherto unimagined by our current traditions of religious life or by our modern world? And even if we want to make a real distinction between marriage and celibacy, it could still be said that vows to Christian marriage—with all its radical demands and joys—nevertheless involve a kind of "virginal" or monastic commitment to the love of God above all.[58] Couples must often exercise immense obedience, poverty and undivided love for God as they fulfill their vows to lifelong, faithful and fruitful love in sacramental marriage. We should, therefore, promote the monastic heart of all the baptized and recognize that the goal of spiritual totality should be common to all Christians, even if the measure and means of our self-gift will differ according to the specific design of God for each member of the Body of Christ. Concretely, many lay men and women live in evangelical obedience,

---

[56] Anselm once counseled someone who had committed himself to the monastic life while in danger of death. He insisted that a resolution made under such conditions is no less valuable than one made freely in a time of health. As the example of St. Paul shows, God does not consider the motivation with which one begins to serve him—Anselm says that St. Paul was "forced" (*coactus*) to convert—but rather the devotion and resolution with which one retains the graces he is given (Ep 335, S V, 271:8–15). He appears to have left behind a form for deathbed professions in fragments of his writings (SS 352–53). A distinct element of this profession is an expression of desire (*voluntatem emendandi*).

[57] *Irascitur enim, si videt ullum ab ullo amari plus quam se* (Ep 117, S III, 253:41–42).

[58] (Prosperi 2018). With my comments in this paragraph, I certainly have not explained clearly or fully the relationship between marriage and celibacy, or a life vowed to the evangelical counsels and one that is not. I am trying to hold two things in tension. First, there does seem to be clear warrant in the words of Christ to see as 'more perfect' (cf. Mt 19) a life that is consciously and totally given over to the love of God, and therefore also to detachment from the world, through vows to evangelical poverty, obedience and celibacy. However, and this is the second side of the tension, it seems to me that married men and women, depending on their intention, can in a way vow themselves to the evangelical counsels. After all, as Christian spouses they profess mutual obedience under God (cf. Ephesians 5:21), and the obedience of family life is totalizing in so many ways; they can profess a material simplicity and solidarity in their union "for better, for worse, for richer, for poorer" until death; and their union "in sickness and in health" until death, as well as their discerning openness to life, would appear to involve a submission of their sexual powers to God that is in fact open to periodic celibacy—even indefinite celibacy, should illness, for example, prohibit their conjugal union.

poverty and celibacy for the sake of love and fidelity to the Gospel. But what some might be missing today is a readiness to gather themselves up with as much totality as they can summon in a conscious and binding (lifelong) act—a vow. There is a difference between living the evangelical counsels de facto day after day and choosing to do so for a lifetime in response to God's call. In the former, we accept passively to give away our present; in the later, we offer to God freely also our future—our totality. Making lifelong vows enacts the greatest commitment to Christian perfection. It is greatest because it is total. Given the primacy of love (cf. Mt 22:36–40), the Church can consider new ways to encourage the faithful to commit themselves entirely to their baptismal call to perfection.

8. The Reach of Reason

For Anselm, monastic vows enact a total commitment to love God above all things. After identifying the specific character of the monastic commitment, we are now ready to consider whether this commitment can shape the way we reason, and especially our ability to apprehend the existence of God.

Does the heart unified in love for God enjoy a special vision of him (cf. Mt 5:8)? Is there an intellectual advantage for those who vow themselves to converting *a vanitate ad veritatem* through monastic life?[59] Anselm seems to think there is, and the reason seems to be rooted in the proportionality between love and knowledge: the more we love the world, the less unified are our desires and therefore the less able we are to apprehend the transcendent *maius* or *melius* relativizing all things; but the more our hearts are unified by love, the more we can reason rightly and apprehend the one Anselm calls God.

Searching for God presupposes our desire actually to see him. This desire cannot be taken for granted. To be sure, in an ultimate sense, all men and women desire God. As St. Augustine so famously said, "our hearts are restless until they rest in you." And yet, God is not a trivial reality; discovering him has absolutely significant consequences. And so long as we want to avoid these consequences, we are, tragically, in a way actively desiring not to see him and so frustrating our search.[60] The discovery of God presumes we are ready to discover what is absolute, or the one who relativizes all things under himself—and thus to give ourselves away to him entirely. In other words, it presupposes our readiness to vow ourselves to him totally in response to his concrete invitation. The most coherent way to search for God is as someone looking to give himself away entirely to the one he discovers.

This is why, as noted above, Anselm begins the *Proslogion* by exhorting his reader to be ready for what is absolute (*vacare Deo*), and therefore to be willing to see everything in her life relativized. This readiness gives us a speculative advantage in our search for God. The reader whose desire is so great that he is existentially ready to commit himself totally is ready to discover what is truly absolute, or the one Anselm calls God. By contrast, the one who prefers to hold on to even a very small measure of independence is trying to carve out a space protected from the comprehensive demands of what is transcendently great (*maius* or *melius*). Such a one is setting up unreconciled loyalties and loves, and therefore dividing his heart. Such a heart ultimately does not *want* to see God—at least not "totally" (*toto corde*)—because it does not want to see all its loves relativized or ordered under what is absolute.

The connection between purity of love and the vision of God can become more intelligible if we consider briefly how Anselm understood human reason. He says reason "ought to be leader and

---

59   This citation is taken from Ep 418 (S V, 363, 5), but the comparison between a love for the world and a love for God in terms of *vanitas* and *veritas* emerges in several letters, such as Epp 46, 99, 101, 117, 120, 133, 169 and 418.

60   This desire is what I think Henri de Lubac calls a "taste" for God. "So, in the matter of God, whatever certain people may be tempted to think, it is never the proof which is lacking. What is lacking is taste for God. The most distressing diagnosis that can be made of the present age, and the most alarming, is that to all appearances at least it has lost the taste for God. Man prefers himself to God. And so he deflects the movement which leads to God; or since he is unable to alter its direction, he persists in interpreting it falsely. He imagines he has liquidated the proofs. He concentrates on the critique of the proofs and never gets beyond them. He turns away from that which convinces him. If the taste returned, we may be sure that the proofs would soon be restored in everybody's eyes, and would seem—what they really are if one considers the kernel of them—clearer than day." (De Lubac 1996, p. 83).

judge of all things which pertain to human beings" (*ratio, quae et princeps et iudex debet omnium esse quae sunt in homine*).[61] Existentially, when Anselm thinks and wills he commits himself to discerning everything in life rationally, that is, to evaluating everything by its relative participation in what is just, true and good.[62] Reason is therefore animated by its apprehension of the transcendent greatness in which all things participate to various degrees and against which they can be measured. The more readily we measure, that is, the more readily we reason, or the more readily we order all things under what is absolutely just, true and good, the more ready we are to apprehend our measuring rod—the transcendent *maius*, or the one Anselm calls God.

But if we make some opposing existential commitment—say, by refusing to order something rationally in relation to everything else—then we deny the transcendental character of justice, truth and goodness, and thereby we also deny the unity of all things under what is absolutely great. In this way, we pretend there are things which concretely cannot be measured against each other, or which cannot be rationally ordered. The unity of all things falls away, or at least not all things can be unified under justice, truth and goodness. If we refuse to subordinate something to God, no matter what it is, or if we deny the transcendental character of values, we handicap our reason and its relation to the real. For reason, as Anselm understands it, is precisely the power to order whatever we encounter by its relative greatness.

When Anselm and other authors in the Christian tradition go searching for God, they are searching for the one who magnetizes their every faculty, the one who gives their every thought and decision a direction. To understand the one for whom Anselm searches, we must understand the way in which this one puts his life into question by inviting him to make the only fully coherent response to its discovery: to give his life away. If we wish to join him and, more broadly, the Christian monastic tradition in this search for God, we must be ready to put ourselves in question as well, and then to give our own lives away.

9. Conclusions

I am not a historian nor am I an expert in sociological and ecclesial trends. I am relatively young in religious life and in the formal study of theology. I write as a millennial, who, following St. Anselm of Canterbury, suspects that true happiness is found only in turning away from the empty loneliness of radical self-determination and toward the spiritual abundance and communion of co-creating our lives by giving them away freely to God. In my approximately ten years as a monk, I think I can understand something of the connection between life and thought that validates Anselm's idea of vows and their connection to the knowledge of God. Depending upon God totally, or trusting in the coherence of a life given away in every thought and action to the benevolent and transcendent ground of all justice, truth and goodness—this is a commitment that can be carried in monastic vows, and it is a commitment that shapes our reason by anchoring it in an intuition of what is absolute, that is, in a vision of God.

The world needs men and women who are ready to give themselves away totally and in this way to testify to the reality of God. If we are honest with ourselves, we long to unify our lives under a single absolute, and yet no one other than God is worthy of a total commitment. How precious it is that we can root ourselves existentially in what is absolute; how precious it is that vows are possible in the Christian dispensation, and that we, by God's tremendous gift, are not so weak as to be unable to give our-*selves* away in love—not just one of our days or our possessions but our whole *selves*. The author of all things is kind and provident, and therefore a life given over entirely to him is one that is indeed lived in a way than which no greater way can be thought. By his grace, we can love "to the end" (Jn 13:1) and give our lives away apart from physical martyrdom. We are not helpless victims

---

[61] *De incarnatione Verbi* 1, S II, 10:1–2.
[62] Thus, in the *Monologion* Anselm defines reason as an ability to discern relative values: *Denique rationali naturae non est aliud esse rationalem, quam posse discernere iustum a non iusto, verum a non vero, bonum a non bono, magis bonum a minus bono* (Monologion 68, S I, 78:21–23).

of sin and circumstance who must always hedge their bets and therefore avoid making a definitive commitment. God can help us to possess ourselves with sufficient freedom to give our lives away in response to his call. We can promise fidelity until our last breath, and the world can take us seriously because of him.

And so, I hope the future of Christian monasticisms includes many lives offering this radical witness to the goodness of God, and that the world will thus be moved to reject all cynical self-reliance and to orient itself under him. These future monks will, I imagine, include many who in some respects do not look like the monks whose traditions are rooted in the middle ages, although I hope many of them will, since these forms still remain relevant. I imagine that the rediscovery of the lifelong vows inherent in Christian baptism and marriage will provoke many to enact more consciously and fully the total gift of self that marks the monastic commitment. These vows, if they are lived authentically, will manifest the prophetic vocation that the monk offers the world: giving himself away purely (*toto corde*), and therefore holding nothing back, he will provoke others to believe in God and to love him with their whole heart.

Funding: This research received no external funding.

Conflicts of Interest: The author declares no conflict of interest.

References

Bayer, John. 2019. The Unity of the Proslogion: Reason and Desire in the Monastic Theology of Anselm of Canterbury. Ph.D. dissertation, Pontifical Gregorian University, Rome, Italy.

Benedict, Saint. 1981. *The Rule of St. Benedict in Latin and English with Notes*. Collegeville: The Liturgical Press, pp. 268–69.

Clayton, John. 1995. The Otherness of Anselm. *Neue Zeitschrift für Systematische Theologie und Religionsphilosophie* 37: 139–40. [CrossRef]

De Lubac, Henri. 1996. *The Discovery of God*. Translated by Alexander Dru. Grand Rapids: William B. Eerdmans, p. 83.

Leclercq, Jean. 1961. Études sur le vocabulaire monastique du moyen âge. *Studia Anselmiana* 48: 29.

Ogliari, Donato. 1991. La vérité comme principe herméneutique de la vie monastique. *Collectanea Cisterciensia* 53: 105–16.

Palmeri, Pietro. 2016. Ricerca della verità, volontà di giustizia e desiderio di felicità nel monachesimo di Anselmo d'Aosta. In *Anselmo d'Aosta e il pensiero monastico medievale*. Edited by Catalani L. and de Filippis. R. Turnhout: Brepols Publishers, pp. 191–209.

Peters, Greg. 2014. *Reforming the Monastery*. Oregon: Cascade Books.

Prosperi, P. 2018. Do Not Hold Me: Ascending the Ladder of Love. *Communio* 45: 210–49.

Schmitt, F. S., and R. W. Southern. 1991. *The Memorials of St. Anselm*. Oxford: Oxford University Press.

Southern, Richard W. 1990. *Saint Anselm: A Portrait in a Landscape*. Cambridge: Cambridge University Press, p. 217.

Walz, Matthew. 2013. *Proslogion: Including Gaunilo's Objections and Anselm's Replies*. South Bend: St. Augustine's Press.

Fröhlich, Walter. 1990. *The Letters of Saint Anselm of Canterbury*. Kalamazoo: Cistercian Publications, 3 vols.

religions

MDPI

Article

Rediscovering Monasticism through Art

Bernard Lukasz Sawicki

Monastic Institute, Faculty of Theology, Pontificio Ateneo Sant'Anselmo, Piazza dei Cavalieri di Malta 5, 00153 Roma, Italy; berosb@gmail.com

Received: 1 June 2019; Accepted: 9 July 2019; Published: 10 July 2019

Abstract: Looking at modern monasticism and its role in society one can see how traditional monastic concepts or values find their new forms. On the other hand, art and artists willingly, though not always consciously, use or refer to some monastic themes. In this paper, on the base of texts of some authors open to the dialogue between monasticism and art, a reading of monasticism in the key of art is proposed, exclusively in reference to the Christian monasticism. Given its present cultural and social context, the thesis of this paper is that through the rediscovering of monasticism through art, one can and should refresh and save it in a more and more secularized society, what may be also a perspective of a new role of monasticism in the modern world.

Keywords: monasticism; art; creativity; monk; artist

The phenomenon of monastic life, though it remains attractive in our times, seems to search for new forms in changed circumstances. The modern perspective gives a particular opportunity to see monasticism in its broad historical and cultural context from a vast distance. It stimulates ever new approaches to monasticism, sometimes resulting in attempts of updating monasticism or its ideals. A recent example is the bestselling book by Rod Dreher, *The Benedict Option: A Strategy for Christians in a Post-Christian Nation*, in which the author presents monasticism as a social proposal with a distinctive political import, particularly valid in a specific historical moment.

In modern approach to monasticism one notices a tendency to express monasticism in other terms. These authors, and theologians among them, use various non-monastic concepts to express monastic ideas today. We present two of them, because they open an interesting perspective for considering our vision of an affinity between monasticism and art. They are proposed by two theologians, Hans Urs Von Balthasar and Elmar Salmann. The first, in his article *Philosophy, Christianity, Monasticism* (Balthasar 1971; Meiattini 2012, pp. 95–126) shows, or rather reminds us of the closeness between monasticism and philosophy. The second, developing this juxtaposition, writes about symbolism, and sees the monk as a symbolic being (Salmann 2000, pp. 278–305). Such an approach to monasticism reflects its rich cultural meaning as one that is characterized by a constant openness towards an integral experience of wisdom, with the natural inclusion of beauty. Recent approaches in philosophy show the closeness of art to its activity as, for example, in Heidegger, who sees the thinker's closeness to poets (Heidegger 1997, p. 139) or in Merleau-Ponty, who does not hesitate to put philosophers among artists (Merleau-Ponty 1945, pp. 220, 248). Today, the mutual interaction between art, philosophy, and spirituality seems inevitable. Jaspers writes about the necessity of referring philosophy to religion, poetry, and art (Jaspers 1996, p. 121). Even Dreher, presenting his strategy of evangelization in the modern world, provides an alliance between goodness and beauty, indicating that they both have a common root—the human, inner desire. At the same time, he notices a need for integrity:

> Art and the saints—material instantiations of beauty and goodness—prepare the way for propositional truth because they appeal to our inner desire. Not every act that pierces our heart and awakens our desire is truly beautiful or good. Reason helps us to rightly order those desires (Dreher 2017, p. 117).

Such integrity requires a right balance, a possibility of reconciliation between different usual oppositions characterizing human existence, such as reason and emotions, body and spirit, freedom and determination, individual growth and the good of community. In such cases the idea of the symbol fits very well. It may lead directly to the vision of a modern affinity of monasticism and art. The symbol appears as a potential connection between different possible levels of human existence. The configuration of such connections is a form of wisdom. Technically, however, the symbol is helped by metaphor.

The connection between symbol and wisdom, which is an essential feature of monasticism, is seen very clearly by William A. Dyrness. According to him, "a symbol better represents what we might call understanding rather than knowledge—reflecting a kind of wisdom about life and the world" (Dyrness 2010, pos. 718). In this way, the symbol may become one of the instruments in seeing, understanding, or even transforming the world. Dyrness sees it as one of the principal functions of art and the artists: "Surely one of the principal functions of art and the artist—at least as we have come to understand this in the modern period—is rendering another world in terms of this one—that is, seeing this world metaphorically" (Dyrness 2010, pos. 3529). This vision opens our eyes and minds to the theological meaning of the world. Therefore, it may be considered not only as a mission, but also as an existential duty, while, as Dyrness continues, "symbolism [...] involves discovering meaning in what is given in creation, which is the theological condition for this process, ascribing significance to objects and actions, and being moved to pursue these as in themselves" (Dyrness 2010, pos. 703). Artists, like monks, stay in between the world and its meaning, between reality and the ideas which make the reality livable. It is an approach of involvement, sometimes drastic and radical, but always challenging in a unique way. The history of monasticism knows radical examples of such forms of monastic life. The first monks described in the Apophthegmata, the behavior of Syrian Stylites are examples of such an active and humble mediation between the world and its sense, between people and the world. A monk is placed in between, sometimes in radically difficult circumstances, but is always determined to live their existential vocation honestly and deeply; so they become a sign, a symbol, and a metaphor. His or her life, health, or social position are to transmit the message about salvation of the world. Being visible, narrated, or described, they carry out and even become a message.

As we remember, etymologically "monos" means "alone". It is a valid observation, which concerns the personal and existential involvement resulting explicitly from the fact of being a monk. This involvement is an existential sign, a symbol, or a metaphor of monasticism. It is a personal choice which sometimes may arrive to a sacrifice. Here we arrive at the very important concept of "performance". We will develop it later. For the moment we can only say that the monk, like the real artist, performs the spectacle of their life radically, to the very end, sometimes at the highest cost. This readiness for an eventual sacrifice distinguishes them, but also sets an ethical barrier from others. As Diana Taylor, a professor of Performance Studies writes: "The ethical considerations of performance are essential. An artist/activist may cut, mutilate, or flagellate herself, but she cannot do it to another person without his consent. She can perform a work that risks her own employment or arrest, but she cannot put others at risk without their permission" (Taylor 2016, pos. 1734). This possibility of sacrifice may bring an artist closer to a radical religious experience and from this perspective it is not difficult to identify the monk with the artist. According to Joan Chittister, the famous Benedictine writer:

> In truth, [...] the monk and the artist are one. Monasticism, in fact, cultivates the artistic spirit. Basic to monasticism are the very qualities art demands of the artist: silence, contemplation, discernment of spirits, community, and humility. Basic to art are the very qualities demanded of the monastic: single-mindedness, beauty, immersion, praise, and creativity. It is contemplation that leads an artist to preserve for us forever, the essence of a thing that takes us far beyond its accidents (quoted after Valters Paintner 2011, p. 161).

Quite often, also the artists emphasize their affinity with monks. Julia Cameron in her bestselling book *The Artist's Way* wrote directly about it and her words are also her personal confession:

Artists throughout the centuries have spoken of "inspiration", confiding that God spoke to them or angels did. In our age, such notions of art as a spiritual experience are seldom mentioned. And yet, the central experience of creativity is mystical. Opening our souls to what must be made, we meet our Maker. Artists toil in cells all over Manhattan. We have a monk's devotion to our work—and, like monks, some of us will be visited by visions and others will toil out our days knowing glory only at a distance, kneeling in the chapel but never receiving the visitation of a Tony, an Oscar, a National Book Award. And yet the still, small voice may speak as loud in us as in any. So we pray. Fame will come to some. Honor will visit all who work. As artists, we experience the fact that 'God is in the details'. Making our art, we make artful lives. Making our art, we meet firsthand the hand of our Creator. (Cameron 2002, p. 231).

Following this direction, one can speak about "anonymous monasticism" characterized by a typical, and radical existential approach of artists living as monks, even not being aware of this (Sawicki 2005, pp. 537–51). As an example may serve different "radical" artists, like G. Gould, the world-renowned Canadian pianist, who at the age of 27 withdrew from the stage to focus on recording in studio (Sawicki 2013), Lubomyr Melnyk, an original Ukrainian pianist and composer, known from his intensively expressive improvisations and called the Prophet of Piano (Quartier 2017, pp. 91–95), or Konstantin Wecker, a German songwriter, who dedicated his songs to social and political problems (Quartier 2018).

This affinity between monasticism and art is the main inspiration of our proposal of rediscovering monasticism through the art, expressed in the title of this paper. It may help us to look again at the main monastic values in a new light, expressing them in a new language. Actually, it also is a matter of a special style of life characterized by a radical and involved relationship to the world. We will present this shortly on the basis of texts written by the authors more or less consciously referring art to monasticism.

The affinity between monasticism and art occurs on two basic levels:

1. Internal life;
2. Mission.

In both cases, the approach and practices are strikingly similar, indicating not only the importance of a personally authentic and deep spiritual life but also the simple necessity of the existence of God. In this context, God seems to be as essential for the monk as for the artist. Moreover, the internal, intimate experience inevitably leads to external action, which has its clear objective and is addressed to other people. Being a monk, as much as being an artist, is a deep internal experience and a service, both to other people and to the whole world. These two dimensions interweave and supplement one another. In each of them one can distinguish some separate themes which explicitly have a spiritual character. For internal life there are:

(a) Necessity of wilderness;
(b) Intimacy with God;
(c) Deep exploration of one's own soul;
(d) Mystical experience;
(e) Meditation;
(f) Contemplation;
(g) Conversion.

Mission may be presented in four fields:

(a) Captivation of imagination;
(b) Communication (also to create a community);

(c)   Formulation of message, namely: expression of God, call for contemplation, sacredness, glorification;

(d)   Style of humility and discretion.

In all these cases the internal attitude is transformed into activities focused on the transmission of internal, spiritual experience. Here, the analogy between artist and monk is very evident—both try to communicate the message resulting from their internal experience. Therefore, they necessarily turn to other people, not only for sharing with them their experience, but also to help them. So, at least in their own opinion, such mission is a service rendered to humankind and even to the world.

1. Internal Life

As classical history teaches, Christian monasticism was born in the desert, first in Egypt, then in Syria, Palestine, and in other countries where persons looking for a radical life according to the Gospel started to populate inhabited, sometimes wild places. It was to be the right environment for personal spiritual growth, protection from distraction, and unnecessary involvement. The motive of importance of the desert was introduced into literature in the fourth century by Saint Athanasius in his famous biography of Saint Anthony—the *Vita Antonii*. The desert offered to the monk the best conditions for his own spiritual work. No wonder then that a radically authentic understanding of an artist's mission must also refer to the desert. So says Geoff Hall, photographer, film maker, mentor, and writer, in his book, *Translating the invisible world*, which connects the experience of wilderness with the sense of sacredness of life and a need of transformation. He writes:

> The Wilderness addresses the fundamental things which need healing in our lives—our fears. As we roam this dry and weary land, our false-consciousness is rectified and our vision re-oriented. We see that all of life is sacred, that our life with God is the one essential thing that will help us see the world correctly—to see ourselves correctly—as we navigate the cultural terrain as artists (Hall 2012b, pos. 943).

As the desert was a master and teacher for monks, so it can (and should) be for artists. Only in this way can we learn and experience what is most essential in our life: "who we are and what we are here for—our calling. The art we make—whether, word, image or performance art—will communicate incoherence if these things are not well-developed in our hearts" (Hall 2011b, pos. 130).

The objective of the experience of the desert is intimacy with God. Hall describes the life of the artist also in these categories. He writes: "The life of the artist is an intimate walk with God" (Hall 2011a, pos. 210). A similar opinion is expressed by Christine Valters Paintner, a Benedictine oblate, theologian, writer, and blogger. She makes the affinity between monks and artists the main inspiration of her writing and activity. She does not speak explicitly about God but about Mystery. Nevertheless, the perspectives, especially for human beings, are similar. For example, she writes that poetry slows us down, moves us into a different way of knowing, changes our breath and demands a more attentive presence, helps us to integrate sorrow and joy, horror and humor, with compassionate awareness. That is why perceiving poetry as a way of being with Mystery is the reason why Valters Paintner sees it as a potent form for spiritual direction (Cf. Valters Painter and Beckman 2010, p. 110).

Here, poetry, like each true spiritual experience, integrates the subject exercising it, authorizing him or her to help others. This is exactly what was mentioned above about the necessity of missions resulting from deep spiritual experience. Such a mission is possible because of the transforming power of poetry. The artist cannot just keep it only for him/herself: "*Poiesis*, the creative act, occurs as the death and re-birth of the soul" (Valters Painter and Beckman 2010, p. 157).

Speaking generally about the arts, Valters Paintner talks explicitly about God: "the arts help expand our ways of knowing God beyond the cognitive level" (Valters Painter and Beckman 2010, p. 143). She sees that creative acts of art have a deep existential and implicitly spiritual meaning: "When we create art, ceremony, or ritual, it is not for the practical purpose of accomplishing a task, but to reflect our deepest meaning and our core values" (Valters Painter and Beckman 2010, p. 180). The evident theological character of such involvement is clear in the book of James Watkins, significantly titled *Creativity as Sacrifice*. To some extent, he confirms the intuition of other Valters Paintner's words: "When we engage in the arts, we dip into our soul to discover deep pools of wonder, breath-taking gifts of beauty, and quiet revelation. As we create, we are invited into playfulness, poignancy, and surprise—energies that renew us and revitalize our sense of purpose" (Valters Painter and Beckman 2010, p. 3). The thesis present in the title of his book shows the theological and even Christological perspectives of creative act.

An artist's deep internal experience has not only an existential character. It is often described in mystical categories. Matthew Fox, writer and the founder of the University of Creation Spirituality in California, when he writes about creativity and its intimate character, mentions mysticism very plainly. According to him, "the intimacy of creativity corresponds to the mystical experience itself. Mysticism bespeaks union, and there is an ongoing union of us and the Divine precisely during the process of giving birth in any form whatsoever" (Fox 2004, p. 9). The relationship between mysticism and art is well known. There were mystics who expressed their mystical experiences in poetic texts (Saint Ephrem of Syria, Saint John of the Cross), in music (Hildegard of Bingen), or in painting (Fra Angelico). Mystical experience as such was also very attractive and inspiring for many artists; it is enough to recall Lorenzo Bernini and his famous *Ecstasy* of Saint Theresa of Avila. The intensity of intimate personal contact with God, being a normal condition of mystical experience, finds its usual medium in meditation and contemplation. Valters Paintner sees a clear analogy between the art-making process and the practice of meditation. For her, the art-making process may become a container for our internal awareness, much as in meditation practice. So monks and artists "are teachers of slowness, of savoring, of seeing the world below surfaces" (Valters Paintner 2011, p. 10). As we can see here, this experience is tightly connected with the perception of the world. In this realm the artist admires, meditates, and contemplates the creature. Beverly Lanzetta (quoted by Valters Paintner) says: "True contemplation always overflows into creation—it becomes a creative act" (Valters Paintner 2011, p. 25).

The personal commitment to a relationship with God does not have merely a spiritual character. It transforms the person involved. Watkins, elaborating his theological model of creativity as Sacrifice, sees it as "a respectful transformation" (Watkins 2015, p. 11). In monastic vocabulary such process is called "conversion", and Valters Paintner finds it "central to creativity because it calls us to begin again and try new things" (Valters Paintner 2011, p. 73). The artist's continuous research and pursuit of ideals has the same dynamism as the spiritual search of monks. As Dyrness explains, "it is the motivation to pursue—the affective attraction—that constitutes the aesthetic element" (Dyrness 2010, pos. 704).

2. The Mission

The seriousness and intensity of the internal spiritual life must inevitably lead towards activity. It is a sign of responsibility which naturally grows from a deep, personal relationship with God. This responsibility, activated by the singularity of spiritual experience, leads towards mission. A monk and an artist cannot resist an imperative of sharing their experience with other people, transmitting to them a message of joy and hope. So they must confront their public (listeners, readers, or visitors in museums or galleries), capturing their attention and communicating a previously formulated message. Surely, the power of authenticity of testimony is unquestionable, but the mechanisms and dynamisms of transmission are everywhere the same and must be, more or less consciously, respected. All this happens in a certain style, marked by a spiritual quality. Even if the message is to be powerful, it is a style of humility and discretion.

The beautiful, as Watkins notes, "is not the product of our own fantasy, nor of our subjective perception, but has an objective existence, being itself the expression of a Divine perfection" (Watkins 2015, p. 51). Thus, the artistic activity is a service. It is a duty. So, it needs effort. Particularly today, in times of so many different proposals and market competition, the artist must make an effort to capture the attention of their public. It is something more than just transmitting a message. First of all, it is a matter of creating bonds and constituting a space for community. Hall describes it very clearly:

> The work of the storyteller, the artist, is not to convict people of error, nor convince people of truth, but to capture the imagination with the possibility of something new being born into the world; a change in the world-order, justice for the afflicted and the disenfranchised, a change in the materialistic concepts of life and the materialistic conceptions of art. Conviction isn't their job, it is something achieved in the heart, by the Spirit (Hall 2012b, pos. 451).

The theological background for this is obvious—monks and artists are messengers of God, they announce His presence and His Grace. Watkins inserts this activity in an important place of the Christian community: "The task of the theologian is to show how a theological model for human creativity in the arts can inform the life of the Christian community" (Watkins 2015, p. 43). A monk acts within the community of the Church. An artist, at least, acts in the community of their public. There may be also a community artist. Hall proposes here the spiritual community of artists—a place of support, solidarity, and mutual inspiration. It is especially important in a fragile social context of artistic activity: "The spiritual community of the artist is a place where the sharing of common brokenness occurs in the hospitality of equality" (Hall 2012a, pos. 434). The base of this community is care. It is a community of inclusion, against all social, economic, or cultural marginalization. Such a community expresses the coherence between internal life and mission, guaranteeing the successful transmission of the message. Hall calls it a prophetic lifestyle, appealing for its restitution:

> We have lost the connection between prophetic communication and prophetic lifestyle. Such art cannot be conducted from the soft-centre of the institution along with its power-base. Prophetic art is always expressed from the margins where the pain, injustice and the angst of life are experienced, where the powerless live. It is subversive, not political or ideological. It is not armchair Prophetic! (Hall 2011a, pos. 373).

With the adjective "prophetic", which often appears in this quotation and has explicitly Biblical origins, one can associate the monastic tradition which has always linked monastic life with prophecy. It is the matter of charismatic life in the Church, complementary to its hierarchical structures.

In such a way we arrive at the figure of the Biblical prophet, who may be regarded as a model for both monks and artist. Usually their task was to communicate something and doing this in an efficient way. This leads us for the second time to the very important, above-mentioned concept of modern art—*performance*, a theme also studied and explored by Thomas Quartier (Quartier 2013). A prophet was a performer, as well as a monk. His or her whole life, in all its gestures and actions, was a sign, a symbol, or a metaphor. In modern art, performance plays a key role. Diana Taylor, quoted above, sees it as a means of communication, as "a doing with and to", as an act of imagination (cf. Taylor 2016, p. 207). In her *Esthetics of Performance*, Erika Fisher-Lichte, among various categories constituting the phenomenon of performance, also mentions those which have an explicitly communitarian character. She writes directly about community (Fisher-Lichte 2016, pp. 90–106), about contact (Fisher-Lichte 2016, pp. 107–19), about embodiment (Fisher-Lichte 2016, pp. 136–64), about presence (Fisher-Lichte 2016, pp. 164–79), and about transformation (Fisher-Lichte 2016, pp. 301–10). Community is first of all a space of encounter. In times of excessive individualism, performance and its symbolic and metaphorical character is actually (or can be, and should be) one of the most efficient tools to achieve it. It offers both interaction and involvement. It permits integration between the corporal and the spiritual, human and divine. As Dyrness observes, "aesthetic and symbolic projects are also spiritual sites where the affections, the goods of the world, and religious longings meet and interact" (Dyrness 2010, pos. 116).

As we mentioned, good communication is only a means to transmit a message. The affinity between monks and artists can be also traced on this level. Following the authors we quote, one can distinguish three main themes of this message: (a) bringing to contemplation; (b) showing the sacredness of everything; (c) calling to glorification.

Geoff Hall, exploring the affinity between art and mysticism, observes that they both help in achieving the contemplative vision of the world: "Art like mysticism, breaks through the screen of objectivity and draws on our pre-conceptual capacities of contemplative vision" (Hall 2012b, pos. 765). As we mentioned above, it is a very important aspect and task of perception. The most ancient, classical monastic tradition connects it clearly with internal spiritual experience seen as a perception of Divine Light, which permits us to see everything in truth. These optics naturally lead towards discovering the sacredness in everything. Valters Painter defines it as essential for monasticism: "This is the heart of the monastic path, of being present to the sacredness of everything—including ourselves" (Valters Paintner 2011, p. 100). This approach is very close to the sensitivity for beauty in everyday life which is becoming more and more popular. Elisabetta Di Stefano, apart from giving an overview of various texts dedicated to this theme (Di Stefano 2017, pp. 11–35), presents it in a wide anthropological and ecological context (Di Stefano 2017, pp. 89–119). In this sense, the monastic approach to the world, born from a deep spiritual and mystical relationship to God and proved by the long history and culture of monasteries of the Benedictine tradition, can find its contemporary continuation, perhaps in new forms, but on the base of the same anthropological principles. It is an approach not of contemplative passivity, but of a wise collaboration in continuation of the divine act of creation. Fox describes it very clearly in the words which smartly combine theology and anthropology:

> God has gifted creation with everything that is necessary. Humankind, full of all creative possibilities, is God's work. Humankind is called to co-create. God gave to humankind the talent to create with all the world. Just as the person shall never end, until into dust they are transformed and resurrected, just so, their works are always visible. The good deeds shall glorify, the bad deeds shall shame (Fox 2004, p. 228).

In this appeal one can find easily an echo of Saint Benedict's amazing conclusion to the chapter dedicated to artists living in the monastery—discussing the possible price for their products, he recommends, quoting the words from the first Letter of Saint Peter Apostle, that in everything God may be glorified (1 Peter 4;11; *The Rule of Saint Benedict* 57: 7).

The final observation which should be added to this short look at the affinity between monks and artists, in view of the further growth of their presence and meaning in the world, concerns the style of being of a monk as an artist and, vice versa, of an artist as a monk. It is a matter of humility, which, more precisely and adequately in the modern context, we would prefer to call "discretion". In this context we refer to the amazingly monastic reflection published recently by Pierre Zaoui, a French philosopher, under the very meaningful title *The Art of Disappearing* (*L'arte di scomparire*). In spite of appearances it is not a nihilistic book. On the contrary, it appears to be a very subtle proposal for a good and honest life in our times. It is a proposal for a style of presence and interaction, for a fresh and updated look at some monastic values. The author describes the main idea of his proposal in the following words:

> Your discreet, unobserved, transparent position opens you up to a new experience: the abandonment of the ghosts of omnipotence, of being indispensable, of being responsible for each and every one. Becoming suddenly discreet means giving up for a moment any will of power. Not that the will to power is negative in itself, but we know too well its dark and tyrannical face, and even the luminous face is sometimes a heavy burden, for its need to overcome itself relentlessly, to always push its forces to their extreme limit. Hence the so soothing joy of being able to download it for a moment on others or on things, to let them appear, not to give them more shade, to take off from their sun (Zaoui 2015, pos. 49).

In this declaration one can see a new melody played with the notes of artist identity, life, and action. The classical, many-centuries-old stereotype of the glorious power of art is here transformed into a new vision, which Zaoui discreetly links to theology and religion:

> The art of discretion seems to depend on an authentically metaphysical gesture, if not actually theological origin, which aims to constitute its concept by differentiating it from proximate

but distinct experiences: the ancient and worldly ones of touch, modesty, demeanor, of courtesy, and religious ones of humility, detachment or withdrawal from the world (Zaoui 2015, pos. 272).

The explanation of this approach is also very meaningful, sensitive, and corresponds to the modern trends in art which really need more humility and discretion. Beauty and truth, particularly seen as gifts from God, are sufficiently powerful to exist and do their work. We should not disturb them. On the contrary, new, quiet, creative spaces are needed to give them opportunity to grow:

> Because a life without secrets, without mystery, without shadows, without interstitial spaces between oneself and others, as well as between oneself, is a life destined to absolute terror and without limits, which in the end destroys every residue in us of humanity (Zaoui 2015, pos. 1047).

3. Conclusions

Concluding this reflection, we hope that the affinity between monasticism and art it outlines may be a helpful way of looking differently at, and perhaps with a larger perspective on, both contemporary artists and monks. The mutual symbiosis, organically and naturally resulting from this affinity, also turns out to be stimulated by our times. If art has always been present, even sometimes struggling for its identity, then monasticism seems to be losing its terrain. The necessity of deep spiritual experience, so important for art, may in fact be a good occasion for rediscovering monastic traditions and practice in collaboration with artists. It seems that this work has already begun. What it needs now is mutual sensitivity, courage, patience, and perseverance. In this way the monastic values which set the course of this reflection (existential necessity of wilderness, prayerful intimacy with God, deep and serious internal spiritual work, openness for mystical experience, practice of meditation, grace of contemplation, and path of conversion) will find their new expression, and so they will be able to be transmitted to people who for different reasons do not know them. At the same time, it could also be a powerful message of evangelization, since, in essence, Christian monks have always been radical practitioners and witnesses of the Gospel. In times when sensibility for spirituality and religion is weakened and only an interest and attraction for beauty remains, it would be good to recall that, in origin, these two spheres went together.

Funding: This research received no external funding.

Conflicts of Interest: The author declares no conflicts of interest.

References

Balthasar, Hans Urs. 1971. Philosophie, Christentum, Mönchtum. In *Sponsa Verbi, Skizzen zur Theologie II*. Einsiedeln: Johannes Verlag.

Cameron, Julia. 2002. *The Artist's Way: 25th Anniversary Edition*. New York: TarcherPerigee, mobi.

Di Stefano, Elisabetta. 2017. *Che cos'è L'estetica Quotidiana*. Roma: Carocci Editore.

Dreher, Rod. 2017. *The Benedict Option: A Strategy for Christians in a Post-Christian Nation*. New York: Sentinel, mobi.

Dyrness, William. 2010. *Poetic Theology: God and the Poetics of Everyday*. Grand Rapids: Eerdmans, mobi.

Fisher-Lichte, Erika. 2016. *Estetica del Performativo. Una Teoria del Teatro e Dell'arte*. Roma: Carocci Editore.

Fox, Matthew. 2004. *Creativity: Where the Divine and Human Meet*. New York: Tarcherperigree, mobi.

Hall, Geoff. 2011a. *The Cultural Way of Being*. Fort Collins: Upptäcka Press, mobi.

Hall, Geoff. 2011b. *The Wilderness and the Desert of the Real*. Fort Collins (CO): Upptäcka Press, mobi.

Hall, Geoff. 2012a. *The Artist's Autobiography*. Fort Collins: Upptäcka Press, mobi.

Hall, Geoff. 2012b. *Translating the Invisible Wind*. Fort Collins: Upptäcka Press, mobi.

Heidegger, Martin. 1997. *Was Heißt Denken?* Tübingen: Niemeyer.

Jaspers, Karl. 1996. *Einführung in die Philosophie. Zwölf Radiovorträge*. München: Piper Taschenbuch.

Meiattini, Giulio. 2012. *Monachesimo e Teologia. La Triplice Prospettiva di Hans Urs Von Balthasare*. Lugano: Eupress FTL.

Merleau-Ponty, Maurice. 1945. *Phénoménologie de la Preception*. Paris: Gallimard.

Quartier, Thomas. 2013. Monastieke performances: Verrassende artistieke uitingen vanuit abdijen. *De Kovel* 30: 38–51.

Quartier, Thomas. 2017. De grot van de pianomonnik. Lubomyr Melnyk speelt onafgebroken. *De Kovel* 48: 91–95.

Quartier, Thomas. 2018. Kunst der Wandermönche—Ars monastica. Available online: https://hinter-den-schlagzeilen.de/kunst-der-wandermoenche-ars-monastica (accessed on 30 June 2019).

Salmann, Elmar. 2000. *Presenza di Spirito. Il Cristianesimo Come Gesto e Pensiero*. Padova: Edizioni Messaggero Padova, Abbazia di Santa Giustina.

Sawicki, Bernard. 2005. *Concept of the Absurd and Its Theological Reception of Christian Monasticism*. Lewiston: Edwin Mellen Press.

Sawicki, Bernard. 2013. Glenn Gould—An Anonymous Monk? On Some Possibilities of Applying Monastic Categories to Modern Culture. In *Monasticism between Culture and Cultures*. Edited by Philippe Nouzille and Michaela Pfeifer. Roma: Pontificio Ateneo S. Anselmo, pp. 427–38.

Taylor, Diana. 2016. *Performance*. Durham: Duke University Press, mobi.

Valters Paintner, Christine. 2011. *The Artist's Rule: Nurturing Your Creative Soul with Monastic Wisdom*. Notre Dame: Sorin Books, mobi.

Valters Painter, Christine, and Betsey Beckman. 2010. *Awakening the Creative Spirit: Bringing the Arts to Spiritual Direction*. New York: Morehouse Publishing, mobi.

Watkins, James. 2015. *Creativity as Sacrifice: Toward a Theological Model for Creativity in the Arts*. Minneapolis: Fortress Press, mobi.

Zaoui, Pierre. 2015. *L'arte di Scomparire*. Milano: Il Saggiatore, mobi.

![religions logo] religions

MDPI

Article

Monasticism, Monotheism, and Monogamy: Past and Present Expressions of the Undivided Life

Martha Elias Downey

Independent Scholar, Montreal, QC H4R 3A7, Canada; mattedowney@gmail.com

Received: 30 May 2019; Accepted: 16 August 2019; Published: 20 August 2019

Abstract: Monasticism first appeared in Christian tradition in the late third and early fourth centuries as a way to practice true religion. Soon after, it also became a way of eschewing the Church's embrace of political power and the divided loyalties which accompanied that union. Contemporary expressions of monasticism in the Protestant tradition (often identified as new monasticism) have interpreted the *mono* (singularity) not as celibacy or living in a cloistered community, but as abandoning cultural promiscuity in order to live out a monogamous spirituality. Though each monastic community has its own distinct characteristics and context, one can identify two common markers which unite both contemporary expressions of monasticism and historical monastic communities: (1) monotheism or a singular devotion to God which is separate from political, societal, and economic ambitions, and (2) monogamy or a commitment to a particular community, neighborhood, and mission. This article explores ancient and contemporary expressions of monasticism by examining their guiding documents and looking for evidence of monotheism and monogamous spirituality. By giving fresh articulation to the *mono* in monasticism, we are better able to identify the heart of the undivided (monastic) life and discern its presence in reimagined forms.

Keywords: monasticism; community; monotheism; spirituality; monogamy

1. Introduction

The singularity at the heart of monasticism, the *mono* in monasticism if you will, is a bit of an enigma. In some ways, it is as simple as translating the Greek word, *monazein*: to live alone. Monasticism of any sort implies a certain amount of separation from society. Yet none of the monastics, not even the early Egyptian hermits, totally eschewed human contact; all were in some way connected to a community of like-minded devotees. Though solitude features significantly in Christian monasticism, the religious life has found expression primarily in a communal setting. In the Benedictine tradition, these communities are characterized by vows of obedience, stability, and conversion of life (which includes chastity and relinquishing private ownership). Instead of life alone, monasticism has come to mean life bound to community. What, then, is the singleness (*mono*) at the heart of this particular expression of Christian spirituality?

I ask this question both as a scholar who studies spirituality and as a practitioner involved in the spiritual formation of various faith communities. While I celebrate the renewed interest in monastic practices and disciplines within my Protestant tradition, I am also wary of appropriation or modernization without due diligence. Critics of the new monastic movement such as Martha McAfee suggest that Protestant intentional communities do not qualify as monastic expressions because they do not practice celibacy as *the* school for loving God.[1] However, it seems clear that monastic celibacy is

---

[1] McAfee (2008) concludes that New Monasticism is not truly monasticism, but a "renewal of the Protestant response to the perceived elitism of the Medieval Monastery," or a renewal of the Free Church tradition (p. 6).

a means, not an end. My goal in giving fresh articulation to the *mono* in monasticism is to identify the heart of the undivided (monastic) life and thereby discern its presence in reimagined forms.

The manner in which one articulates monastic tenets has implications for the teleological instinct of the community. Is spirituality framed positively or negatively? Is hatred for sin primary or is it compassion for the world? Are discipline and correction viewed as deserved punishment or doorways to restoration? Does a monastic Rule foster fear or love? If we view monasticism as primarily a *turning to* instead of a *rejection of* (though the second will necessarily follow the first), the vows of obedience and renouncing personal property might be better framed as monotheism (love of God), a life of devotion to the Divine Source as revealed in Jesus. Similarly, the monastic vows of stability and chastity could be framed as a type of monogamy (love of neighbor), a call to faithful, loving relationship(s).[2]

In order to trace the presence of these markers of monasticism (monotheism and monogamy), I engage with the Rules governing two monastic expressions: the Monastery of Monte Cassino in Italy (founded around 529) and the Order of Sustainable Faith in Ohio (2014), a missional monastic expression of the Vineyard movement. In many ways, these communities represent opposite ends of the spectrum in the tradition: ancient and contemporary, Catholic and Protestant, cloistered and integrated, celibate and family-inclusive. Benedict's Rule is established, its merit proved through centuries of practice. By comparison, Boyd's Rule is still a work in progress, not yet fully tested in community life. Practices differ as well. Benedict combatted fleshly temptation by taking off his garments and throwing himself into a patch of briars (Gregory the Great 1911, p. 55). A member of the Order of Sustainable Faith states that living under the Rule allowed her to have greater compassion for herself, especially her shortcomings and mistakes.[3]

Despite the variance in methods, a common thread runs through the monastic storyline: a desire to pursue an undivided life and find a measure of wholeness. By engaging with two monastic Rules separated by fifteen hundred years, I seek to establish that the heart of the undivided life in monasticism has been and still is expressed through a pronounced singular devotion to the divine (monotheism) and an emphasis on fidelity to a specific community (monogamy).

2. Context

Within the Christian tradition, the idea of singular devotion is not limited to monasticism. Before Christ entered history, statutes and ordinances written to the nation of Israel in seventh century B.C.E. featured repeated invocations to monotheism.[4] Faithful relationships were also introduced early on in the story of Israel, most notably in the recurring refrain, "I will be your God and you will be my people"[5] and in the identifying ritual of circumcision which represented the life-long covenant between YHWH and Abraham's descendants.[6] While all followers of YHWH are called to singular devotion, Christian monasticism represents an intensification and intentionality which goes above and beyond common religious practice.

In both ancient and contemporary contexts, the monastic vocation is a call to an alternate way of living, what Thomas Moore (1998) calls "making a life apart from the crowd, in a style at odds with the norm" (p. xv). Saint Antony of Egypt (c. 251–356) is often cited as the seminal example of the monastic impulse, fleeing to the desert in order to renounce sin and encounter God. Historian Marilyn Dunn (2003) notes that Antony's life in the desert was characterized by solitude, self-denial, and asceticism (p. 3). Aspects of these same elements can be identified in what is known as new monasticism. In 2004, a group of Protestant "practitioners, scholars, and dreamers" (Stock et al. 2007, p. 4) gathered in North Carolina and composed the twelve marks of new monasticism. The list begins with a call to "relocate to the

---

2 Jesus identifies the love of God and love of neighbor at the core of the law and the prophets (Matt. 22:40).
3 Interview with a member of the Order of Sustainable Faith, July 2019.
4 Exodus 20:1–2 and Deuteronomy 6:4–5 are two well-known examples.
5 Exodus 6:7, Ezekiel 36:28, Jeremiah 7:23, Jeremiah 30:22, Jeremiah 31:33.
6 Genesis 17:10–14.

abandoned places of Empire" (Claiborne 2006, pp. 363–64). This phrase intentionally echoes what has been understood as part of the early monastic mindset: a belief that the Church in the fourth century was losing its way, transitioning from being the oppressed to becoming the oppressor (Dunn 2003, pp. 1–2). Similarly, those who identify as new monastics condemn unholy alliances between politics and religion, calling their adherents to denounce empire-building and dedicate themselves to building the kingdom of heaven (see Rutba 2005). Like Antony, the new monastics seek to affirm monotheism by turning away from the cultural gods of their time.

For the monastics, rejecting unholy pursuits is not an end in itself, but the means by which one becomes free to embrace that which is holy and good.[7] Dunn (2003) observes that, "For Antony, the life of an ascetic or *monachos* was a constant struggle for self-knowledge, self-purification, and through these, the return of the soul to unity with God, in whose image it was created" (p. 4). The monastic desire for unity and wholeness is articulated in slightly different language by contemporary adherents. Joan Chittister (2015), a Benedictine nun, identifies the main pillars of Benedict's Rule as community, peace, stewardship, and equality, invoking the idea of faithful, loving relationships (monogamy). Jon Stock (Stock et al. 2007) identifies the common elements shared by ancient and new forms of monasticism as being that of close proximity and daily accountability (p. 8), both of which are vital to fidelity. In a 2015 interview, Chittister links monasticism to honoring others: "[A] monastic outlook … says that what we all share in common is this obligation, this desire to live together in a global community in a way that does honor to the will of God for all of humankind. It requires hospitality. It is inclusion. It takes everybody in. It requires accountability to one another as well as to the goods of the universe and of the community itself." One could take Chittister's words to be a dynamic description of monastic fidelity: the monk evolves from individual accountability to communal responsibility to dealing honorably with all of humanity and creation. The paradox of monastic monogamy is that in pledging oneself to a particular community, one becomes increasingly connected to the world. Chittister confirms this idea when she goes on to say: "The Rule of Benedict says that you are to treat all things as if they were the vessel and the altar."

In looking at the history of monasticism, there is a sense of continuity and stability even in the midst of reform and change. In several instances, monastic reform was not an updating of practices to reflect a contemporary context, but an attempt to recapture monastic values. Influenced by Bernard of Clairvaux (1090–1153), the Cistercians branched off from the Benedictines in 1098 in order to return to a more literal interpretation of Benedict's Rule (Merton 1949). Teresa of Avila founded the Discalced Carmelites in 1562 intent on recovering the order's commitments to contemplation and poverty (Bilinkoff 1989). Chittister notes that recycling is part of what makes monasticism sustainable: "Benedictine poverty requires you to use everything in such a way that it is, in essence, recycled for centuries." I believe this principle applies not only to material goods, but to the very tenets of monasticism. As we examine the *Rule of Benedict* and the *Rule of Life* for the Order of Sustainable Faith, we find that faithful reinvention continues to be part of the monastic story.

3. The Rule of St. Benedict (Monte Cassino)

Benedict of Nursia (480–547) crafted his influential monastic rule shortly after he became Abbot at Monte Cassino. Before this, Benedict had spent many years as a monk, becoming intimately familiar with the austerity and solitude characteristic of the Christian hermits. Drawing on his experience and several existing monastic rules (Rule of the Master, Rule of St. Basil, Rule of St. Augustine, writings of John Cassian), Benedict penned a governing document which reflected the strictness of the eremitical practice but tempered it with the stability of communal life (Sheldrake 2007, p. 51). Unlike the eremitical tradition where each monk was viewed as a spiritual athlete, Benedict's Rule established interdependence and a family spirit at its center.

---

[7] Kallistos Ware (1998) argues for a positive interpretation of asceticism.

3.1. Monotheism

Benedict fled the trappings of Rome when he was twenty in order to pursue a simple, pure life, so it is no surprise that the themes of purity and simplicity are woven throughout the Rule (Okholm 2001, p. 301). Every directive is meant to help the monk keep his focus on the divine love at the heart of all things. Thomas Merton, a twentieth-century Trappist monk, made this point clear when he explained the Rule to novices.

> St. Benedict did not call us to the monastery to serve him, but to serve God. We are not here to carry out the prescriptions of men, but to love God. The purpose of the Rule is to furnish a framework within which to build the structure of a simple and pure spiritual life, pleasing to God by its perfection of faith, humility and love. The Rule is not an end in itself, but a means to an end, and it is always to be seen in relation to its end. This end is union with God in love, and every line of the Rule indicates that its various prescriptions are given us to show us how to get rid of self-love and replace it by love of God. (Merton 2009, p. 6)

The Rule of Benedict (RB)[8] covers a variety of topics, many concerned with mundane communal matters such as meals, times of prayer, clothing, discipline, and work. For those of us living in a culture obsessed with self-determination, the tightly scheduled order of each day seems excessively restrictive. Similarly, our heightened sense of individuality, particularly in the West, is in marked contrast to the over-arching authority granted to the Abbot, an authority verging on the absolute. However, Benedict's Rule claims that it requires "nothing harsh, nothing burdensome" but leans toward strictness in some instances in order to "amend faults and to safeguard love" (RB Prologue). The good of all is cited as central, and Benedict urges those in the community not to be "daunted by fear" but to have "hearts overflowing with the inexpressible delight of love" (RB Prologue).

There are many instances in the text, some more direct than others, where the monk is called to love God with singular devotion. I will mention but two. The first is rather counterintuitive to modern sensibilities: the pervasive authority and care of the Abbot or Superior. For Benedict, devotion to God is conterminous with a Rule and an Abbot (RB 1). Chapter 2 refers to the Abbot as a representative of Christ in the monastery; he is to be an exemplar of all that is good and holy, he is to love all in the community equally, and he is to govern souls with both gentleness and severity, accommodating the variety of persons in his care. In every way, the Abbot is to embody God's interactions with his beloved subjects. For Benedict, obedience to Christ is primarily practiced through obedience to the Superior as the agent of Christ. In Chapter 4, Benedict writes: "First of all, love the Lord God with your whole heart, your whole soul and all your strength," and in Chapter 5, he links this love to obedience as a way of "cherish[ing] Christ above all."

A second indicator of monotheism in Benedict's Rule appears in the spiritual practices associated with humility. Benedict lists twelve degrees of humility, which include rather severe measures such as accepting hard and distasteful commands, confessing evil thoughts to the Abbot, believing oneself to be the lowest and vilest of men, practicing silence, avoiding laughter, and keeping one's head bowed and eyes on the ground (RB 7). Benedict compares these degrees of humility to climbing a ladder, the purpose being that "the monk will quickly arrive at that perfect love of God which casts out fear" (RB 7). As Merton so astutely observes, the Rule (including the somewhat harsh steps to humility) is but a means to living in the love of God and freely reciprocating that love.

It is interesting to note how freedom is associated with the constraints of the Rule. While we are accustomed to equating freedom with autonomy, twentieth-century theologian, Hans Urs von Balthasar (1990), notes that there is a second type of freedom to consider, and that is the freedom to consent (pp. 227–42). Basically, a person has the freedom to align their will, their desires, their very

---

8 Unless otherwise noted, quotations from the *Rule of Benedict* are from the 1998 edition published by the Order of St. Benedict (St. Benedict 1998).

life, with another person. It is this type of freedom that Benedict is alluding to when he calls the monks to practice humility and obedience. Similarly, Thomas Moore (1998) notes that the Rule can be harsh but it is also liberating because "It frees a person from the unspoken rules of the society at large and offers an alternative" (p. xvii). The alternative to self-will or the pressures of society is to align one's life and will to a community dedicated to loving and serving God.

In the Benedictine Rule, obedience to an Abbot and the practice of humility are two ways one expresses undivided devotion to God, two practices which place love of the divine above all other loves. However, it is important to note that this hard-won liberation to love God fully and freely does not happen in isolation. There is a related love which naturally flows out of divine devotion: faithful love of the other.[9]

3.2. Monogamy

In the biblical text, idolatry and unfaithfulness are closely linked. Devotion to God is enacted through covenants, promises, and vows. Hebrew scholar Robert Alter (2004) observes: "Monogamy, of course, is a reiterated biblical metaphor for monotheism, and so worship of the goat-demons and other deities is an act of promiscuity, 'whoring'" (p. 617). Faithfulness is a recurring theme in the Scriptures: God is described as a covenant-making, promise-keeping God (Genesis 6:18; 17:7; Jeremiah 32:40). Because covenants and promises are by nature relational, we also find commands and directives for the people of God to be faithful, to keep vows made not only to God but to each other.

When a monk takes the vows of stability, fidelity to monastic life, and obedience in a Benedictine community, it is considered a serious matter, not to be undertaken quickly or lightly (RB 4, 58, 60). In Chapter 58 of the Rule, Benedict indicates that when someone arrives at the monastery seeking entrance, he is to be given a room in the guest quarters for four or five days. If he responds well to "bearing his harsh treatment" and the "difficulty of entry," the man is allowed to live with the novices. After two months in the community, the newcomer is read the Rule and given the option to leave. If the man chooses to stay, he is granted another period of six months in the community before the Rule is read to him again. If the man still desires to remain, the Rule is read to him after a further four months of residence. This year-long trial period highlights the solemnity of the promises made to God and to the community.

Benedict dedicates numerous chapters to guidelines meant to protect the integrity of the monastic community. In particular, he addresses corrective discipline and causes for excommunication (RB 23–29, 44–46). No doubt, Benedict writes about these matters in such detail because he experienced the many ways in which community life could go wrong. According to Gregory the Great (1911), in Benedict's first attempt at leading a monastic community, the monks tried to poison him (pp. 56–58). Abbot Philip Lawrence of Christ in the Desert Monastery in New Mexico observes that the vow of stability (fidelity to a particular group of people) proves difficult for some. "So many monks and nuns come to the Monastery and begin to want the life of another Monastery . . . Part of the task of formation is simply accepting the life of this community, under whoever is the present superior, with these brothers who are here today" (Lawrence n.d.). When circumstances become challenging, one must continue to accept those to whom one is joined by a promise. This type of faithfulness is not achieved through sheer determination but is meant to stem from relationship with a God who keeps promises.

What does this fidelity look like? Benedict indicates that monks are to treat other members of the community with honor, preference, and love, engaging in mutual obedience (RB 72). "Obedience is a blessing to be shown by all, not only to the abbot but also to one another as brothers, since we know that it is by this way of obedience that we go to God" (RB 71). A 1949 translation of the Rule frames the

---

9   It should be noted that the distinction between monotheism (love of God) and monogamy (love of neighbor) is somewhat artificial; the love of God is shown primarily through love of neighbor and those who love their neighbor are, in many ways, loving the divine image reflected in the other. Nevertheless, I address each one separately.

monks' love for each other as a form of chastity: "Let them practice fraternal charity with a chaste love" (RB 73).

One of the primary ways in which this vow of chaste, fraternal love is enacted is through the vow of poverty by which monks renounce what Benedict calls the "vice of private ownership" (RB 33, 55). Before a monk becomes part of the community, he is required to divest himself of all possessions including personal garments (RB 58). The vow of poverty is often viewed as a form of asceticism, but it is first a demonstration of fidelity to the community, an immersion so total that self-will and self-sufficiency have no place. Merton (2009) observes that "it is a poverty in which proprietorship is renounced in favor of the community (or of the whole Church). The monk becomes poor in order to share whatever earthly goods he may have had with the poor and with the community" (pp. 148–49).

I will mention one final imperative found in Benedict's Rule which fits under the heading of monogamy or faithful love and sacrificial commitment to the other. Though the cloistered nature of monasteries is meant to preserve the sanctity of the monastic vows, especially that of stability, Benedict directs the closed community to receive all guests as if they are Christ (RB 53). Members of the Church and travelers alike are to be welcomed, and monks are instructed to "let Christ be adored in them as He is also received" (St. Benedict 1949, p. 53). The Abbot and the brotherhood are called on to pray for the guests, read them edifying literature, show them every kindness, feed them, and wash their feet. The monk's commitment to the community is chaste but not insular; love and hospitality are meant to flow out of the strength and stability the community has cultivated through bonds of fidelity. This is the dynamic monastic mindset which Chittister speaks of. It echoes the covenant YHWH made with Abraham: to live in the divine blessing so that all the peoples of the earth might benefit from the relationship (Genesis 12:1–3).[10] Fidelity to the community (monogamy) is meant to be fruitful, to produce radical hospitality.

4. The Order of Sustainable Faith

Having traced the presence of singular devotion in an ancient Rule, I turn now to a contemporary Rule: *Invitations and Commitments: A Rule of Life* written by Jared Patrick Boyd in 2014 for the Order of Sustainable Faith. Boyd is part of the Vineyard movement, a charismatic denomination rooted in traditional evangelicalism, which began in 1980 in Southern California. In crafting a monastic Rule, Boyd draws from various ancient traditions (mostly Benedictine and Ignatian) and merges them with Vineyard values and distinctives. Boyd affirms that Benedict's Rule has impacted the *Rule of Life*. In addition, vows of poverty, chastity, and obedience, taken by mendicants and other vowed religious as early as the twelfth century, figure prominently. In reinterpreting each of these commitments, Boyd seeks to honor monastic tradition while reflecting the community's Vineyard context.[11]

A modified approach such as this must be done with care in order to avoid selecting only those parts of ancient traditions which are palatable to modern sensibilities. However, done well, the practice of taking the best and leaving the rest can capture the heart of a tradition in ways which resonate with contemporary culture (Boyd 2014, p. iii). Moore (1998) indicates that this kind of adaptation is common in the monastic tradition: "Just as civil laws can be interpreted strictly or in a relaxed fashion, so the monastic rule is open to fresh consideration and readings. Here again we can see the rule as a pattern or model instead of a literal list of dos and don'ts. It is the embodiment of a vision and a philosophy that is perhaps better lived in the spirit of its origins than as a legal document" (p. xvii). A spiritual practice which is both faithful and creative is imperative to the continued viability of monasticism, whatever form it may take.

---

[10] See also Deuteronomy 6:18–19.
[11] Interview with Jared Patrick Boyd, July 2019.

4.1. Monotheism

Informed by a range of monastic expressions, Boyd (2014) manages to forge a unique yet familiar monastic path for the Order of Sustainable Faith. By classifying the community as both missional and monastic, he seeks to bridge the gap between traditions which are cloistered (such as the Benedictines and Carmelites) and mendicant traditions, whose members move more freely in the world (such as the Jesuits and the Franciscans) (p. 1). As a result, missional language is at the forefront in the opening pages: "The Order of Sustainable Faith is a distinctly monastic expression committed to the work of the Kingdom of God" (Boyd 2014, p. 1).

The Rule is divided into sections which address mission and vision, leadership structures, membership, life rhythms, and commitments expected of its members. Though Boyd notes that for each member of the Order, "there is an invitation to seek after God in the consecrated life" (Boyd 2014, p. 3), direct mention of monotheism is mostly muted in the document. I suspect this is because its target audience is those already committed to some form of Christian spirituality. The most overt mention of undivided loyalty and love to God comes in a call to recognize and surrender disordered desires or attachments in order to enter into God's great love and to journey in God's way (Boyd 2014, p. 29).

Similar to Benedict's insistence on obedience to the Abbot as a way of loving God, Boyd (2014) positions engagement with a Spiritual Director and subjection to a Discerning Community as means of practicing faithful devotion to God (p. 39). Thus, monotheism is articulated not so much as undivided loyalty to Christ, but as a commitment to journey through life with people who assist one another in being attentive to the presence and revelation of God. Boyd (2014) writes: "For every other commitment we are making—be it to align ourselves to this rule of life, or to align ourselves toward something to which the Spirit is leading—spiritual direction will provide a context for conversation and discernment" (p. 28).

Boyd's Rule is deeply influenced by Ignatian spirituality which seeks to find God in all things.[12] Therefore, the Rule includes mostly indirect talk about encountering God: "In prayer, in silence, in work, and in relationship—God is speaking and inviting us into his great love and into his way. The contemplative life is a life that is listening" (Boyd 2014, p. 29).

The language of contemplation and action roughly equates to loving God and loving neighbor, but the line between the two is rather fuzzy in Boyd's Rule. Though there is little overt reference to monotheism, the practices hint at an undivided devotion to God which underlies all the community's commitments. For example, it is noted that each member "should think of his or her possessions as belonging to the Lord" (Boyd 2014, p. 40). In a section on hospitality, Boyd (2014) echoes Benedict's directives toward visitors when he asks, "Where do I see the face of Christ in the needs of others?" (p. 43).

The clearest statement of monotheism comes at the very end of the document when Boyd articulates the Order's relationship with the Vineyard movement. Not surprisingly, it is immediately followed by a reference to mission. For Boyd, contemplation is always linked to action. A commitment to the theology and practice of the kingdom of God is a core value of the Vineyard. Thus, the Order of Sustainable Faith also cites this as a guiding premise. "We view the kingdom of God (God's rule and reign with Jesus as King) as the overarching and integrating theme throughout the Bible. God's mission to the world (*missio dei*) is also our mission to the world. We join God in the work of nurturing life in this world, partnering with God to bring all things under the rule and reign of Jesus" (Boyd 2014, p. 46).

4.2. Monogamy

I have already noted that it is difficult to precisely separate devotion to God from devotion to the community in Boyd's Rule for the Order of Sustainable Faith. I believe this is intentional, a deliberate effort to confront the ubiquitous individualism and self-determination of our age. Boyd clearly views a

---

12 Ignatius of Loyola (1491–1556) sought to cultivate a life of Christlikeness through the use of spiritual exercises, self-examination, and reflecting on the life of Christ.

commitment to stable, communal life as the means by which one practices devotion to God. In a world where people are increasingly mobile, many new monastic expressions place significant value on stability, making it one of the primary markers of love of neighbor (monogamy). Jonathan Wilson-Hartgrove (2010), co-founder of Rutba House, an intentional Christian community in Durham, North Carolina, states: "If we really want to make a difference, stability's wisdom says to our ambition, we must learn what it means for each of us to do the knitting of life together with God's people" (p. 115).

Fidelity to a particular community and place reflect the monastic belief that Christ is present in every person and God can be found in all things. Wilson-Hartgrove (2010) observes: "Careful attention to the mundane tasks of daily life is the process by which we exorcise ambition and grow in love" (p. 115). In Boyd's rule, just as in Benedict's, much space is dedicated to articulating the details of community, leadership, and rhythms of life. The section called Commitments includes the traditional monastic vows of poverty, chastity, and obedience. Boyd reframes them for a contemporary context: poverty is interpreted as an invitation to greater simplicity with regard to clothing, food, possessions, and technology, as well as participation in a shared economy (pp. 30–34). Chastity is viewed as sexual expression with one person or consecrated celibacy (pp. 35–37).[13] Obedience is associated with humility and vulnerability as part of a discerning community. Boyd invites members to ask: "Do I trust my community? Do I trust that God can speak in a significant way through others?" (p. 37).

The section on Commitments includes other subjects such as shared work, shared economy, hospitality, restorative peacemaking, and the expression of faults and admirations (a communal form of confession). One substantial difference between traditional monasticism and most forms of new monasticism is the inclusion of married couples and families in the community. For new monastics, celibacy is not seen as the ultimate expression of devotion to God. Instead, marriage is celebrated as a means of experiencing divine fidelity and love. Boyd writes: "For those whom God has invited into a marriage relationship, it is also a place where God's grace and Spirit are working. In marriage, one is committed to another, as an expression and demonstration of Christ's love for the church as well as an expression of love and companionship" (p. 36).

Boyd's articulation of the undivided, monogamous life focuses on mutual submission, mutual love, mutual commitment, mutual sacrifice, and mutual mission (p. 48). It is a constant turning toward the other, day after day, in good times and in bad, in order to knit a life together.

5. Analysis

The governing documents of the monastery at Monte Cassino and the Order of Sustainable Faith represent the breadth of monastic expression within the Christian tradition. In them, we find evidence of the undivided life, the *mono* in monasticism, in two positive fidelities: monotheism (love of God) and monogamy (love of neighbor). Both Rules incorporate commitments to obedience, to stability, and to aspects of poverty and chastity. For Benedict, poverty is the renunciation of all earthly possessions. For Boyd, poverty is reflected in the choice to forgo self-sufficiency and self-will by stepping away from consumerism and sexual gratification. Benedict calls the monks to love God through submission to the Abbot and through striving for humility. Boyd's call to monotheism is more indirect, inviting members of the order to practice their devotion to God through participation in the mission of God (kingdom of God).

In Benedict's Rule, obedience stands at the forefront of one's commitment to the monastic community. In Boyd's rule, mutuality is a recurring theme. In Benedict's Rule, the language is characterized by compulsion and command. In the contemporary rule, the language is much more invitational (Boyd 2014, p. 27). Each commitment listed in Boyd's document includes questions for the reader to consider, an invitation for members to engage with the Rule as a conversation partner.

---

[13] Interview with Boyd, July 2019.

One of the main differences between the two Rules is the leadership structure. Benedict follows a more hierarchical model where decision-making, confession, and discipline fall under the purview of the Abbot. Boyd reflects a more flattened, shared approach to leadership. The language of "we" permeates Boyd's Rule, and the posture is relational. The community acts as the discerning body, and members submit themselves to the guidance of a spiritual director.

The impact of Benedict's Rule is evident in Boyd's governing document, especially in three areas: (1) the membership process requires that one spend time as a novice and a postulant before being received as a full member of the community, (2) the rhythm of the community includes prayer, work, study, and rest, and (3) the commitments of community members highlight a shared life characterized by contemplation and action.

6. Conclusions

The *Rule of Benedict* and the *Rule of Life* for the Order of Sustainable Faith were written over fifteen hundred years apart. The cultural differences are obvious, yet important similarities bind them together across centuries and traditions, specifically, the call to love God and love neighbor in an intentional, communal, counter-cultural way.

For the most part, new monastic expressions seek to use the gifts of traditional monasticism, such as the *Rule of Benedict*, in such a way that they are, as Joan Chittister says, "recycled for centuries." Intentional communities such as Wilson-Hartgrove's Rutba House and Boyd's Order of Sustainable Faith have sought to embrace ancient monasticism as a "template for spirituality" (Chittister 2015). The form may change. The structures of the communities may vary. The specifics of the Rules may differ, but at the heart of these various expressions of Christian monasticism, we find a commitment to the undivided life: a devotion to one God and to one community; monotheism and monogamy. This is the positive posture of monasticism, a stance which should serve it well for another fifteen hundred years.

Funding: This research received no external funding.

Conflicts of Interest: The author declares no conflict of interest.

References

Alter, Robert. 2004. *The Five Books of Moses: A Translation with Commentary*. New York: W.W. Norton & Co.
Bilinkoff, Jodi. 1989. *The Avila of Saint Teresa: Religious Reform in a Sixteenth-Century City*. Ithaca: Cornell University Press.
Boyd, Jared Patrick. 2014. *Invitations & Commitments: A Rule of Life*. Columbus: The Order of Sustainable Faith.
Chittister, Joan OSB. 2015. Interview. "Sr. Joan Chittister Talks About St. Benedict". Meditation and Spirituality at Wisdom Center. Available online: https://www.youtube.com/watch?v=_agXGmezOzE (accessed on 16 August 2019).
Claiborne, Shane. 2006. *Irresistible Revolution: Living as an Ordinary Radical*. Grand Rapids: Zondervan.
Dunn, Marilyn. 2003. *The Emergence of Monasticism: From the Desert Fathers to the Early Middle Ages*. Malden: Blackwell Publishers.
Gregory the Great. 1911. *Dialogues*. Translated by Philip Warner. London: Philip Lee Warner.
Lawrence, Philip. n.d. OSB, Abbot of Christ in the Desert. Commentary on *Rule of St. Benedict*. Prologue, verses 8–14. Available online: https://christdesert.org/prayer/rule-of-st-benedict/prologue-verse-8-14/ (accessed on 16 August 2019).
McAfee, Martha. 2008. "New Monasticism: It's New, but is it Monastic?". Paper presented at the Annual Meeting of the American Academy of Religion, Chicago, IL, USA, October 31–November 3.
Merton, Thomas. 1949. *The Waters of Siloe*. New York: Harcourt, Brace.
Merton, Thomas. 2009. *The Rule of Saint Benedict: Initiation into the Monastic Tradition 4*. Collegeville: Liturgical Press.
Moore, Thomas. 1998. "Preface.". In *The Rule of St. Benedict*. Vintage Spiritual Classics. Collegeville: The Order of St. Benedict, pp. xv–xxv.
Okholm, Dennis. 2001. "Benedict of Nursia (480–547)". In *Dictionary of Christian Spirituality*. Edited by Glen G. Scorgie. Grand Rapids: Zondervan, pp. 301–2.
Rutba, House, ed. 2005. *School(s) for Conversion: 12 Marks of a New Monasticism*. Eugene: Cascade Books.

Sheldrake, Philip. 2007. *A Brief History of Spirituality*. Malden: Blackwell Publishing.

St. Benedict. 1949. *The Holy Rule of St. Benedict*. Translated by Rev. Boniface Verheyen. OSB of St. Benedict's Abbey. Available online: http://www.ccel.org/ccel/benedict/rule.html (accessed on 16 August 2019).

St. Benedict. 1998. *The Rule of St. Benedict*. Vintage Spiritual Classics. Collegeville: The Order of St. Benedict.

Stock, Jon, Tim Otto, and Jonathan Wilson-Hartgrove. 2007. *Inhabiting the Church: Biblical Wisdom for a New Monasticism*. Eugene: Cascade Books.

von Balthasar, Hans Urs. 1990. *Theo-Drama: Theological Dramatic Theory, vol. 2, Dramatic Personae: Man in God*. Translated by Graham Harrison. San Francisco: Ignatius Press.

Ware, Kallistos. 1998. "The Way of the Ascetics: Negative or Affirmative?". In *Asceticism*. Edited by Vincent L. Wimbush and Richard Valantasis. Oxford: Oxford University Press, pp. 3–15.

Wilson-Hartgrove, Jonathan. 2010. *The Wisdom of Stability: Rooting Faith in Mobile Culture*. Brewster: Paraclete Press.

religions

MDPI

Article

Future of Catholic Monasteries on New Monastic Continents: The Case of Africa

Isabelle Jonveaux

Institute of Religious Studies, University of Graz, 8020 Graz, Austria; isabelle.jonveaux@uni-graz.at

Received: 4 July 2019; Accepted: 31 August 2019; Published: 4 September 2019

Abstract: Catholic monasticism in Europe is often associated with a crisis of vocations, of credibility and sometimes the question of closing down. Looking at monasteries outside Europe, especially in Asia and Africa, we observe a dynamic of new foundations and young entrants into the communities. What are the challenges for monasteries in Africa in future decades? To what extent does monasticism experience a gravitational shift from Europe to other continents in the next thirty years? This article seeks to explore the challenges of African monastic communities now and in the future. The first part gives some demographic data which shows the dynamism of African monastic communities. The second part deals with the adaption of monastic life in the local environment; for instance, concerning the liturgy but also the role of the development of monastic communities. In the last part, I discuss the challenges of African monasticism, which is becoming autonomous from its European founders and developing more and more indigenous foundations. This article is based on field inquiries conducted in monastic communities in five countries in Africa between 2013 and 2019.

Keywords: Catholic monasticism; Africa; cultural transfer; development

1. Introduction

Monasticism in Europe is often associated with a crisis of vocations, of credibility and sometimes the question of closing down. Demographical statistics of congregations show a high average age with a significant proportion being over 70 and a low rate of new members joining. A monk in Belgium, whom I met in 2008 during a field inquiry, spoke about the end of monasticism and, in another community, a plan B for the moment when the community will be too small to live in the big building. Will Catholic monasticism die? Indeed, according to the Alliance Inter Monastique, we can count 68 closures of monasteries in Europe between 2000 and 2014. This apocalyptic description has nevertheless to be moderated, taking into account the 41 new foundations in Europe in the same period and the dynamism of some new monastic communities (Palmisano 2015).

Studying Catholic monasticism, it is important to take a look at monasteries outside Europe. Today, Roman Catholic monasticism exists in all countries where Catholicism is widespread, even if it is officially forbidden, such as in China. The Order of Saint Benedict (OSB) catalogue lists 1185 Benedictine communities spread across 80 countries. Trappists include 102 male and 76 female monasteries[1]. Looking at monasteries outside of Europe, a different situation presents itself. For instance, in Asia or Africa, vocations do not appear to constitute a problem.

Will Catholic monasticism experience a gravitational shift from Europe to other continents within the context of religious modernity? Demographic statistics of communities and foundations seem to be particularly dynamic in Africa, where monastic life is still new. Actually, Roman Catholic monastic life has its origin in the monasticism of the deserts of Syria and Egypt during the first centuries of our

---

[1] For 2015. http://www.ocso.org/monasteres/current-statistics/?lang=fr.

era. The institutionalization of monastic life in regulated communities began with Pachomius († 346) in Egypt and the redaction of his rule (Cousin 1956). As Casier notes, "we must not forget that eremitic life and monasticism, during the first centuries of Christianity, took place in Africa, and more especially in Egypt. Saint Augustine, an African too, was one of the pillars of monasticism" (Casier 1974, p. 137). But the institutionalization of the present form of Roman Catholic monasticism occurred effectively in Europe during the sixth century with the Rule of Benedict in Italy, which spread rapidly. Charlemagne imposed the Rule of Benedict for all monasteries of the empire, and also for nuns (Hasquenoph 2009, p. 458). In this sense, the long history of European Catholic monasticism left its mark on Catholic monasticism itself.

The evangelization of sub-Saharan Africa in its present form occurred especially in the nineteenth century but the Catholic Church remains very young in many of these countries. If we take countries I especially deal with in this article, we observe different religious situations. Senegal is predominantly Muslim with 94% Muslim and only 4% Roman Catholic. In Togo and Benin, approximately 30% of the population is Christian and traditional religions are still practiced by a majority of people. The first diocese was founded in 1892 in Togo and, in 1883, in Benin. But north Benin, where I studied two monasteries (in the region of Parakou), has been evangelized for less than 80 years. This means that the first generation which was evangelized is still alive and presents priests, nuns and monks who often come from families who converted to Catholicism or where the parents belonged to a traditional religion. The diocese of Parakou was founded in 1948. At last, the predominant religion in Kenya is Christianity (85%), with 23% of Christians identifying as Catholic. The religious situation of a country is important to take into account in order to better understand the challenges for a community to accept, in the local environment, the role of monastics for the acculturation of the Catholic religion.

This article endeavors to explore monastic life outside of Europe in newly founded communities in Africa. What is the future of these new foundations in Africa? What are the present challenges, so that they manage to build a monastic tradition in Africa? To what extent do the monastic dynamics in Africa renew the monastic charisma, compared to Europe?

Inquiry

So far, I have studied contemporary Catholic monastic life in seven countries in Europe, Argentina, and five countries in Africa, but I will focus here on African monasticism. This article is based on multilocal empiric inquiries with half-structured interviews and participant observations in Catholic monasteries in Togo, Kenya, Burkina Faso, Senegal and Benin. Field inquiries were carried out between 2013 and 2019, mainly in 12 communities from the Benedictine and Trappist orders. I conducted 50 interviews with monks, nuns, abbots and abbesses of these communities. Within the scope of my field inquiries outside Europe, I limited the focus to monasteries under the Rule of Benedict in order to investigate specific phenomena within a particular socio-cultural context and the cultural transfers thereof. The Benedictine family can be seen as a representative example for such research as it is the most widespread monastic rule worldwide for Roman Catholic monasteries and includes both male and female communities. It comprises three main orders: Benedictine, Cistercian and Trappist. Here, I will especially use interviews of field inquiries in six monasteries:

- The monastery of Agbang, belonging to the Benedictine Congregation of Saint Ottilien, was founded by a local monk, Father Boniface Tiguila in 1985. I spent more than two weeks there for a field inquiry in April 2013. I conducted six interviews and ethnographical participant observation.
- Our Lady of Mount Kenya, a Benedictine priory of the Congregation of Saint Ottilien, founded in 1979 by German monks, where four monks live. I visited in March 2014.
- The Benedictine abbey of Keur Moussa, founded by the French abbey of Solesmes in 1962. I conducted two field inquiries: the first in July 2016, when I conducted nine interviews; and the second, in cooperation with Dr. Muhammad Bâ (University of Saint Louis, Senegal), in March 2017, when we conducted six interviews.

-    My last inquiry in March 2019 included three monasteries in Benin: the female Benedictine monastery of Toffo, founded by the French monastery of Saint Bathildes of Vanves in 1966 (four interviews); the male Trappist monastery of Kokoubou, founded by the French abbey of Bellefontaine in 1972 (four interviews); and the female Trappist monastery of L'Etoile Parakou, founded by the French abbey of Notre-Dame des Gardes in 1960 (nine interviews).

2. From a Statistical Point of View

2.1. Demographic Shifts in European Communities

For demography in Europe, the main question concerns the future of monasticism, which actually hides other challenges of present monastic life (Jonveaux 2018b, p. 121). If we consider demographic statistics for Western Europe, we observe that communities often have a high average age and a low rate of entrants. For instance, in the Benedictine Congregation of Subiaco in France in 2014, four of the five female communities and four of the seven male communities have an average age over 70. This naturally has consequences about the dynamic of community life and economy, for instance, but also about the form(s) of asceticism (Jonveaux 2018a, p. 80). For Italy, where the number of nuns and monks is the highest in Europe, Giovanni Dal Piaz identifies a radical decline in the last fifty years: "The number of cloistered nuns has decreased from 12.863 to 5.828 by 2011, a decline of 55%" (Dal Piaz 2014, p. 40). Concerning the rate of entry, I could calculate for the monastery of Kremsmünster in Austria that the community had on average two stable entrants each year in the 1950s, then one stable entrant in the 1960s and 1970s and 0.5 each year since the 1980s. Bernhard Eckerstorfer, a monk of this abbey, notes: "In my own abbey of Kremsmünster, during the last decade, more monks have left than have entered and remained. We are now fifty-six, while thirty years ago we were over ninety." (Eckerstorfer 2013, p. 527)

Linked to this demographic evolution, a new phenomenon can be observed—long-established European communities no longer send members to their foundations abroad but call members of these foundations home to overcome the reduction and the ageing of their community. Dal Piaz noticed for female monasteries in Italy that "forty-two percent of cloistered communities currently include foreigners" (Dal Piaz 2014, p. 43). Especially for nuns between 20 and 29 years old, 60.2% are foreigners (Dal Piaz 2014, p. 43).

If we compare this with other continents, we note younger average ages for Asia and Africa for many communities and a high rate of entry. I could not create statistics for the population of the Benedictine order as a whole, but the communities of the Benedictine Congregation of the Annunciation can serve as an example[2]. The average age in communities in Africa is 42 and almost 40 in Asia. Compared to Europe (62), this is very low. The minimum age is lower in Asia (19) and Africa (21), which indicates that people enter monastic life at a younger age than in Europe (23). The maximum age is also lower in Africa (77) due to the general life expectancy being lower than in Europe (95). According to the 2004 OSB Catalogue, the Benedictine monastic population is still concentrated in Europe as 55% of Benedictine monasteries are in Europe, 9% in Africa and 11% in Asia. But the lower average age and higher numbers of new members in Asia and Africa predict a *coeteris paribus*, a shift in global monastic dynamics in future decades.

2.2. Dynamic of Foundations

It would be wrong to consider that Christian monasticism is a totally novel import of the nineteenth and twentieth century in sub-Saharan Africa. According to the legend of the Nine Saints, native monasticism in Ethiopia emerged in the fourteenth century as introduced by Orthodox Christian

---

2   These statistics are based on official catalogues of orders and/or congregations. Each Benedictine congregation has a list of communities and members, including date of birth, of entry, profession, etc.

monks. The biggest monastery was founded in the fourteenth century in the forest of Waldebba and still counts over a thousand monks today. Nevertheless, concerning Catholic monasticism, the first monasteries were founded by German monks of the Congregation of Saint Ottilien in Tanzania at the end of the nineteenth century. In 1887, the Holy See had asked the Congregation of Saint Ottilien to evangelize East Africa. In other parts of Africa, especially in West Africa, a new wave of foundations appeared in the 1960s after the encyclical *Fidei Donum* (1957) was published, in which Pope Pius XII urgently called people to the missions in Africa (Zorn 1994, p. 57). Monastic foundations in Western Africa were often the result of a request of the local bishop and the possibility for a community or the project of one community to found a new community. One condition is that the founding community has enough members to send to the foundation. For instance, the foundation of the Benedictine monastery of Keur Moussa in Senegal was founded at the request of the bishop of Dakar, who was at the time Monseigneur Lebfevre. The foundation of the female Benedictine monastery of Toffo in South Benin was called for by Bishop Gantin (who was made a cardinal in 1977), as he was native to this region. The aim of the bishops is often to establish a contemplative monastic presence in their diocese. A French sister of the monastery of L'Ecoute Pèporiyakou, the second to last monastery founded in Western Africa, explains: "The idea of Mgr Pascal, when he called us, was to have a monastery in his diocese. It was one of his three objectives when he was appointed bishop, to have a monastery, a diocesan Marian center and to initiate work for a new cathedral." (03.2019).

As illustrated in Figure 1, according to the statistics from the Alliance Intermonastique (AIM), foundations of Roman Catholic monasteries in Asia and Africa are a fairly recent phenomenon:

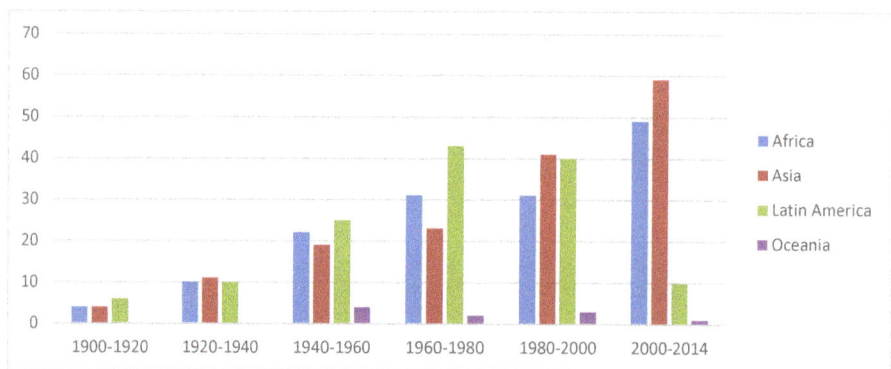

Figure 1. New foundations 1990–2014. Martin Ney, 2000, Geraldo Gonzales y Lima, AIM, 2014.

We can see here that there were 49 new foundations in Africa in the last period—the second continent with the most foundations after Asia.

3. How to Adapt Monastic Life in Another Culture

3.1. To Build Monasticism in a New Cultural Context

Following Jean Séguy, we consider the monastery as a utopia which he defines as "a complete ideological system aiming to transform radically the existing global system implicitly or explicitly, by appealing to an imaginary vision of the world or by applying it in practice" (Séguy 2014, p. 288). A utopia inevitably exists in a state of tension, as it tries to embody the eschatological, which has not yet happened, in the present. Monasteries are confronted with the "fatal dilemma of each utopia" (Hervieu-Léger 2017, p. 232). Practiced utopia is never stable and needs to justify itself with respect to written utopia and society. Justification to society refers to its plausibility. Thus, a utopia is in a constant renegotiation of compromises between the real world and the ideal model. These negotiations can be observed in particular in the case of foundations or re-foundations, as monasteries need to justify themselves with regard to existing monasticism and establish their plausibility within society. In this respect, newly founded monasteries during the first charismatic period or the routinization period serve as laboratories to examine the creation of a utopia and its integration into society.

African monasticism was established in a context where monastic life was, most of the time, not known, whereas apostolic religious life was present in the public space. A lot of these congregations came with European colonization and developed social engagements like schools and a dispensary. When they arrived in a region, monks and nuns are often considered by the local population as apostolic brothers and sisters from whom they awaited social activity. Father Catta, one of the first monks of Keur Moussa in Senegal, explains that they had to affirm at the beginning: "we are not missionaries, we are contemplative monks" (Interview 07.2016). The first challenge of monastic life is, therefore, to establish the specificity of monasticism.

Monastic communities in Africa are, therefore, confronted with the question of constructing a monastic utopia. The main challenge for monastic life is to distinguish itself from the apostolic religious. It is a characteristic of monasticism to be, according to Max Weber, "out of the world" (Weber 1972), so as not to be active for the world. In other words, monastic life has to affirm its contemplative dimension and its "usefulness" (Merton 1975, p. 23). When they arrive, monks and nuns often have to answer to a local demand for social needs, even if they consider that it is not their vocation. As a monk of Keur Moussa said in an interview: "Women came to the monastery to find help for a birth, and the monks had to do it although it is not a mission of a monk to do it!" (Interview 07.2016). Similarly, in the Benedictine monastery of Toffo in Benin, a French nun who was sent to the community two years after the foundation, in 1968, explains: "It was not our vocation, but it was a necessity" (Interview 03.2019). Another sister of the same community explains:

> They began [to have social activities] but they said, over time, it will be forgotten, or it will be said that we are not here for something else. To want to live a monastic life. It will be said, they never were like that, it will not be understood by the new generations. So, we have to get it right from the start. They asked the cardinal to bring a religious community to the parish. They also built the church in the parish. […] Otherwise, at the end, people will come to the monastery and no longer to the parish. It will be ambiguous. So they have wished clarity from the beginning. […] And they managed to do it. […] For first aid, it was clarified since the beginning. There are communities, which had to open a dispensary. And they are no longer able to cut it. Our sisters did the transition well. (Interview 03.2019)

In the female Trappist monastery of L'Etoile Parakou in North Benin, the situation was different. Three monks of the same congregation were sent one year before, in 1959, in order to build the monastery before the nuns came. A French nun who came in 1962 explains: "The first nuns arrived the first Advent Sunday in 1960. They could start monastic life right away, the very next day, correctly because they found all the buildings. […] They found a chapel, a refectory and places to sleep." (Interview 03.2019) However, at the beginning, they had a small dispensary, which was developed into a real hospital, but which was transferred to the next city as it became bigger. The sister says, "We called a male nurse, so that we do not need to work in the dispensary so that the monastery stays a monastery, without confusion in the mind."

Another challenge in the construction of a utopia is acceptance in the local environment. Monasticism has not, as a first goal, to be a part of society but to contest some dimensions of present society and to build itself as different. Nevertheless, a monastery has to be accepted to limit the tensions with the surrounding area. Conflicts with the local population sometimes happen, especially land disputes. This was the case of the Trappist monastery of Our Lady of Victoria in Kenya[3], which had

---

3 I met a monk of this community, in 2014, at the Benedictine student house in Nairobi.

to move to Uganda in 2008 because of violent tensions with the local population. Koudbi Kaboré[4] observed the same kind of tensions for the monastery of Diabo and Anne Diah for the monastery of Bafor, both in Burkina Faso, when the sisters tried to extend their land. Monastic utopia has, therefore, a geographical dimension, which can conflict with the non-utopian space.

3.2. Cultural Transfers to Root Monasticism in the Local Environment

The development of monasticism in Africa is only possible if monasticism is permanently anchored in the local culture and environment. Monasteries in Africa have often been initially founded by European communities. If we consider African monasteries listed on the homepage of the AIM, the majority were founded by European communities from 10 different countries, especially France and Belgium (20 each) in their ancient colonies. The founders brought their way of life and culture as well as the monastic model of their respective country with them. At the beginning, monasteries were not always open to local novices. In Tanzania, the first monastery founded by the Congregation of Saint Ottilien in 1898, Peramiho, only started to accept African monks into their community in the 1980s (Tiguila 2011). Cultural transfers to adapt monastic life in the local context are nevertheless necessary to embed monastic life in the African context, when the founder communities from Europe no longer send monks to the foundations.

I choose here not to use the term "acculturation," as this notion can be ambiguous due to its having been developed in Europe in the context of decolonization. At the same time, the Church developed the emic concept of "inculturation", which considers traditional religions as a preparatory precursor for Christianity (Metogo 1985), and which, therefore, takes place in a context of domination. This is the term nuns and monks use in the interviews. The concept of cultural transfer is used herein, as it does not consider each cultural space as inherent, but as a product of previous hybridizations and mutations (Espagne 2013, p. 3). It is necessary to consider that the confrontation between two cultures is a process, not a result (Ripert 2010, p. 9).

It is not possible here to describe all dimensions of cultural transfers in monastic life, but I will focus on the question of liturgy. Liturgy is one of the dimensions of monastic life where we can observe cultural transfers with the most intensity. Monastic communities which were founded at the beginning of the 1960s came to Africa with their own liturgy, so did the Latin language and Gregorian chant as it was also in Europe at this time. As Father Catta of Keur Moussa in Senegal explains it in an interview (07.2016), it was not the aim at the beginning to change the liturgy. Latin and the Gregorian chant were considered the monastic liturgy for the whole Catholic Church. But the Second Vatican Council opened the door first to use vernacular languages and second to adapt the liturgy to the local culture, so to the African culture. The Abbey of Keur Moussa, which was founded by the French abbey of Solesmes in 1963, is the most well-known example of the adaptation of Gregorian liturgy in West African culture (see Sarr 2013, 2015). The abbey of Solesmes is itself famous in France for its Gregorian liturgy, which was reintroduced by Dom Guéranger, founder of the monastery, at the end of the nineteenth century. After the publication of the documents of the council encouraging the adaptation of the liturgy to the local culture, the abbot of Solesmes asked a monk of Keur Moussa, Father Dominique Catta, to carry out the work of the adaption of the monastic liturgy in the African culture. He travelled through different countries of West Africa and collected melodies of traditional music, which he combined when composing the tones for the psalms. According to him, this adaptation was possible because there is a connection between Gregorian music and traditional African music. The monks of Keur Moussa also developed and improved a traditional instrument, the kora, which they started to make in the monastery as one of their main economic activities. The kora is a Mandinka harp with

---

[4] Koudbi Kaboré, University of Ouagadougou I, and Anne Diah, University of Bobo, took part in the project "Contemplation and social engagement of monasteries in Western Africa". Dr. Katrin Langewiesche, project leader, invited me twice to Ouagadougou for a workshop with the students and asked me to accompany the students in their research.

21 strings, which is made of a half calabash covered with a cow skin and a long neck of *vène* wood. It was traditionally played by men for religious ceremonies. This liturgy has become widespread in the whole of West Africa as I could observe it during my inquiries in Togo, Benin and Burkina Faso. It does not mean that these monasteries adopt the liturgy as a whole but they are taking some elements, especially the use of the kora of Keur Moussa. As the monks and nuns explained to me in Benin this year, they could have sessions to learn the kora either with a monk of Keur Moussa who came to Benin or by going to Senegal themselves.

Yet we have to note that this work of the adaptation of the liturgy was not carried out by a local monk but by a French monk. As Father Catta died in August 2018, the question arises as to whether there will soon be a second wave of adaptation led by local monks. Indeed, young monks of Keur Moussa told me that they think it would be important to have more songs in local languages and to further include local adaptations. Kabasele Lumbala underlines that the conception of "inculturation" by the Catholic Church itself "consists in giving the initiative to the Africans people" (Lumbala 2011, p. 433). An association to reflect on acculturation in monastic life was founded in Togo and the Ivory Coast with the help of the ethnologist Clémentine Madiya Faik-Nzuji (UCL): Association Monastique de Réflexion sur les Symbolismes dans les Cultures Africaines. This association works on the composition of liturgical texts and music, the translation of spiritual texts into local languages and the integration of religious life into the African traditions (Adom 2001, p. 29). Parallel to this, the network Répertoire Monastique d'Afrique de l'Ouest (REMONAF) for work on the liturgy has been developed in Togo, the Ivory Coast, Benin and Burkina Faso. With the help of a French music teacher, communities work on the cultural adaptation of their liturgy by composing new songs in French with local music intonations. This work is, therefore, an ongoing process, especially concerning the local languages when the monastery is located in a context with a lot of local languages. As there are more than 70 languages in North Benin, the common language of the liturgy in the monasteries is French. In the Trappist monastery of Kokoubou, none of the monks come from the ethnic group where the monastery is situated. According to a monk of this monastery, the challenge for the adaption of the liturgy in future decades is the language. He says, "we like to speak French, but it is not our mother language. [...] So we have this concern that our liturgy becomes really enculturated" (Interview 03.2019).

Socio-cultural transfer not only happens in a single direction but can be a two-way exchange. Indeed, more and more monasteries in Europe are using the kora of Keur Moussa for their liturgy and some communities in France are also using the liturgy of the African monastery in order to renew and give a new dynamic to their liturgy. In addition, more koras of Keur Moussa were sold in Europe (942 until 2014) than in Africa (899).

3.3. Monasteries as Actors of Development

Monastic life in Africa plays an important role in the development of its region, as we can observe it in the long history of monasticism on other continents; for instance, in Europe in the Middle Ages (see Schmitz 1949). In developing countries, monastic communities often have to meet the demands of society regarding education and healthcare.

Monasteries from the Benedictine family have in their tradition developed, in and around the monasteries, the kinds of activities that can provide for the subsistence of the community. For a new foundation in Africa, it often means at the beginning that monks and nuns will develop the possibilities of agriculture. For instance, the motto of the abbey of Keur Moussa in Senegal is, "And the desert will start flowering" (Isaiah 35:1), and indeed they transformed the desert in which they are in into arable lands, introducing also a lot of new species to this environment. The employment of local salaried workers also contributes to local development, giving work to people around the community. It also helps to integrate the monastery into its environment. For a Kenyan Benedictine monk of Our Lady of Mount Kenya, the employment of local people is the main dimension of their development activity. The formation of monks and nuns is another part of direct development, which is also necessary for monastic life. As Katrin Langewiesche notes for female monasteries in Burkina Faso: "It is very difficult to make the monastic lifestyle understandable and clear for young girls if they have no school education" (Langewiesche 2017, p. 68).

Civil society also becomes interested in the role of the development of monasteries. For instance, in Senegal, the president of the Republic, who is himself Muslim, showed interest in cooperating with the Benedictine monastery to further the development of the country. He gave a solar dryer he received as a gift from the president of Thailand to the monastery, as he thought the monastery was the best place for it. Katrin Langewiesche also notes for the female monastery of Koubri in Burkina Faso where NGOs have begun to support some activities of the monastery: "[...] International organizations like the World Bank and small NGOs have identified the potential of the monasteries as catalysts for economic development, and support monastic projects in the area of sustainable development, food self-sufficiency, and the protection of biodiversity. For example, Koubri received support from an international program (Global Environment Facility (GEF), United Nations Development Program (UNDP) and United Nations Office for Projects Services (UNOPS)) for the conservation of biodiversity." (Langewiesche 2015, p. 139)

Contrary to an apostolic congregation, such social development is not included in the definition of monastic life, but even monasteries are not acting directly for the development it "comes with," as the abbot of Keur Moussa put it. It is, therefore, a positive external force which changes the social and economic environment of the monastery. However, some monasteries have a direct action plan for development. Speaking about his monastery in Uganda, Father Isaac, whom I met in Nairobi in the Benedictine Student House, explains:

> The activities of the monastery, they have a school. The orientation wants to bring basic human development on the background of agriculture and schools and medical services. So you open a school to train them to do something for themselves so that they can come and get the skill, maybe of building, carpentry; maybe repairing bicycles or motor vehicles, then they go and establish themselves to do something on their own. [...] So these were the basic projects which started to bring basic human development, which helps people who did not go high in their academic levels to at least find a way of living well, to establish themselves. (Interview 03.2014)

According to the charisma of the community, this development activity can be more or less direct, but a monastery is always a center of development and improvement of life conditions for the surrounding populations. For instance, in all monasteries I visited in Togo and Benin, Peul people around the monastery come to charge their mobile phone in the monastery as they have no electricity in the bush and communities let them dig wells for safe drinking water near the camps.

4. Challenges for African Monasticism in Future Decades

Despite the apparent dynamism of its communities, African monasticism is presently confronted with diverse challenges which will decide whether this monasticism can really take root in this continent in future decades. The statistics of the new foundations given above do not occlude the closing down of other houses. According to AIM[5], 49 communities were founded in Africa between 2000 and 2014, and 12 were closed. These were often mission houses. This means that the social role of monasteries is changing in these countries and that a new foundation does not necessarily mean that it will stay and develop itself. In fact, not all foundations in Africa manage to live longer than thirty years.

4.1. Turning Point of African Communities

Nowadays, African communities are at a turning point. They are progressively moving away from European influences and are founding their own communities. European people who came to

---

5   http://www.aimintl.org/fr/2015-05-29-13-29-48/2015-06-23-12-55-30/fondations-fermetures.

found these communities will no longer be seen in the communities either because they returned to Europe for health reasons or because they passed away. In addition, European communities no longer send members to Africa because they are already too small and too old.

The fact that African communities, which were founded by European communities, will soon have no European members has at least two important consequences. The first concerns continuity. European founders assured the continuity of monastic tradition between the "mother abbey" and the "daughter community" in the long "chain of memory"[6]. According to Delpal, unlike the Church, monasticism cannot base itself on a divine foundation and requires a tradition to establish its legitimacy (Delpal 1998). In this process of evolution from the "mother abbey" to the "daughter abbey", which in turn also founds new communities in their respective or neighboring countries, the question of which processes are faithful and which break with tradition arises. During my field inquiry in Argentina in 2015, I observed that monasteries, such as Niño Dios (Entre Rios), adapted the Gregorian Latin liturgy in the last decade to affirm their affiliation with traditional European monasticism. I could note the same situation in the female Trappist monastery of L'Etoile in North Benin, which began to use again Latin in the liturgy. For the nuns, it is a sign to integrate their community into the monastic tradition. On the other side, the whole Africanization of the communities give them the opportunity to carry out a second step of the adaptation process, which is no longer performed by European monastics but by the African monastics themselves. Now almost all communities in West Africa have a local abbot or abbess. A French Benedictine sister of Notre Dame de l'Ecoute in Benin, the second to last monastery founded in West Africa, explained that there are only two European people at the meeting of the masters of novices for West Africa. The situation can be yet different between male and female monasteries. Field research in Kenya in 2014 showed that male monasteries of the Benedictine congregation of Saint Ottilien are led by an African monk, while the female community from the congregation of Tützing in Nairobi has no African nuns in positions of responsibility. The prior comes from the USA, the master of novices from Germany and the cellerer from China.

The second consequence is economic. In France, monks and nuns have to pay for social security contributions and they then receive a pension. African communities which were founded by French communities still benefit from these pensions either because some French monastics are still in the community or because monastics who returned back to France still send their pension to the communities. Compared to the local buying power, these pensions are an important part of incomes for a community. For instance, in the Benedictine female monastery of Toffo in Benin, the pensions represent 36.9% of all the revenue of the community in 2015. It is the same in the Trappist male community of Kokoubou, also in Benin, where the pensions are the first source of income, accounting for 38.9% of the revenue. They come from four French monks, one of whom is now in France[7]. This means that these communities have the urgent need to find new sources of incomes in order to replace the pensions in the near future, ideally before the French monks die. The economy of African monasteries has also to find new ways of development as some activities were initiated by European monks and nuns with their own conception of a monastic economy. Studying different countries in Europe, I observe that monastic economy is directly influenced by the political and religious history of individual countries (Jonveaux 2011, 2018b). This means that European communities often brought their monastic economic model to Africa. For instance, all monasteries I visited in Benin are producing jam, whereas this product does not belong to the local culture and is purchased only by rich people. This turning point will, therefore, also mean a development of new forms of activities for African communities.

---

[6] I refer here to the title of the book of Danièle Hervieu-Léger: Religion as a chain of memory (Hervieu-Léger 2000).

[7] Thank to André Ardouin, a French monk, who conducts controls finances for European and African monasteries, I had access to the accounting reports of 15 communities.

4.2. Towards an African Monasticism?

The second turning point of African monasticism today is that communities which are presently being founded in Africa are, most of the time, founded by African communities or individual African people. It means that the communities that were founded by European or American communities are now becoming themselves mothers of new communities. For instance, the abbey of Keur Moussa founded, in 2011, the monastery of Segueya in Guinea Conackri. An interesting example comes from Togo with the project of Father Boniface Tiguila of founding "an African monasticism by an African monk, for African people". At the beginning of his monastic life, he entered the only Benedictine monastery in Togo at the time, Dzobegan, which was founded in 1961 by the French Benedictine monks of En Calcat. According to him, this form of monasticism, which is influenced by the French contemplative model, was not adapted to African society. He says that he was "looking for a kind of monastic life which is very simple, closer to the people and more African"[8]. After spending six years in this community and travelling through Europe to observe different forms of monastic life, he left his community to pursue the project of establishing a new African community. To explain his project, he wrote a "small book for African monastic life", which takes Benedictine spirituality and tries to adapt it to the African cultural context and to local needs. Here, we observe the affirmation of a breaking away from the model of the French founders. The new monastery was institutionalized by entering the German Congregation of Saint Ottilien in 1991, followed by the erection as an abbey in December 2016.

The monastery of Agbang has as an explicit goal to root monasticism in the local culture. In this case, cultural transfer takes place as a conscious act of adaptation. Adaptation to the local culture occurs in different domains. Firstly, the local language (kabyè) and African music (kora from Keur Moussa, jumbeeaso) are integrated into the liturgy. Then, the habit is adapted to the climate and socio-economic environment: kaki habit for the liturgy and white habit for special occasions. Particularly interesting is the chest tattoo monks get upon their solemn profession with a cross and the name of their monastery. According to a monk of this monastery, it refers to the "seal of the living God" (Revelation 7:2). This is as much a symbol of the Monastère de l'Incarnation as it is a traditional rite in the kabyè culture, where young men are tattooed as part of their initiation. Monks can then show that they belong to Christ and that their new family is the monastery (Adom 2001, p. 35). The architectural design of the monastery is a dialogue between African architecture (round buildings) and traditional monastic architecture (cloister, water tower in the center, etc.).

The example of Agbang shows a case of a monastery which was, from the beginning, founded by a local monk. Boniface Tiguila himself belongs to the local ethnic group of kebyè. In this sense, we might consider that the acceptation of monastic life in the local environment is easier when compared with the monastery founded by foreign people. But monastic life is also a utopian "micro-society" (Séguy 2014, p. 288), which builds itself in contradiction with the surrounding society, as already said. This means that some dimensions of monastic life can, nevertheless, cause tensions with the local culture or population. For instance, in Agbang, when the first monk died in the community, a conflict occurred with the family as they wanted to take the body because it is important in the local tradition, although the monastic tradition states that monks are buried in the cemetery of the monastery. Some conflicts also appear because of the wood in the forest surrounding the monastery.

This model of indigenous foundation—in Africa from African people—may be the model of monastic foundations in the near future. Father Tiguila has, for instance, a project to found a community in the Central African Republic.

---

[8]   Website of the monastery: http://www.agbang.org/welcome.html [consulted on 2 June 2019].

4.3. Towards the Autonomy of African Monasticism

Until the 1990s, monasteries in southern countries were not considered as independent monasteries but overseas establishments of European or US-American monasteries. This took place within a context of missions, which could be linked with some forms of domination (Habermas 2008). Today, African monasteries are becoming more and more independent; firstly because European monks and nuns are no longer present or in fewer numbers, and secondly because these monasteries also found new communities on their own.

In this sense, we can observe a form of the globalization of monasticism understood as "transnational interdependencies" (Metzger 2012). Metzger distinguishes between three levels of consideration in a sociology of globalization: the supranational level, the transnational level and the local level. Monastic life is becoming a global reality, not only because it is present in nearly every country of the world, but because each local institution is becoming an equal part of the transnational and supranational institution. This means that young monasteries in southern countries are becoming more and more independent of their occidental founders and are taking part in transnational organizations and decision-making processes as equal members. Access to positions of abbatial authority for local monks, and access to obtaining the status of abbey by local communities are part of this process. The creation of local transnational associations or networks in countries where monasticism has recently been introduced can also be observed, like REMONAF for the liturgy as discussed above, or Saint Anne initiated by Keur Moussa for the training of young monks and nuns in Western Africa.

Another aspect of the autonomy of African monasticism is economic. I already discussed the question of pensions, but it concerns the whole African monastic economy when it deals with spending for buildings or investment as an economic activity. Katrin Langewiesche notes that African monasteries "can survive only with the help of money from the North" (Langewiesche 2015, p. 140). African monks and nuns are aware of this problem and are trying to change this fact. A Trappist monk in Kokoubou told me it is important for him that they become self-sufficient, and do not "hold out the hand beyond the ocean when [they] need to do construction" (Interview 03.2019). This question is all the more important for him because European communities have less and less possibility to help. The prior of the monastery of Agbang in Togo told me that he is aware that his monastery could not survive without the help of the congregation, but he hopes that it will be able to help German monasteries in future decades when the communities there will be too old to have sufficient revenues.

5. Conclusions

The future of Catholic monasticism has to be considered with a global perspective and not only concerning continents with older traditions of monastic life.

At first glance, monastic communities in Africa present exactly what European communities no longer have: a young and dynamic community, a high rate of entrants, a present dynamic of foundation, etc. But monastic communities in Africa are also confronted with different challenges which are as a result of the routinization of monastic life. The foundation of a monastery is a charismatic time where the founders—or the individual charismatic founder like the case of Agbang—are animated by a special enthusiasm. After this charismatic step, the time of routinization comes, where the monastery has to be rooted in daily life to develop a sustainable way of life. "According to Weber, all legitimate social authority is rooted in charisma, but because charisma is founded on a personal relationship between a followership and a leader, charismatic authority is inherently unstable; that is, it cannot directly survive the loss of the leader. If the social organization is to survive, some form of *routinization* must take place; an orderly (or routine) determination of who legitimately wields power must be determined." (Swatos 1998, online)

Some monasteries in Africa are already beyond this turning point, whereas others are now arriving at it. Monastic life in Africa will, therefore, be a very interesting topic to study in the next thirty years in order to observe its evolution. The same work could be performed in Asia, where Catholic monastic life is rooted in a context where monasticism already has a tradition in the local culture.

Funding: This research was founding for a part by the Mariann Steegmann Foundation (Switzerland).

Conflicts of Interest: The author declares no conflict of interest.

References

Adom, Johannes. 2001. Monastère de l'Incarnation d'Agbang: Un essai d'inculturation de la vie monastique en Afrique. Mémoire de Quatrième année de Théologie. Master's thesis, University of Lomé, Lomé, Togo.

Casier, Jacques. 1974. Entry "Africa". In *Dizionario degli Istituti di Perfezione*. Edited by Guerrino Pelliccia and Giancarlo Rocca. Rome: Edizione Paulina.

Cousin, Patrice. 1956. *Précis d'histoire monastique*. Paris: Bloud et Gay.

Dal Piaz, Giovanni. 2014. Female Monasticism in Italy: A Sociological Investigation. In *Sociology and Monasticism, Between Innovation and Tradition*. Annual Review of the Sociology of Religion. Edited by Isabelle Jonveaux, Enzo Pace and Stefania Palmisano. Leiden: Brill, pp. 34–54.

Delpal, Bernard. 1998. *Le silence des moines. Les trappistes au XIXème siècle*. Paris: Beauchesne.

Eckerstorfer, Bernhard. 2013. Monasticism and contemporary culture: Where are we going? In *Monasticism between Culture and Cultures*. Edited by Philippe Nouzille and Michaela Pfeifer. Rome: Studia Anselmiana, pp. 527–42.

Espagne, Michel. 2013. La notion de transfert culturel. *Revue Sciences/Lettres* 1: 1–9. [CrossRef]

Habermas, Rebekka. 2008. Mission im 19. Jhd. Globale Netze des Religiösen. *Historische Zeitschrift* 28: 631–79.

Hasquenoph, Sophie. 2009. *Histoire des ordres et congrégations religieuses en France du Moyen Age à nos jours*. Paris: Champs Vallon.

Hervieu-Léger, Danièle. 2000. *Religion as a Chain of Memory*. Chicago: Rutgers University Press.

Hervieu-Léger, Danièle. 2017. *Le temps des moines*. Paris: PUF.

Jonveaux, Isabelle. 2011. *Le monastère au travail. Le Royaume de Dieu au défi de l'économie*. Paris: Bayard.

Jonveaux, Isabelle. 2018a. *Moines corps et âme. Une sociologie de l'ascèse monastique contemporaine*. Paris: Le Cerf.

Jonveaux, Isabelle. 2018b. *Mönch sein heute. Eine Soziologie des Mönchtums in Österreich im europäischen Dialog*. Würzburg: Echter.

Langewiesche, Katrin. 2015. Transnational monasteries: The economic performance of cloistered women. *Social Compass* 62: 132–46. [CrossRef]

Langewiesche, Katrin. 2017. Economic Management under a Vow of Poverty: Monastic Management in Burkina Faso. In *Monasticism in Modern Times*. Edited by Isabelle Jonveaux and Stefania Palmisano. London: Routledge, pp. 63–78.

Lumbala, Kabelase. 2011. L'inculturation comme antidote à la violence en Afrique. *Revue des Sciences Religieuses* 85: 427–46. Available online: http://rsr.revues.org/1752 (accessed on 15 May 2019). [CrossRef]

Merton, Thomas. 1975. *Le Retour au silence*. Paris: Desclée de Brouwer.

Metogo, Eloi Messi. 1985. *Théologie africaine et ethnophilosophie. Problèmes de méthode en théologie africaine*. Paris: L'Harmattan.

Metzger, Jean-Luc. 2012. Que pourrait-être une sociologie de la mondialisation? *Recherches sociologiques et anthropologiques* HS: 87–103. [CrossRef]

Palmisano, Stefania. 2015. *Exploring New Monastic Communities. The (Re) Invention of Tradition*. New York: Routledge.

Ripert, Balndine. 2010. Entry "Acculturation". In *Dictionnaire des Faits Religieux*. Edited by Régine Azria and Danièle Hervieu-Léger. Paris: PUF.

Sarr, Olivier-Marie. 2013. «La musique liturgique en Afrique: l'expérience de Keur Moussa (Sénégal), genèse et évolution (1963–2011)». In *Atti del Congresso Internazionale di Musica Sacra in occasione del centenario di fondazione del PIMS Roma, 26 maggio–1 giugno 2011*. Città del Vaticano: Libreria editrice vaticana, pp. 1347–59.

Sarr, Olivier-Marie. 2015. L'inculturazione liturgica: Fra fede celebrata e fede incarnata. *Urbaniana University Journal* 58: 51–75.

Schmitz, Philibert. 1949. *Histoire de l'ordre de saint Benoît*. Maredsous: Editions de Maredsous.

Séguy, Jean. 2014. A Sociology of Imagined Societies: Monasticism and Utopia. In *Sociology and Monasticism, between Innovation and Tradition*. Annual Review of the Sociology of Religion. Edited by Isabelle Jonveaux, Enzo Pace and Stefania Palmisano. Leiden: Brill, pp. 71–86.

Religions **2019**, *10*, 513

Swatos, William. 1998. Entry "Routinization". In *Encyclopedia of Religion and Society*. Edited by William Swatos. Walnut Creek: AltaMira Press, Available online: http://hirr.hartsem.edu/ency/Routinization.htm (accessed on 30 May 2019).

Tiguila, Boniface. 2011. L'AIM, un Baobab dans le paysage africain! *AIM Bulletin* 102: 137–45.

Weber, Max. 1972. *Wirtschaft und Gesellschaft, Grundriss der verstehenden Soziologie*. Tübingen: Mohr Siebeck Verlag.

Zorn, Jean-François. 1994. Les espaces de la mission. *Autres Temps* 43: 47–62. [CrossRef]

religions

MDPI

Article

Beyond Gender: Reflections on a Contemporary Case of Double Monastery in Orthodox Monasticism—St. John the Baptist Monastery of Essex in England

Maria Chiara Giorda [1,*] **and Ioan Cozma** [2]

[1]   Department of Humanities, Roma Tre University, 234 Via Ostiense, 00146 Rome, Italy
[2]   Faculty of Eastern Canon Law, Pontifical Oriental Institute, 7 Piazza di S. Maria Maggiore, 00185 Rome, Italy
*   Correspondence: mariachiara.giorda@uniroma3.it

Received: 18 June 2019; Accepted: 21 July 2019; Published: 26 July 2019

Abstract: This paper focuses on the contemporary controversy in the Orthodox Church regarding the non-existence of the monasteries, where monks and nuns cohabit (so-called "double-monasteries"), which were prohibited by the Byzantine legislation and the Seventh Ecumenical Council (Nicea 787). The article attempts to demonstrate that, in spite of the centuries-old prohibition, the Orthodox Monastery of St. John the Baptist is an exceptional contemporary case of such cohabitation: monks and nuns live under the roof of the same monastery, sharing common places and certain activities. Furthermore, the paper envisions a possible accommodation in the monastic vision and practice regarding gender cohabitation in Orthodox monasticism. The research employs the historical-critical method, which is based on literary, archeological, and documentary sources, as well as interviews.

Keywords: double monasteries; gender cohabitation; Orthodox monasticism; monastic rules

---

1. Introduction

This paper is a part of a broader research project on contemporary Orthodox monasteries that was initiated in January 2017 with the aim of analyzing the gender relationship in the Orthodox monasticism (Cozma and Giorda 2018a, 2018b; Giorda 2019). In particular, the project stems from the need to respond to the repeated affirmations of certain insiders (with, or without, roles of responsibility) of the Orthodox community regarding total separation of men and women within monasteries and the non-existence of monastic double communities, i.e., monasteries, including both communities of men and women, which were prohibited *illo tempore* by canonical and Byzantine law. Furthermore, this is a useful perspective in comparing Orthodox monasticism to Catholic monasticism, since the "lens" on gender relationship permits one to stress the historical differences between the two traditions. While the term "double monastery" and the corresponding prohibition is well-known and still in force in Orthodox monasticism, the term has not been used in Catholic monasticism. However, the practice of monasteries with double communities lasted for centuries in the Catholic west in practice, as multiple cases show, especially in France, Spain, Italy, and the United Kingdom (Elm and Parisse 1992).

From this standpoint, the St. John the Baptist Monastery of Essex, England presents a case, both for its architectural structure and its mixed composition, which constitutes an evident exception to the canonical norms that regulate the organization of Orthodox monastic life. Insiders affirm that this monastery is an example of an anecdotal reproduction stimulated by ancient monastic forms of organization and able to form a collective precept, as well as a cultural and social memory that have been sedimented and transmitted over the centuries (Fentress and Wickman 1992). Thus, despite the presence of monks and nuns residing in the same place at St. John the Baptist, we often hear from its defenders: "it is not a double monastery, because double monasteries do not exist".

The history of the *de jure* formalization process of the category of double/mixed/twin monasteries, and their relationship with the variety that *de facto* characterizes the coexistence of men and women in the same monastic place, is turbulent. The result has been the survival of different forms of this cohabitation since the very origins of monasticism, through the Byzantine period, and until today.

Therefore, this paper adds to the contemporary research regarding double monasteries in the Orthodox Christianity ambit (Bateson 1899; Pargoire 1906; Stoney 1915; Hilpisch 1928; Trone 1983; Konidaris 1990; Stramara 1998a, 1998b; Schipper 2005; Melvani 2016; Jugănaru 2018; Beach and Jugănaru forthcoming), and its main aims are (1) to demonstrate the vitality of a typology of gender monastic cohabitation, despite the canonical norms that prohibit it, as well as (2) to explore the arguments that defend/support the evidence of a phenomenon that is not only prohibited, but also denied.

2. Methodology

Before considering the history and sociology of the St. John the Baptist Monastery of Essex, it is first necessary to provide a methodological note in order to frame all of the research opportunities and difficulties encountered. The absence of both a complete bibliography and a well-structured website, as one would expect from an attractive and spiritual center of this kind, is notable (Jonveaux 2013).

Taking into consideration its genesis and objectives, this essay is based on an experimental methodology, both for the diachronic arc that led us to consider the phenomenon over a long period of time—more than 15 centuries—and for the instruments that were used for this research: historical and critical reading of sources (i.e., literary, documentary, and archaeological sources), interviews that were conducted to define the object of the research, and direct and indirect ethnographic investigations (Diéz et al. 2014).

The only official online information about the monastery can be found on the website of the Ecumenical Patriarchate of Constantinople, to which it belongs (www.patriarchate.org/monastery-essex), and on the Facebook page of the monastery (www.facebook.com/monasterystjohnbaptistessex). Some scattered information can also be found on different websites and blogs.[1]

Faced with this quite fragmented information, we decided to contact the monastery by traditional mail, asking some general questions regarding the organization of the monastery and its daily monastic life. The answer came to us through a letter, which was dated 13 January 2018, and signed by Archimandrite Kyrill, abbot of the monastery, in which he refused to reply to the questions of external inquires (Kyrill 2018).

Therefore, this article draws upon written sources, and personal statements of visitors and frequent pilgrims of the monastery, as well as on a conspicuous bibliography that was produced within the monastic environment. Here, we also employ the concept of "indirect observation" that is based on analyzing textual material generated from narratives (i.e., letters, blogs, and emails) as well as interviews with people who frequented the monastery (Anguera et al. 2019). The most notable volume of this bibliography is the special issue of *Buisson Ardent* (Revue de l'Association Saint Saint Silouane l'Athonite), called *Cahiers Saint Silouane l'Athonite, Hommage à l'Archimandrite Starez Syméon* (2012). Important details regarding the genesis and the activities of the monastery have been deduced from the testimonials of several monks of the monastery, which include Rafail Noica, Syméon Brüschweiler, and Zacharias Zacharou (Drăgoi and Tugui 2002; Zacharias 2003; Syméon 2012). Lastly, the experiences of some people who have either visited the monastery as pilgrims, or that are linked to it through spiritual bonds (spiritual guidance, confession), were extremely helpful. We note especially here the testimonies

---

[1]   www.thyateira.org.uk/monastery-of-st-john-the-baptist; www.patheos.com/blogs/orthodixie/2014/05/essex-monastery-of-st-john-the-baptist.html; www.rafailnoica.wordpress.com/2008/12/09/manastirea-sfantul-ioan-botezatorul-essex-anglia-unde-a-vietuit-par-rafail-noica-sub-obladuirea-arhim-sofronie;   www.londinoupolis.blogspot.it/2015/01/patriarchal-stavropegic-monastery-of-st.html; www.greekamericangirl.com/a-pilgrimage-to-st-john-the-baptist-monastery-in-essex-england/.

of Daniela Dumbravă—a "spiritual daughter" of the monastery for almost 16 years (Dumbravă 2018a, 2018b, 2018c, 2019).

We consider this article to be a preliminary introduction to both the topic and case study due to the impossibility at this time to have direct interviews with monks and nuns of the monastery. It is also useful for framing some topics and to prepare the fieldwork, since we believe that it would be very important to know first its historical and theological background.

3. History of the Monastery

The monastery of St. John the Baptist was founded in 1959 at Tolleshunt Knights, within the area of Maldon District, in Essex county (northeast of London), England, by the Russian Archimandrite Sophrony Sakharov, disciple of the monk Silouan—canonized as a saint in 1987 by the Holy Synod of Ecumenical Patriarchate of Constantinople (Sophrony 1999).

Archimandrite Sophrony—Sergei Symeonovich Sakharov—was born on 23 September 1896 in Moscow. He studied art and painting at the Academy of Arts (1915–1917) and the Moscow School of Painting, Sculpture, and Architecture (1920–1921). In 1921, he left Russia and he settled in Paris in 1922 after a short journey to Italy and Germany. At that time, Paris was one of the major European cities with a large population of Russians, many of whom had escaped from Russia after the 1917 Revolution (Menegaldo 1998). The first phase of Sergei's sojourn in France was characterized by a period of spiritual research, including even some yoga courses. In 1924, on the Saturday before Easter, Sergei decided to change his life by moving towards a pragmatic Christianity that was centered on the efforts of man to know Jesus through prayer. In 1925, he began studying theology at the Saint Sergius Orthodox Theological Institute in Paris, but after a short time, in 1926, he abandoned his theological studies for the St. Panteleimon's Monastery in Mount Athos, Greece (a monastery with a dominant Russian ethnicity), wherein he received the monastic tonsure as Sophrony. In 1930, he was ordained to the diaconate, and in 1941 to the priesthood by Serbian bishop Nicolai Velimirovič of Zicha. In 1930, Sophrony began a close spiritual relationship with the *staretz* Silouan, which lasted until the staretz's death on 24 September 1938 (Sakharov 2002).

With regard to its canonical status, St. John the Baptist is a *stavropegial* monastery (Thomas 1987; Morris 1995), being directly subject to the Ecumenical Patriarchate of Constantinople and organized as a monastic community for both men and women. As far as we know, it is the only instance in the Orthodox Church recognized *de jure* and *de facto* as a monastery where two communities—male and female—share the *topos* and the roof of the same monastery.

The proto-history of the monastery goes back to the Athonite period of Sophrony, originating from his spiritual relationship with Silouan. Before his death, Silouan gave his disciple various writings that described his spiritual experiences. Although different semantically, but not spiritually, the handwritten texts of Silouan were similar to those that comprised in the spiritual testament left by Theodore Studites to his disciples in the IX century (Miller 2000; Giorda 2017b).

In Silouan's writings, a central theme was a practical ascetic life that was understood as "Adamic life". This theological term refers to the period of Adam and Eve before the Fall in Paradise when sexual attraction did not exist. Thus, monastic gender cohabitation is also a challenge that aims to reduce the passions and carnal desires by replacing them with communication and communion in spirit. That is why the notion of "Adamic life" is important, since it offers to us a better understanding of the other expressions often encountered in the Orthodox monastic *typika*, such as "the masculinization of the nuns", with reference here to a double monastery of the late 13th century, where its founder, Patriarch Athanasius I of Constantinople, accepted into monastery women who came to him *"pour se viriliser"*, i.e., to be strengthened with masculine qualities (Delehaye 1897, p. 57).

The main idea of Silouan's ascetic path is that the love of God brings believers to the knowledge of God's will. In his thinking, knowing God means the experience of an organic communion, a real union with the Divine Light. Throughout this process, a man must have his heart preserved from all external influences, renouncing his own will and preparing himself for every sacrifice, "like Abraham—even like Christ Himself" (Sophrony 1999, p. 77). The exercise of pure prayer, especially the so-called "Prayer of Jesus" or "Prayer of the heart" (that is a prayer chiefly composed of invocation of the name of Jesus, accompanied by a confession of faith and the cry for mercy: "Lord Jesus Christ, Son of God, have mercy on me, a sinner"), is essential in this process, allowing for the mind to descend into the heart, filling it with the grace of the Holy Spirit, and transforming man into a true "theologian".

According to Silouan, the word "theologian" is not to be understood in an academic sense, but in a spiritual sense—namely, a theologian is anyone who practices pure prayer. He stated: "If you are a theologian, your prayer is pure. If your prayer is pure, then you are a theologian" (Sophrony 1999, p. 138). This recalls the teaching of Evagrius Ponticus on prayer: "If you are a theologian, you will pray truly. And if you pray truly, you are a theologian" (Evagrius 1983, p. 63). The maxim that constantly has accompanied Silouan's teaching has been, "keep your mind in hell and despair not" (Sophrony 1999, p. 210).

Sophrony immigrated back to Paris in 1947 due to health reasons, but also because of the situation that was created in Mount Athos after World War II, which led to a drastic limitation of the number of non-Greek monks at the Athonite monasteries (Sakharov 2002, pp. 28–29). This post-Athonite period was important for him. He settled in an old house in the Parisian suburb of Sainte Geneviève des Bois, which was then used at the time as a home for elderly Russian emigrants. In this period, Sophorny's main concern was making known, publishing, and putting into practice Silouan's teachings. His efforts came to fruition in September 1948, when the first edition of the staretz's notes was printed using the cyclostyle process. Ample comments with an impressive hermeneutic, dogmatic, and philosophical background, and brief bibliographic notes accompanied Silouan's writings. This edition was followed by a second one in 1952, in which Sophrony added a theological introduction to the writings of Silouan (Syméon 2012; Hierotheos Vlachos). This last edition, which was translated into English, German, French, and Greek, depicts the staretz Silouan as one of the most important contemporary spiritual fathers, while conferring significant credibility and spiritual authority to Sophrony.

The Parisian period gave Sophrony the opportunity to begin a spiritual journey that would culminate in the organization of an initial ascetic nucleus of men and women in 1956, and subsequently the transfer of this group to England and the foundation of the St. John the Baptist Monastery. Thus, for Sophrony, the prophetic words of Silouan that he received when he lived as a hermit in Karoulia, in the heart of Mount Athos, were coming true: "One day you yourself will distribute the obedience" (Monastere St. Jean Baptiste 2012, p. 11).

The move to England was mainly determined by several factors, as follows: the precarious conditions of the monastic community in Sainte Geneviève; the linguistic heterogeneity of the monastic group, which was increasing; and, not least, the attempt of some Orthodox theologians and intellectuals to isolate Sophrony due to his refusal to openly condemn the political complicity of the Moscow Patriarchate, whose leaders abandoned political opposition to the communist regime and pledged their loyalty and support (Bociurkiw 1959). He was also rejected by the St. Sergius Institute for his sympathies toward the Russian church and never completed his theological training (Sakharov 2002, pp. 30, 41–42).

Syméon Brüschweiler—who one of the first monks of Sophrony's community—and Rosemary Edmonds—who later became a nun at Essex—played an important role in the relocation of the community to England. It was Edmonds who recommended the place of the future monastery to Sophrony in 1958. The site was an ancient presbytery (the Old Rectory), which was located at Tolleshunt Knights, in the English county of Essex, an isolated place, put up for sale at a modest price due to its advanced state of deterioration. In the same year, Sophrony went to England to see the place and, with the blessing of Patriarch Alexy I of Moscow, he immediately decided to begin the formal purchasing process. The young monastic community of six people (four men and two women) moved from Paris to the new location on 5 March 1959 (Sakharov 2002, p. 34). Nevertheless, the advanced state of degradation did not allow for the use of the entire property; thus, the small community settled in the old parish house.

In spite of the monastic discipline of the group, they initially chose not to call themselves a monastery, but rather a community: The Community of Saint John the Baptist. Only a few months later, the Orthodox bishop Anthony Bloom, suffragan of the Patriarchate Exarchate of Western Europe (Moscow Patriarchate), blessed and approved the foundation of the monastery. In 1962, the monastery entered under the canonical jurisdiction of the newly established diocese of Great Britain and Ireland—that was known as the Diocese of Sourozh—to which Anthony was appointed as titular bishop. In 1964, due to some disagreements with Anthony, Sophrony asked Patriarch Alexy I of Moscow for his blessing to transfer the monastery to the jurisdiction of the Ecumenical Patriarchate. We have not found any explicit information regarding this crucial point of Sophrony's community. Nonetheless, it seems that the disagreement between them was more personal than institutional, and it was primarily determined by their different spiritual positions and monastic experiences (Dumbravă 2019). Thus, the monastery entered under the jurisdiction of the Ecumenical Patriarchate in 1965, and later received the status of stavropegial monastery (Sakharov 2002, p. 34; Sarni 2012, pp. 57, 61). Sophrony was the superior of the monastery until his death on 11 July 1993. Since 1993 the staretz and superior of the monastery has been Archimandrite Kirill, one of the disciples of Sophrony since his Athonite period.

4. Liturgical Asceticism and Practice: A Monastic *Habitus*

In monasticism, the word "habitus" expresses a spiritual sense, since it refers to a way of life common to both monks and laypersons, monastic families, and traditional families (Alciati and Giorda 2010; Giorda 2015, 2017a). As Greg Peters has recently shown, this way is rooted in baptism for it unifies all believers, whether monks or laics, essentially propelling them towards the same overall Christian goal: deification and union with God (Peters 2018, p. 110).

In Silouan's teachings, hesychasm does not necessarily mean living like a recluse, isolated in the desert, but primarily means living uninterruptedly with God, which should be a common way of life for all believers (Sophrony 1999, p. 141). The first spiritual group around Sophrony in Paris was formed on such ascetical reflection. Therefore, Sophrony did not seek to establish a formal monastic community, but rather to promote a type of asceticism that was focused on meditation of the mind and heart, in which the primary means are the Liturgy and the recitation of the Prayer of Jesus. Within this framework, the meaning of the monastic life was understood as a gift of the Holy Spirit, an imitation of the angelic life in the world (Zacharias 2003, pp. 127–29), and a school of life through which a man "passes from the individual status—i.e., from the fallen, divided, and atomized state—to the unity of the hypostasis of the person in communion with God and neighbor" (Syméon 2012, p. 45).

Therefore, from the beginning, Sophrony did not follow the regular structure of the Orthodox liturgical *typikon*, since he considered the inner perfection that was derived from the freedom of the person to be more important than the external conformity to a rule, which could cancel or suppress such freedom (Sakharov 2002, p. 34). In his words, "any spiritual act, performed under an external pressure and with no freedom, has no value before God's eyes. Therefore, everything we do in the monastic life must be wholly inspired by the love of God and neighbor, not simply derived from the observance of an external rule" (Syméon 2012, pp. 45–46).

In our view, such a spiritual life has attracted, and continues to attract, people with different cultural background, since it opens the possibility of expressing themselves in a liberal way, freely adapting the monastic rule, that is, a kind of (re)invention of the monastic tradition in everyday life, as Stefania Palmisano has demonstrated (Palmisano 2015).

During the Parisian period, the *typikon* included a simple rule of prayer as follows: O Heavenly King (a prayer addressed to the Holy Spirit), O most Holy Trinity, Our Father, some Psalms (of which including Psalm 50[51]), the Symbol of Faith, and the Jesus Prayer. This short rule of prayer is older than Silouan or Sophrony, and it is sometimes called the "Rule of St. Pachomius", (Brianchaninov 2005, p. 33), or "The Little Rule of St. Seraphim of Sarov" (2000; Puretzki 2017).

At the beginning of the English period of the monastery, the *typikon* included the Vigil (Hours, Vespers) and the Matins recited in Slavonic, followed by the Jesus Prayer, which was recited in Old Slavonic. The liturgical rhythm was completed by the celebration of the Divine Liturgy on Sundays, Saturdays, and on the most important feast days. In addition to the linguistic diversity in liturgical celebrations (Slavic, Ancient Greek, English, French, and Romanian), this *typikon* is currently completed by the recitation of the *Paràklisi* to Theotokos on Sundays, and by the special Lenten Hours during the Great Lent, which has slightly different liturgical rhythms from the ordinary liturgical period.

The liturgical life *tout court* is organized in two periods: the weekends and weekdays. On the weekends, the schedule is as follows: on Saturday at 7:00 a.m., the Matins, is celebrated, followed by the Divine Liturgy, and the Vigil is at 5 p.m. (Evening Hours, Vespers, and an Akathist Hymn); Matins and the Divine Liturgy are celebrated on Sunday, in two separate sets and places: from 7:00 a.m. to 10:30 a.m. in the St. Silouan Church (the former All Saints Chapel), and from 10:15 a.m. to 12:00 p.m. in the Old Church. The Vespers and Paràklisi to Theotokos are celebrated from 03:00 p.m. to 05:00 p.m. on Sundays. The weekday celebrations (from Monday to Friday), which are held from 6:00 a.m. (7:00 a.m. on Mondays) to 8:30 a.m. and from 5:30 p.m. to 8:00 p.m., are mainly based on the unceasing recitation of the Jesus Prayer in different languages. On Tuesday and Thursday, the Jesus Prayer is followed at 7:00 a.m. by the Divine Liturgy (Filip 2010; Dumbravă 2018b; Visiting St. John the Baptist Monastery, England. Orthodox in Malaysia 2018).

On feast days during the week, the celebration begins on the evening of the day before with the Vigil (Evening Hours, Vespers, and the Akathist Hymn to the saint or for the feast that is being celebrated), followed in the morning of the next day by Matins and the Divine Liturgy (Sokolof 2001, p. 35).

The linguistic and national heterogeneity of both the monastic group, which includes people from over 17 nationalities, and those attending the monastery have contributed to the implementation of the Jesus Prayer as a liturgical *ritus* (a form of common prayer), which is loudly recited by everyone in his own language up to four hours each day (except on Saturdays and Sundays), even replacing the usual ritual of the Hours.

With this *typikon*, Sophrony imparted his own spiritual rule of prayer (the Divine Liturgy and the Jesus Prayer) to the monastic community (and to others beyond the monastery) from his time as a monk at Mount Athos (Monastere St. Jean Baptiste 2012, p. 13). Nicholas Sakharov, who is Sophrony's nephew and a monk at Essex, noted that the substitution of the regular common services of the Hours in church (Matins, Vespers, Compline, Midnight Office) with the Jesus Prayer has a practical utility and it was not an unspoken invention of Sophrony. This *typikon* of prayer was indeed practiced by other Athonite monks, among which he recalled Nicodemus the Hagiorite and Paisy Velichkovsky. Nicholas emphasized: "this pattern was more appropriate to a small multinational community: reading services in one particular language would have excluded some (members as well as visitors) from full participation in the service" (Sakharov 2002, p. 34). Furthermore, we should have always in mind that the so called "Orthodox Diaspora" has a dominated ethnic character with multinational jurisdictions. This fact creates a particular situation within the Orthodox Church without precedent, which is characterized by two tendencies: (1) the affirmation of the Western local Orthodox Churches and (2) the preservation of specific national-ethnic Orthodox traditions. The latter is quite widespread at the local level (i.e., parishes and monasteries), not only in Western Europe, but also in the United States as well as over the Orthodox Diaspora. This best exemplified especially by liturgical celebrations held exclusively in the language of the national group which makes up that parish and frequents church events. Such tendency often transforms the church into an "enclave" only available to those who use the same language and share the same cultural and national traditions, i.e., Russians for Russians, Romanian for Romanians, Greeks for Greeks, Georgians for Georgians, Bulgarians for Bulgarians, etc. (Cozma 2018; Cozma and Giorda 2018c). In such instance, according to Alexander Schmemann, the Church becomes an "instrument of nationalism" (Schmemann 1964, p. 77), losing its missionary aim.

Therefore, in addition to promoting a spiritual unity, the Jesus Prayer as a common prayer is very important, because it intends to offer a unique identity to all participants, overcoming the inherent complications that are posed by a congregation of different linguistic, national, and gender identities. It is a monastic way of life that is not only reserved for monks, but it can be practiced in any place and by anyone: at the monastery, at home, by a whole family, by a group, or in private. Sophrony advised non-monastics to bring the monastery—with its goals, ideals, purity, faith, and experience—into their homes and their own lives, transforming their houses into churches (Dahulich 1997). This practice echoes John Chrysostom's teaching, who considered that every Christian family is in fact a "small Church" (PG[2] [Migne 1857–1866] 62, coll. 135–150).

Dumbravă (2018a, 2018c) emphasized that this identity is also designed to create a kind of spiritual familiarity, in which the binomials of monk/layman and male/female become an integrated part of a normality that clearly reflects the doctrine of the two staretzes (Silouan and Sophrony). According to this doctrine, cohabitation is simply a detail of the monastic life, as compared to the requirements that they have to fulfill as monastics. The spiritual quality of the monastic existence puts the form of cohabitation of this monastic community in second place. In this sense, the answer of sister Mikhaila—one of the oldest nuns, and among the first in the Essex monastic community—to the question regarding the presence in the same place of a community of men next to one of women, is quite relevant: "Where do you see men around here? I do not see any man, but only brothers" (Dumbravă 2018b). This affirmation reveals that the monastic life is perceived by the St. John the Baptist monastic community as an angelic life, which the monk strives to reach in this world through continuous prayer, fasting, and repentance. The result of such a commitment is a highly spiritualized vision, in which men and women are perceived as angels, a status that precludes any sexual temptation.

Some monks and nuns do not follow the complete liturgical rhythm, but rather live in a semi-idiorrhythmic condition that frees them from regular participation at liturgical celebrations from Monday to Friday, in order to be able to dedicate themselves to translations and other writing works. This was Syméon's *modus vivendi*, but the Archimandrite Zacharias Zacharou and other senior members of the community (monks and nuns) also follow this program.

Among the activities within the monastery are the so-called *Talks*, which are organized every Sunday evening after the evening prayer (Vespers and Paràklisi): two lectures, each one hour long, one in Greek held in the St. Silouan Church, and one in English held in the vestibule of Hylands Refectory, which are followed by tea offered to all the participants. The topics of the lectures are usually chosen by speakers—typically a well-prepared nun, or a hieromonk.

Regarding the attendance of the non-monastics, every Sunday the monastery is visited by about 150–200 people, with most of them coming from nearby areas, including London and Colchester, and some from different countries. On average, around 10,000 people visit on Sundays throughout the year. According to interviews conducted within the monastery, both the new members of the monastic community and pilgrims have declared that they are attracted to this sacred place, due to its existential and pragmatic spirituality, which is more practical than theoretical and discursive. For who attends the monastery, this pragmatism gives to the place a unique spiritual legitimacy that is rarely found in other similar places (Filip 2010; Archos 2018; Dumbravă 2018c; Visiting St. John the Baptist Monastery, England. Orthodox in Malaysia 2018). Two months a year, the monastery is closed to the public for renovation and construction work on the pilgrim accommodations.

5. Complexity of the Monastic Sacred Space

This research is concerned with the peculiarity of the double structure of the community: men and women living together in the same monastery, sharing the same *typikon*, and, in certain cases, the same spaces. This is not only a simple restoration of an ancient monastic typology, but is also a

---

[2] Jacques-Paul Migne, ed., *Patrologiae Cursus Completus. Series Graeca* (Parisiis: Migne 1857–1866).

modern way of living the monastic ascetical experience in the contemporary world, which—according to Sophrony—is characterized by the sobriety of the spirit and the silence of the intellect, as well as by *hesychia*, where the monastery, as *topos*, becomes a common place of prayer and penitence (Zacharias 2003, p. 129; Syméon 2012, p. 46; Burgat 2012, p. 192). Within this context, all of the details related to the genesis of the Essex monastic community are fundamental in understanding the reasons for gender cohabitation and the architectural partition of the monastic buildings.

The living spaces within the monastery were built and organized according to the evolving needs of the people living there, and were mainly determined by the increase in number of the monastic community, and only secondarily by the stream of pilgrims. Sophrony aimed not to draw attention to the monastery within the surrounding natural and architectural landscape since the beginning, neither as a cluster of buildings nor as a new form of organization. All of the buildings, including the places of worship, have a modest architectural form that is consistent with the urban planning style of the area and is also completely atypical when compared to the Orthodox churches and monasteries in Greece, Cyprus, Russia, Romania, Serbia, Bulgaria, Georgia, and Ukraine. Rather, extreme simplicity characterizes the monastery's buildings. Nonetheless, Sophrony's contribution to the architectural and aesthetic geometry of the monastery was quite significant. Sophrony's art and painting studies in Moscow, his brief experience as a painter in his youth, the lessons on iconography and church painting he took in Paris from the famous Russian icon painter and historian Léonide Ouspensky (Doolan 2008), and his Athonite experience, all served as inspiration as he reconfigured and adapted the buildings of the Old Rectory to Orthodox monastic needs. He painted icons first, and then painted the inside chapel walls and the refectory (*trapeza*) in fresco. On the refectory's walls he painted the main narrative scenes from the Gospel (i.e., the Transfiguration of Jesus, the Last Supper, the Crucifixion, the Resurrection, and the Pentecost) and some Old Testament scenes, including the appearance of the Holy Trinity to Abraham at the Oak of Mamre.

On the iconostasis of the Old Rectory chapel are icons painted by Léonide Ouspensky and monk Grégoire Krug (Syméon 2012, p. 42). Thanks to sister Maria, whose field of expertise is the art of mosaic making, there are mosaics that portray various Orthodox saints, such as St. Nicholas, and some biblical scenes, like the ark of Noah, St. Symeon of the Wonderful Mountain, and St. Kirill, on the external walls of the churches and some other buildings.

From an architectural perspective, the monastery is comprised of two structures: the male quarters and the female quarters, which a road separates. The male area contains the following buildings: the St. Silouan Church, the hegumen house (used for the accommodation of bishops and elderly guests), the Old Rectory (for young guests), the All Saints Chapel (with the tomb of Sophrony, and the house where he lived—currently inhabited by his nephew Nicholas), the rooms for the monks, various rooms for the work of the monks (ateliers), various gardens, the Bookstore, and a small trapeza, where breakfast is eaten. In the gardens, there are also various small houses where the monks can work or host male visitors. Today the male monastic community has 20 people, most of whom are novices. Men entering the community are prepared to be priests, spiritual fathers, and deacons, as well as witnesses and diffusers of the spiritual heritage of Sophrony and Silouan.

In the nuns' quarters, behind the gates that open each morning before 6:00 a.m. and close each night around 10 p.m., is the main refectory of the monastery, the nuns' dwellings, the working places for nuns, and the female guest rooms, which are located on the opposite side of the house and without connections to the nuns' rooms. In addition, for young women, there are two other guest houses that are located about one mile from the monastery, which are comprised of rooms for both nuns and female guests. For the female guests that are hosted there, the monastery provides a van driven by a nun. Women come to the monastery for liturgical offices, and beyond this, during their sojourn to the monastery, they offer a helping hand in the kitchen or in the garden. Forty women live in the female monastic community, of whom about half are novices (Dumbravă 2018a).

As it has already been emphasized, the double community was formed *in nuce* during the Parisian period, when Sophrony accepted both men and women to be part of his group. However, no information is available about the cohabitation form and the architectural structure of the buildings where this first community lived. It is only known that when the community moved to England, it was comprised of six people: four men (three of whom were monks) and two women.

The English location has permitted the organization of monastic life respecting gender separation: nuns and laywomen are not allowed to enter the monks' and male guests' spaces, and vice versa. Concerning this essential aspect of the monastic life, Archimandrite Syméon emphasized that, as in the Pachomius monastery, where men lived on one side of the river and women on the other side, the *potamos* (river) of Tolleshunt Knights Monastery is a road that separates the two communities (Syméon 2012, p. 45).

However, there are also common areas where men and women encounter each other daily to pray, eat, work, or socialize, including the St. Silouan Church; the All Saints Chapel; the two refectories (there is a convivial five o'clock meeting with biscuits, coffee, and herbal teas); some spaces on the first floor of the Old Rectory, including a small kitchen, the chapel, a small confession room, and Sophrony's office; Sophrony's crypt; the gardens; the parking lot; and, the rooms that were used for various activities and works.

The monastery's rules do not allow for children to be hosted on the monastery premises. Nonetheless, children are an integral part of the religious and social life that takes place on Saturdays, Sundays, and during the main feasts of the year. About 30–35 children attend the liturgical celebrations, together with their parents, and receive communion. Many of them come from London and its suburbs. The monastery is an international environment that is mostly dominated by the ethnic communities of Greeks, Cypriots, Romanians, Russians, and Ukrainians. Every year, more and more British people attend religious services, coming either through conversions to Orthodoxy, or as part of a mixed family. Sister Magdalena, a nun of British origin, is in charge of the children. She organizes various activities for them in the monastery. They often receive gifts, and special attention is given to each of them on their birthdays, when the entire monastic community joins with the guests to celebrate them.

The monastery environment, besides being adorned with a great variety of flowers and trees, is also characterized by the presence of cats, rabbits, squirrels, and birds, which are generously fed by monks and visitors. This is an ecological practice that perfectly integrates with the life of the monastery, together with the cultivation of organic vegetables and legumes (Theokritoff 2009).

6. Monastic Gender Cohabitation in Antiquity: The Norms that Shaped the Ban

St. John the Baptist Monastery's configuration refers to a history of relations between genders that is retraceable in a variety of *de facto* forms of proximity and coexistence, dating back to the very origins of Christian monasticism. Among all the renunciations that are required by those aspiring to monastic life, which inherent to matrimony has been the most evident, because it is based on the idea and practice of celibacy, sexual abstinence, virginity, and physical separation between men and women. Although the renunciation of family ties rivals the severity of that of matrimony, this kind of relationship has been correspondingly preserved and replicated inside of what has been defined as "the monastic family", in which kinship ties have been replaced by spiritual connections. This imitation has been most evident in the monastic language (i.e., brother, sister, spiritual father, spiritual mother) (Wipszycka 2009), but has also been present both in administrative organization, (i.e., communion and division of goods and works) and the architectonic structure of the monastic buildings (i.e., men and women devoted to ascetic living together either in the same house or separate buildings—canonically belonging to the same monastic community; the same worship place for both male and female communities).

The ancient monastic sources, e.g., *Apophthegmata Patrum* (PG 65, coll. 71–440), and *Historia Lausiaca* (PG 34, coll. 991–1260; Palladius 1964), reveal numerous cases of men and women (who were in many cases spouses, brothers, and sisters) sharing the monastic life, either living together or in close proximity to each other, in a multifaceted variety of mixed forms, differently explained and justified. In this approach, the starting point for all historical reflections on ancient monasticism is definitively the late period of ancient Egypt. It is the well-known ascetic path of Antony of Egypt (251–356), who, after giving to the poor all possessions, entrusted his sister to "some faithful women" (the virgins) and lived his initial ascetical experience in a village in close proximity to the house of the virgins (Athanasius 2003).

In *Historia Lausiaca*, Palladius tells the story of Amoun (HL 8: Palladius 1964)—a contemporary to Antony and one of the most famous monks of the Nitrian Desert—who, after being forced by his uncle to marry, managed to persuade his wife to live together in chastity. They decided to separate after 18 years of cohabitation: Amoun went into the inner mountain of Nitria, to the south of Lake Mareotis, where he built two rounded cells, while she founded a convent in her own house. Another remarkable case that was described by Palladius is that of Ammonius (HL 11), a contemporary to the bishop Timotheus of Alexandria (381–385), who, along with his three brothers and two sisters, went down to the desert, each living the monastic life in separate cells and keeping a distance from the others. It would not be right to pass over in silence Olympias: Palladius said of her that, although she was married for a few days, "she died a virgin, wife only of the Word of Truth" (HL 56).

These examples indicate that, in Late Antiquity, the monastic life did not necessarily imply the total separation and annihilation of family ties. Often, a simple family house became a common place of asceticism, a *domus monastica* for a man and a woman.

The figure of Pachomius (287–346/7) is decisive in the construction of a monastic typology technically that is defined by the term "cenobitism" (*koinos bios*), which is centered on the spiritual relationship between the master and his disciples, assuming peculiarities that have endured for many centuries (Giorda 2010, p. 86). This relationship was pivotal in the foundation of the first monastery at Tabennisi, a "deserted village" (Chitty 1995; Goehring 1996; Rapp 2006) that was situated on the bank of the Nile, which included both male and female communities, the latter established a short distance from that of men's community and under the leadership of Maria, Pachomius's sister (Bo 27 [The bohairic life of Pachomius]; G1 32 [The first Greek life of Pachomius]: Veilleux 1980). James Goering underscored that the female monastery of Tabennisi was not included in the number of monasteries that were listed by his sources, but instead was seen as a sister monastery of the male establishment (Goehring 1996, p. 278). Within the monastic federation (*koinonia*) that reinforced Pachomius's paternity, other female monastic communities were established (incorporated into the community) in close proximity to the male foundations, as follows: the convent of Tsmene (Tkahšmin), which was located on one side of the Nile river opposite the male monastery of Panopolis (Šmin) and founded by Pachomius himself (HL 33.1; G^1 134); and, the convent of Bechné, about a mile from the male monastery of Phbew (Pbow/Faou), this last being founded by Theodore, Pachomius's disciple and successor (G^1 134; Rapp 2011; Goehring 2017). According to the *Life of Pachomius*, "These monasteries were able to do the weaving of woolen garments, blankets, and other things, and also the spinning of raw flax for tunics" (G^1 134).

As described in Pachomius's biographies and rules (G^1, 32; HL 33; Precepts 143/Boon 1932; Veilleux 1981), the monastic life was often embraced by an entire family: the men entered a male monastery and the women a female convent. Notwithstanding the proximity of two communities, the contacts between men and women were substantially limited. No men, except for the appointed monks (e.g., the priest and the deacon, whose visits were limited to Sundays), were allowed to visit the women's monastery. A brother was permitted to visit his relatives (i.e., mother, sister, wife, daughter, or cousin) for a limited period of time only if he had a chaperone with him (a man of proven age and life) and in the presence of another sister, but he could not bring them anything, receive anything, or speak "about worldly matters" (G^1 32; Precepts 143; HL 32).

Another important figure in this period was Basil of Caesarea (329/30–379), who is considered to be the legislator of cenobitic monasticism (Špidlik 2007, p. 262); the one "who brought order into the chaos of experimentation by creating communities and written precepts that were to set the standards for generations to come" (Elm 1994, p. 61). The first monastic settlement (called "fraternity/brotherhood" [*adelphótes*]) that was founded by Basil was around 358 in the region of Neocaesarea (in Pontus), in a mountain area surrounded on three sides by the river Iris and located very close (about five miles) to the monastery of Annesi where his sister Macrina and their brother Peter lived (Silvas 2007). These two monastic settlements, which were separated by the crest of the mountain but adjacent to each other, formed a monastic pole, becoming models for the monastic regulations that were laid out in his writings (Morison 1912, pp. 98–99).

However, because of the lack of literary descriptions and archaeological evidence, the only starting point in picturing how Basil's monasteries were architecturally structured is the monastery of Macrina, which was summarily described by Gregory of Nyssa in the *Life of St. Macrina* (PG 46, coll. 976–996; Gregory of Nyssa 2001). It was a monastery with one church and two separate communities: the virgins' quarters led by Macrina, and the men's quarters under the leadership of her brother Peter. From Gregory's testimonies, it appears that each of these quarters was comprised of several houses. For example, he talks about the house of the "great Macrina" (c. 16), and the house close to the house of Macrina (c. 24).

Although Basil promoted this system of monastic double communities, the gender relationships within monasteries were carefully outlined in his *Rules* (55 Longer Rules/*Regulae fusius tractatae*, and 318 Shorter Rules/*Regulae brevis tractatae*), clearly prescribing a segregationist approach. One example of this monastic typology is Rule 33 of the Longer Rules (PG 31, coll. 997–1000; Basil 1962), which deals with the meetings between monks/brothers and nuns/sisters, as well as between them and the laity. The meetings were only allowed after the time, the necessity, and the place were properly established. To avoid any suspicion, no less than two, and no more than three, had to be present on each side participating in the discourse. If one of the brethren had to speak of or listen to something bearing on some private matter, the issue had to be first communicated to the chosen representatives (persons of advanced age), who were then required to discuss the business with selected older members of the sisterhood (a Pachomian *dejà vu*), and the conversation could take place if it was deemed necessary only after their mediation.

The same approach appears in Rule 108 of the Shorter Rules (henceforth SR): the superior of the male quarters was not allowed to meet and talk to a nun from the female quarters without the knowledge of the superior mother, even though their conversations were required to be about faith (PG 31, col. 1156). Furthermore, SR 109 set limitations that were aimed at minimizing the meetings and the conversations between even the superior of the male community and the superior mother of the female community (PG 31, col. 1156).

Despite all of these prohibitions, the nuns' quarters were not completely isolated from the monks'; instead, it could be argued that the two communities were interdependent. The dependence of the female community on the male one was especially highlighted in the spiritual field, as confession was administered by senior brothers that were chosen to serve the spiritual needs of the female community—cf. SR 110 (PG 31, col. 1157), and also included an economic component—cf. SR 154 (PG 31, col. 1184).

However, SR 111 is of particular importance, as it underscores that the relationship between the superior mother and the superior father should not be one of subordination, but of harmonious cooperation, both being assisted and controlled by the council of elders of the brotherhood (PG 31, col. 1157).

Therefore, the location of the Basilian fraternities (or monasteries) within or on the outskirts of cities, and the double composition of the monastic communities (quarters for men and quarters for women), as well as the terminology that is used to describe intra-monastic and extra-monastic relationships (i.e., brothers, sisters, and fraternity) demonstrate that Basil's intent was not to isolate monasticism from the world, but rather to propose the monastic ideal as a spiritual model for the entire Church. Basil did not ever use the concept of "double monastery" for his fraternities. Moreover, words, such as "monk", "nun", and "monastery", which were in use in Egypt, are completely absent from his monastic rules (Morard 1974; Girardi 1981). However, in the years that followed, the Basilian cenobitism became more and more preeminent within the Byzantine monastic landscape.

The intervention of the Byzantine Emperor Justinian I (527–565) in monastic matters was also pivotal for both the organization and internal discipline of monasteries. On 18 January, 529, the emperor issued a law enforcing monastic segregation in order to prevent abuse and eliminate any suspicion of monks and nuns (Codex. Just. I.3.43: Krueger 1892, CIC I: pp. 29–30). The law forbade cohabitation, meetings, and conversations between laymen and nuns, as well as the cohabitation of monks and nuns in the same location. If there were more monks than nuns in a given location, the nuns had to move from that place to another (either to an existing female monastery, or a new one built for them). However, the monks had to move if the number of the nuns was greater or equal to the number of monks. In such cases, the common movable and immovable properties were proportionally divided between the two communities. Moreover, the decree forbade priests and deacons from living in the monasteries of nuns for which they were assigned by the bishop to perform liturgical services and pastoral activities.

The prohibitions regarding gender segregation in the monasteries were completed in 533 with new more explicit provisions in Novella 133: "No woman shall enter into a monastery for men, or a man in one for women, either out of respect of a descendent buried there or for any other reason, and especially if it is said that they have, perchance, a brother in the monastery, or a sister or any other relative. For monks have no relations on earth, since they are seekers of a celestial life (c. 3)". However, the novella allowed for two or three *aprocrisiarii*—preferably eunuchs, or advanced in years—to enter into the convents of women to conduct "business matters and administer the ineffable communion when it is time for that (c. 5)" (Schöll and Kroll 1963, CIC III: pp. 669–71; 672–74; Justinian 2008).

The norm had an imperative character: its motivation was expressed at the beginning of chapter 1, as follows: "But since some things have been reported to us which need a more comprehensive and firmer law [Decree of 529], we have justly come to make this law to perfect and supplement the former one (c. 1)" (Schöll and Kroll 1963, CIC III: pp. 667–68; Justinian 2008).

In 546, Justinian once again interfered with monastic matters by issuing a new decree—Novella 123. In chapter 36 of this new law, the emperor reiterated the previous prohibitions concerning monastic gender cohabitation (i.e., Decree of 529, Novella 5, and Novella 133), but, above all, he introduced a previously unused technical term: "double monasteries" (*dipla monastéria*). Through this term, the emperor appears to have summarized the various monastic typologies of cohabitation that existed in that time (Cozma and Giorda 2018a). However, Justinian does not clearly explain what this term, "double monasteries", means, and what elements would define such an arrangement, which was henceforth prohibited. The prohibition of such monasteries is absolute: "We do not permit monks and nuns to live in the same monastery anywhere in our empire and do not permit the so-called *double monasteries* [emphasis mine] to exist" (Schöll and Kroll 1963, CIC III: p. 619; Justinian 2008).

The ambiguity of the expression "double monasteries" made the norm less effective in its practical application despite the decree's imperative character. Jules Pargoire noted that, beyond Constantinople and the neighboring areas, Justinian's law remained unenforced in the other provinces of the Byzantine Empire (Pargoire 1906, p. 22). For Ioannis Konidaris and Friedrich Schipper, the prohibition referred rather to mixed monasteries only, namely to those communities of monks and nuns that were living together in the same place without an effective mechanism for gender segregation (Konidaris 1990; Schipper 2005).

The intervention of the Church in the monastic cohabitation matter was explicitly considered at the Council in Trullo of 692. Canon 47 of this council, echoing Novella 133 of Justinian (women were prohibited to enter into male monasteries), prohibited women from sleeping in male monasteries, and vice versa, under the penalty of excommunication (Agapios and Nicodemos 1957, p. 347). The Trullan norm was later repeated in Canon 18 of the Seventh Ecumenical Council of Nicea (787), which forbade women from dwelling at diocesan headquarters, as well as in men's monasteries (Agapios and Nicodemos 1957, p. 446). However, the significance of the Council of Nicea is above all given in Canon 20. The Justinian term "double monastery" is used for the first time in this canon: "As from now on we decree that no *double monastery* [emphasis mine] is to be made, because this becomes a scandal and offense to many persons" (Agapios and Nicodemos 1957, p. 448).

This canonical provision—which it is still in force in the Byzantine Orthodox Churches—has prevented the cohabitation (permanent or temporary) of monks and nuns in the same monastery, and also the foundation of new monasteries with double communities (even if segregated), or, according to Ioannis Zonaras (Rhallis and Potlis 1852, pp. 868–69), the founding of two monasteries (one of monks and one of nuns) that are close to each other. However, the norm appears to refer not to a single form of monastic cohabitation, but to diverse typologies, among which, according to Theodore Balsamon, did not exclude mixed monasteries (Rhallis and Potlis 1852, pp. 639–40).

Despite Canon 20 and further prohibitions mandated by the patriarchs of Constantinople, such as Nicephorus I (806–815) and Alexios Studites (1025–1043)—both decreeing that the monk communities had to be moved far away from those of nuns (Janin 1964, p. 8; Parrinello 2012, p. 144; Garland 2013, pp. 31–32)—double monasteries have continued to exist in Byzantine monastic practice in the centuries that followed. In the late IXth century, Euthymius the Younger (824–898) founded a double monastery near Thessaloniki that was directed by his family: his nephew was abbot of the male monastery and his niece of the female convent (Talbot 1990, p. 123).

In Constantinople, in the early 12th century, there were two contiguous monasteries that were separated by a wall: one for men (*Christos Philantropos*) and one for women (*Panagia Kecharitomene*), founded around 1100–1007 by the emperor Alexios I Kommenos (1081–1118) and his wife Irène Doukaina, and situated on the northwest of the city (Janin 1964; Talbot 1998; Stramara 1998b). However, from the *typicon* of the female monastery (dating around 1110–1116), it appears that the two monasteries, despite their proximity, shared nothing, except for the separation wall and a water pipe.

Another example of a double monastery in Constantinople was the *Christos Philantrophos Soter* monastery, which was established in 1307 by Irène Choumnaina Palaiologina and situated on the eastern side of the city (Melvani 2016). This monastery was a legal entity with two segregated communities (male and female), under a single administration, and it shared some activities (Trone 1983; Talbot 1985, 2000).

Patriarch Athanasius I of Constantinople (1289–1293/1304–1310) at first condemned double monasteries, but later founded two similar monasteries: *Nea Mone* in Mount Ganos in Thrace (west of the Sea of Marmara) and *Xerolophos* in Constantinople (Talbot 1985; Mitsiou 2008).

After the fall of Constantinople in 1453, the only information regarding the existence of a double monastery is found in the life of St. Philotheos of Mount Athos. Philotheos and his brother received the monastic tonsure in the monastery of Neapolis (now Kavalla in Greece) around 1540, and their mother, Eudokia, also lived in the female quarters of this monastery (Talbot 1990, p. 123).

The Post-Byzantine and Modern periods, at least according to the plan prescribed by the Orthodox Canon Law, have both been characterized by an exclusive monastic typology in which gender segregation has been enforced and the foundation of monasteries with double communities has not been allowed by the Church authority.

However, places of cohabitation and encounter between monks and nuns have not ceased to exist in the Orthodox Church, albeit in limited numbers and in various forms: cohabitation of monks and nuns at bishoprics; monks and nuns working together at hospitals, nursing homes for the elderly, homes for orphans, and help centers for addicts, inside or outside of monasteries; and, monks and nuns living in segregation at a certain distance from each other, while affirming the spiritual paternity of the same founder or spiritual father (Cozma and Giorda 2018a, 2018b; Giorda 2019). Within this framework, the Essex monastery is an obvious expression of physical and spiritual proximity between monks and nuns in the contemporary world.

7. Conclusions

The proximity of men and women in the monastic environment can be found in a variety of typologies of cohabitation, which can hardly be described by formulated definitions and proposed rigid delimitations. Despite the difficulties of defining the forms, the monastic language has, from the beginning, sanctioned terms and concepts that intended to facilitate a better understanding of the life of those who, in abandoning the world and the family, were faced with a new life, moving from a blood (i.e., socio-institutional) family to a spiritual one.

This perspective is vital in understanding the modalities through which cohabitation has been justified in both ancient and present-day Orthodox monasticism. The dignity of both sexes has never been understood through the modern lens of gender equality, namely in terms of equality of woman with man, but rather as a joint pathway toward the recovery of the original state of the first humans, prior to the Fall (Barone Adesi 1989, p. 272).

Byzantine (Justinian) and the Church norms (i.e., canons of the ecumenical councils, and monastic rules) both did not exclude the spiritual aspect of cohabitation; indeed, the prohibitions regarding the external form of cohabitation (whether mixed or double) were envisioned in order to safeguard the spiritual pathways of both genders. In this civil and canonical structure, total segregation was established as a rule, and gradually the double, mixed, and twin monasteries, as well as the places of proximity and cohabitation between monks and nuns began to diminish, only surviving in a fossilized condition. The Post-Byzantine period was characterized by a strong observance of the canonical norms, confidently stated in terms of the "Tradition of the Orthodox Church", which were considered, without question, not to be ignored, modified, or reinterpreted.

In the contemporary period, due in part to the desire to re-evaluate the *modus vivendi* of the ancient Fathers, but also to the widespread interest in the ascetic practice and ways of living of many people in the Orthodox Church, there has been an attempt to return to the spirit and practice of the Church of the early centuries. It is in this context that we must view the (re)foundation of monasteries with double communities, such as that of St. John the Baptist of Essex in England, with the same *typikon* and in certain cases sharing in a *de facto* form both liturgical or common spaces, or such as that of the New Skete in Cambridge, New York (1966), under the jurisdiction of the Orthodox Church in America, which is comprised of a community of monks and one of nuns that are located a couple of miles away from each other (https://newskete.org), or of two monasteries—one for men (1972) and one for women (1987)—being very close to each other, such as those of Panorama in Greece, under the jurisdiction of the Church of Greece (http://www.agia-triada-panorama.gr), or the most recent Our Lady and St. Laurence Monasteries in Cañon City, Colorado (2015), which is a Western rite monastic double community of monks and nuns under the Antiochian Orthodox Christian Archdiocese of North America (http://saintlaurenceosb.org).

Rather than rigidly interpreting this trend as a violation of Church laws (holy canons, imperial laws, and patriarchal decrees), it can be seen as a pastoral way of interpreting and employing the canonical norm, which is known in the Orthodox Church as *oikonomia*. Such a pastoral method allows for the authority of the Church to apply a permanent or temporary derogation from a canonical prescription (Erickson 1977).

In spite of a still-active canonical ban, and a certain formal duplicity, and notwithstanding those who are aligned with these traditions, and thus deny the existence today of double monasteries or of those monasteries that are characterized by a form of *mixité*, the *de facto* reality demonstrates the presence of such forms of cohabitation, which are theologically and canonically justified through spiritual terms, such as obedience, humility, and a struggle against the passions, as well as utility, and mutual spiritual and material interdependence. For this reason, St. John the Baptist Monastery can be traced back to the diverse forms of cohabitation between men and women of ancient monasticism, as the sources abundantly demonstrate. The example analyzed in this article is emblematic, because it is the only Orthodox monastery with two monastic communities that live in the same space, which is also active in the lives of the faithful both at the local/national and transnational level (Roudometof 2015), in that both male and female visitors live temporarily at the monastery and attend the liturgical services. Furthermore, the widespread devotion to monasticism in Orthodoxy makes the monastery a model to follow for the Christian family, since the monastic pattern (characterized by prayers, penances, fasting, and sexual abstinence) is encouraged for the sanctity of the spouses.

An in depth-analysis of the collective narratives and theological arguments that support this monastic pattern of cohabitation (despite the Church rules) would be an important research path in the future for justifying the contemporary reasons for accepting this reality and analyzing the (possible) transformations of the monastic vision and monastic practice as regards the female gender (Jonveaux 2015).

Furthermore, it will be interesting to compare the history and sociology of some ancient and contemporary double monasteries (Orthodox and Catholic) in order to analyze similar practices in diverse monastic contexts, as well as to reflect on the continuity and discontinuities from both a chronological and comparative point of view.

Author Contributions: M.C.G. conceived the research project, elaborated the main ideas, and established the methodology; M.C.G. and I.C. collected the data, investigated and performed the analysis as well as wrote and reviewed the original draft. All authors read and approved the final manuscript.

Funding: This research received no external funding.

Conflicts of Interest: The authors declare no conflict of interest.

References

Agapios and Nicodemos. 1957. *The Rudder (Pedalion): Of the Metaphorical Ship of the One Holy Catholic and Apostolic Church of the Orthodox Christians or All the Sacred and Divine Canons.* Translated by Denver Cummings. Chicago: Orthodox Christian Educational Society.

Alciati, Roberto, and Maria Chiara Giorda. 2010. Famiglia cristiana e pratica monastica (IV-VII Secolo). *Annali Di Storia Dell'esegesi* 27: 265–90.

Anguera, M. Teresa, Mariona Portell, Salvador Chacón-Moscoso, and Susana Sanduvete-Chaves. 2019. Indirect Observation in Everyday Contexts: Concepts and Methodological Guidelines within a Mixed Methods Framework. *Frontiers in Psychology* 9: 1–20. Available online: https://doi.org/10.3389/fpsyg.2018.00013 (accessed on 25 June 2019).

Archos, Irene. 2018. A Pilgrimage to St. John the Baptist Monastery in Essex, England. *Greek American Girl (blog).* March 22. Available online: https://greekamericangirl.com/a-pilgrimage-to-st-john-the-baptist-monastery-in-essex-england/ (accessed on 10 May 2019).

Athanasius. 2003. *The Life of Antony.* Translated by Tim Vivian. Kalamazoo: Cistercian Publications.

Barone Adesi, Giorgio. 1989. *Monachesimo Ortodosso d'Oriente e Diritto Romano Nel Tardo Antico.* Milano: Giuffrè.

Basil, Saint. 1962. *Ascetical Works.* Translated by Monica M. Wagner. Washington, DC: The Catholic University of America Press.

Bateson, Mary. 1899. Origin and Early History of Double Monasteries. *Transactions of the Royal Historical Society* 13: 137–98. [CrossRef]

Beach, Alison, and Andra Jugănaru. forthcoming. The Double Monastery as an Historiographical Problem. In *The Cambridge History of Medieval Monasticism in the Latin West.* Edited by Alison Beach and Isabelle Cochelin. Cambridge: Cambridge University Press.

Bociurkiw, Bohdan R. 1959. Church and State in the Soviet Union. *International Journal* 14: 182–89. [CrossRef]

Boon, Amand. 1932. *Pachomiana Latina: Règle et Épitres de s. Pachome, Épitre de s. Théodore et "Liber" de s. Orsiesius.* Louvain: Bureaux de la Revue.

Brianchaninov, Ignatius. 2005. *On the Prayer of Jesus: The Classical Guide to the Practice of Unceasing Prayers Found in The Way of a Pilgrim.* Translated by Father Lazarus. Boston and London: New Seeds.

Burgat, Pierre. 2012. Le Starets Syméon à La Côte-Aux-Fées, in Cahiers. In *Cahiers Saint Silouane l'Athonite, Hommage à l'Archimandrite Starez Syméon (1928–2009).* Edited by Jean-Claude Polet. Buisson Ardent. Horse-Série. Paris: Cerf, pp. 183–93.

Chitty, Derwas J. 1995. *The Desert a City: An Introduction to the Study of Egyptian and Palestian Monasticism under the Christian Empire.* Crestwood: St. Vladimir's Seminary Press.

Cozma, Ioan. 2018. Canonical and administrative issues relating to the Parish in the Romanian Orthodox Episcopate of America. In *Patrimoniul Cultural Religios—Legislatie si Jurisprudenta (Religious Cultural Heritage–Legislation and Jurisprudence).* Edited by Marius Balan and Emilian Iustinian Roman. Iasi: Editura Universitatii "Alexandru Ioan Cuza" Iasi, pp. 225–42.

Cozma, Ioan, and Maria Chiara Giorda. 2018a. Uomini e donne nei monasteri: La genesi tardo antica di un equivoco. *Rivista Di Storia Del Cristianesimo* 15: 25–56.

Cozma, Ioan, and Maria Chiara Giorda. 2018b. Sede episcopale e monastero: Un caso inedito di coabitazione istituzionale e amministrativa nel monachesimo ortodosso contemporaneo. *Annali Si Studi Religiosi* 19: 115–39.

Cozma, Ioan, and Maria Chiara Giorda, eds. 2018c. *Ortodossi Romeni d'Italia.* Torino: Quaderni di Benvenuti in Italia 13.

Dahulich, Michael G. 1997. A Modern-Day Saint and His Disciple: Saint Silouan and Father Sophrony. Alive in Christ. *The Magazine of the Diocese of Eastern Pennsylvania* 13: 55–61.

Delehaye, Hyppolite. 1897. La Vie d'Athanase, Patriarche de Constantinople (1289–1293; 1304–10). *Mélanges d'archéologie et d'histoire de l'Ecole Française de Rome* 17: 39–75.

Diéz, Javier Gonzales, Maria Chiara Giorda, and Sara Hejazi. 2014. Studying Monasticism in Italy: An Anthropological and Historical Perspective. *Annual Review of The Sociology of Religion, Sociology of Monasticism, Between Innovation and Tradition* 5: 241–60.

Doolan, Patrick. 2008. *Recovering the Icon: The Life and Work of Leonid Ouspensky.* Crestwood: St. Vladimir's Seminary Press.

Drăgoi, Eugen, and Ninel Țugui. 2002. Celălalt Noica: Mărturii Ale Monahului Rafail Noica Însoțite de Câteva Cuvinte de Folos Ale Părintelui Symeon, 3rd ed.București: Anastasia.

Dumbravă, Daniela. 2018a. Email to Ioan Cozma and Maria Chiara Giorda: "Domande Essex: St. John the Baptist Monastery". January 24.

Dumbravă, Daniela. 2018b. Email to Ioan Cozma and Maria Chiara Giorda: "Stavropegiac Monastery of St. John the Baptist". February 13.

Dumbravă, Daniela. 2018c. "Monastic life at Essex: Interview with Daniela Dumbravă." By Ioan Cozma. Roma. November 22.

Dumbravă, Daniela. 2019. Email to Ioan Cozma and Maria Chiara Giorda: "Essex". July 3.

Elm, Susanna. 1994. *Virgins of God: The Making of Asceticism in Late Antiquity.* New York: Oxford University Press.

Elm, Kaspar, and Michel Parisse, eds. 1992. Doppelklöster und Andere Formen der Symbiose Männlicher und Weiblicher Religiosen im Mittelalter: (Ordensstudien VIII), 1st ed. Berlin: Duncker & Humblot.

Erickson, John H. 1977. Oikonomia in Byzantine Canon Law. In *Law, Church, and Society.* Edited by Kenneth Pennington and Robert Somerville. Philadelphia: University of Philadelphia Press, pp. 225–36.

Evagrius, Ponticus. 1983. On Prayer. In *Philokalia.* Edited by Nikodimos of the Holy Mountain and Makarios of Corinth. vol. 1, Translated by Gerard Eustace H. Palmer, Philip Sherrard, and Kallistos Ware. London and Boston: Faber and Faber. Available online: https://archive.org/details/Philokalia-TheCompleteText/page/n33 (accessed on 21 May 2019).

Fentress, James, and Chris Wickman. 1992. *Social Memory.* Cambridge: Blackwell.

Filip, Gabriela. 2010. Cu Nepsis La Londra Si in Pelerinaj La Manastirea Sfantul Ioan Botezatorul, Essex. *Apostolia.* Available online: https://www.apostolia.eu/articol_67/cu-nepsis-la-londra-şi-in-pelerinaj-la-manastirea-sfantul-ioan-botezatorul-essex.html (accessed on 12 April 2019).

Garland, Lynda. 2013. Till Death Do Us Part?: Family Life in Byzantine Monasteries. In *Questions of Gender in Byzantine Society.* Edited by Bronwen Neil and Lynda Garland. London: Ashgate, pp. 29–56.

Giorda, Maria Chiara. 2010. *Monachesimo e Istituzioni Ecclesiastiche in Egitto.* Bologna: Dehoniane.

Giorda, Maria Chiara. 2015. Familles du «monde», familles monastiques. Une économie du capital dans l'Égypte chrétienne (Ve–VIe Siècles). «*Archives Des Sciences Sociales de Religions*» 17: 263–87.

Giorda, Maria Chiara. 2017a. *Famiglie Monastiche. Il Dominus Tecum Di Pra'd Mill.* Torino: Aragno.

Giorda, Maria Chiara. 2017b. Writing Monastic Testaments: A Communication from Generation to Generation. In *Writing and Communication in Early Egyptian Monasticism.* Edited by Malcom Choat and Maria Chiara Giorda. Texts and Studies in Eastern Christianity 9. Leuven: Brill, pp. 129–50.

Giorda, Maria Chiara. 2019. Monaci e Monache Presso Le Sedi Vescovili. Alcuni Casi Di Convivenza Nel Monachesimo Ortodosso Romeno. *Studi e Materiali per La Storia Delle Religioni* 85: 244–69.

Girardi, Mario. 1981. Αδελφότης Basiliana e Scola Benedettina. Due Scelte Monastiche Complementari? *Nicolaus* 9: 3–61.

Goehring, James E. 1996. Withdrawing from the Desert: Pachomius and the Development of Village Monasticism in Upper Egypt. *The Harvard Theological Review* 89: 267–85. [CrossRef]

Goehring, James E. 2017. The Pachomian Federation and Lower Egypt: The Ties That Bind. In *Christianity and Monasticism in Northern Egypt: Beni Sueff, Giza, Cairo, and the Nile Delta*. Edited by Gawdat Gabra and Hanny N. Takla. Cairo and New York: The American University in Cairo Press, pp. 49–60.

Gregory of Nyssa. 2001. *The Life of Saint Macrina*. Edited by Kevin Corrigan. Toronto: Peregrina Publishing Co.

Hierotheos (Vlachos). 2015. *I Know a Man in Christ: Elder Sophrony the Hesychast and Theologian*. Levadia: Holy Monastery of the Birth of the Theotokos.

Hilpisch, Stephanus. 1928. *Die Doppelklöster; Entstehung Und Organisation*. Münster in Westf: Aschendorff.

Janin, Raymond. 1964. Le Monachisme Byzantin Au Moyen Âge. Commende et Typica (Xe-XIVe Siècle). *Revue Des Études Byzantines* 22: 5–44. [CrossRef]

Jonveaux, Isabelle. 2013. *Dieu En Ligne: Expériences et Pratiques Religieuses Sur Internet*. Montrouge: Bayard.

Jonveaux, Isabelle. 2015. Les Moniales et l'emprise Du Genre. Enquête Dans Des Monastères Catholiques de Femmes. *Sociologie* 6: 121–220. [CrossRef]

Jugănaru, Andra. 2018. Family Double Monasteries in the Fourth and the Fifth Centuries: An Inquiry into the Theological Roots, Social Context, and Early Evolution of an Old Practice. Ph.D. dissertation, Central European University, Budapest, Hungary. Available online: http://www.etd.ceu.edu/2018/juganaru_andra.pdf (accessed on 12 April 2019).

Justinian. ; Translated by Justice Fred H. Blume. 2008. *Novels*, 2nd ed. Available online: http://www.uwyo.edu/lawlib/blume-justinian/ajc-edition-2/novels/121-140/novel%20133_replacement.pdf (accessed on 30 May 2019).

Konidaris, Johannes M. 1990. Die Novelle 123 Justinians und das Problem der Doppelklöster. *Subseciva Groningana (Studies in honor of Nicholas van der Wal)* 4: 105–16.

Krueger, Paulus, ed. 1892. *Corpus Iuris Civilis. Codex Iustinianus*. Berolini: Apud Weidmannos, vol. 2.

Kyrill. 2018. Personal Letter to Maria Chiara Giorda. January 13.

Melvani, Nicholas. 2016. The Duplication of the Double Monastery of Christ Philanthropos in Constantinople. *Revue Des Études Byzantines* 74: 361–84.

Menegaldo, Héléne. 1998. *Les Russes à Paris: 1919–39*. Paris: Autrement.

Migne, Jacques-Paul, ed. 1857–1866. *Patrologiae Cursus Completus. Series Graeca*. Parisiis: Migne, vols. 26, 31, 34, 46, 62, 65.

Miller, Timothy. 2000. Theodore Studites: Testament of Theodore the Studite for the Monastery of St. John Stoudios in Constantinople. In *Byzantine Monastic Foundation Documents: A Complete Translation of the Surviving Founders' Typika and Testaments*. Edited by John Ph. Thomas and Angela Constantinides. Dumbarton Oaks 35. Washington, DC: Dumbarton Oaks Research Library and Collection, pp. 67–83.

Mitsiou, Ekaterini. 2008. Das Doppelkloster Des Patriarchen Athanasios I. in Konstantinopel: Historisch-Prosopographische Und Wirtschaftliche Beobachtungen. *Jahrbuch Der Österreichischen Byzantinistik* 58: 87–106. [CrossRef]

Monastere St. Jean Baptiste. 2012. Moine à Tolleshunt Knights. In *Cahiers Saint Silouane l'Athonite, Hommage à l'Archimandrite Starez Syméon (1928–2009)*. Edited by Jean-Claude Polet. Buisson Ardent. Horse-Série. Paris: Cerf, pp. 11–24.

Morard, Françoise. 1974. *Monachos, Moine Histoire du Terme grec Jusqu'au 4e Siècle: Influences Bibliques et Gnostiques*. Fribourg: Paulus-Verlag.

Morison, Ernest Frederick. 1912. *St. Basil and His Rule; a Study in Early Monasticism*. New York: H. Frowde.

Morris, Rosemary. 1995. *Monks and Laymen in Byzantium, 843–1118*. New York: Cambridge University Press.

Palladius. 1964. *The Lausiac History*. Edited by Robert T. Meyer. New York: Newman Press.

Palmisano, Stefania. 2015. *Exploring New Monastic Communities: The (Re)invention of Tradition*. Burlington: Ashgate.

Pargoire, Jules. 1906. Les monastères doubles chez les Byzantins. *Revue des Études Byzantines* 9: 21–25. [CrossRef]

Parrinello, Rosa M. 2012. *Il Monachesimo Bizantino*. Roma: Corocci.

Peters, Greg. 2018. *The Monkhood of All Believers: The Monastic Foundation of Christian Spirituality*. Grand Rapids: Baker Academic.

Puretzki, Nikolai. 2017. *Life and Teaching of Saint Seraphim of Sarov*. The Hague: Gozalov Books.

Rapp, Claudia. 2006. Desert, City, and Countryside in the Early Christian Imagination. *Church History and Religious Culture* 86: 93–112. [CrossRef]

Rapp, Claudia. 2011. Early Monasticism in Egypt. In *Female Vita Religiosa between Late Antiquity and the High Middle Ages: Structures, Developments and Spatial Contexts*. Edited by Gert Melville and Ann Müller. Wien and Berlin: Lit, pp. 21–42.

Rhallis, Georgios Alexandros, and Michael Potlis. 1852. *Syntagma tōn theiōn kai hierōn kanonōn*. Athens: Chartophylakos, vol. 2.

Roudometof, Victor. 2015. Orthodox Christianity as a Transnational Religion: Theoretical, Historical and Comparative Considerations. *Religion, State and Society* 43: 211–27. [CrossRef]

Sakharov, Nicholas V. 2002. *I Love Therefore I Am: The Theological Legacy of Archimandrite Sophrony*. Crestwood: St. Vladimir's Seminary Press.

Sarni, Michael. 2012. *The Russian Church in London. From Peter the Great to the Present Day*. London: Arefa.

Schipper, Friedrich. 2005. 'Wir Erlauben Nicht, Dass in Einem Kloster Mönche Und Nonnen Wohnen' (Just. Nov. 123.36): Doppelklöster Im Spätantiken Ostmediterranen Raum. *Kanon* 17: 56–77.

Schmemann, Alexander. 1964. Problems of Orthodoxy in America. 1. The Canonical Problem. *St. Vladimir's Seminary Quarterly* 8: 67–85.

Schöll, Rudolf, and Wilhelm Kroll, eds. 1963. *Corpus Juris Civilis. Novellae*. Berlin and Zürich: Weidmann, vol. 3.

Silvas, Anna M. 2007. In Quest of Basil's Retreat: An Expedition to Ancient Pontus. *Antichthon* 41: 73–95. [CrossRef]

Sokolof, Dmytri. 2001. *A Manual of The Orthodox Church's Divine Services*. Jordanville: Holy Trinity Monastery.

Sophrony, Archim. 1999. *Saint Silouan, the Athonite*. Crestwood: St. Vladimir's Seminary Press.

Špidlik, Thomas. 2007. *Il Monachesimo Secondo La Tradizione Dell'Oriente Cristiano*. Roma: Lipa.

Stoney, Constance. 1915. *Early Double Monasteries a Paper Read before the Heretics' Society on December 6th, 1914*. London: G. Bell & Sons.

Stramara, Daniel F. 1998a. Double Monasticism in the Greek East, Fourth through Eighth Centuries. *Journal of Early Christian Studies* 6: 269–312. [CrossRef]

Stramara, Daniel F. 1998b. Double Monasticism in the Greek East: Eighth through Fifteenth Centuries. *The Greek Orthodox Theological Review* 43: 185–202.

Syméon, Archim. 2012. Génération Du Monastère Saint Jean Baptiste. In *Cahiers Saint Silouane l'Athonite, Hommage à l'Archimandrite Starez Syméon (1928–2009)*. Edited by Jean-Claude Polet. Buisson Ardent. Horse-Série. Paris: Cerf, pp. 40–47.

Talbot, Alice-Mary Maffry. 1985. A Comparison of the Monastic Experience of Byzantine Men and Women. *The Greek Orthodox Theological Review* 30: 1–20.

Talbot, Alice-Mary Maffry. 1990. The Byzantine Family and the Monastery. *Dumbarton Oaks Papers* 44: 119–29. [CrossRef]

Talbot, Alice-Mary Maffry. 1998. Women's Space in Byzantine Monasteries. *Dumbarton Oaks Papers* 52: 113–29. [CrossRef]

Talbot, Alice-Mary Maffry. 2000. Philanthropos: Typikon of Irene Choumnaina Palaiologina for the Convent of Christ Philanthropos in Constantinople. In *Byzantine Monastic Foundation Documents: A Complete Translation of the Surviving Founders' Typika and Testaments*. Edited by John Ph. Thomas and Angela Constantinides. Dumbarton Oaks 35. Washington, DC: Dumbarton Oaks Research Library and Collection, pp. 1383–88.

The Holorogion, or Book of Hours. 2000. South Canaan: St. Tikhon's Seminary Press.

Theokritoff, Elizabeth. 2009. *Living in God's Creation: Orthodox Perspectives on Ecology*. Crestwood: St. Vladimir's Seminary Press.

Thomas, John Philip. 1987. *Private Religious Foundations in the Byzantine Empire*. Dumbarton Oaks 24. Washington, DC: Dumbarton Oaks Research Library and Collection.

Trone, Robert. 1983. A Constantinopolitan Double Monastery of the Fourteenth Century: The Philanthropic Savior. *Byzantine Studies* 10: 81–86.

Veilleux, Armand, ed. 1980. *Pachomian Koinonia: The Life of Saint Pachomius and His Disciples*. Kalamazoo: Cistercian Publications, vol. 1.

Veilleux, Armand, ed. 1981. *Pachomian Koinonia: Pachomian Chronicles and Rules*. Kalamazoo: Cistercian Publications, vol. 2.

Visiting St. John the Baptist Monastery, England. Orthodox in Malaysia. 2018. Available online: https://orthodoxinmalaysia.wordpress.com/2018/06/24/visiting-st-john-the-baptist-monastery-england/ (accessed on 4 July 2019).

Wipszycka, Ewa. 2009. *Moines et Communautés Monastiques En Égypte (IVe-VIIIe Siècles).* Journal of Juristic Papyrology Supplement 1. Varsovie: Raphael Taubenschlag Foundation.
Zacharias, Archim. 2003. *Christ, Our Way and Our Life. A Presentation of the Theology of Archimandrite Sophrony.* South Canaan: St. Tikhon's Seminary Press.

religions **MDPI**

Article

New Monasticism: An Answer to the Contemporary Challenges of Catholic Monasticism?

Stefania Palmisano [1],* and Marcin Jewdokimow [2]

[1]   The Department of Cultures, Politics and Society, University of Turin, 10153 Torino, Italy
[2]   Faculty of Humanities, Cardinal Stefan Wyszyński University in Warsaw, 01-815 Warszawa, Poland
*   Correspondence: stefania.palmisano@unito.it

Received: 4 June 2019; Accepted: 26 June 2019; Published: 28 June 2019

Abstract: New Monasticism has been interpreted by its protagonists as an answer to the challenges of the future of Christian monasticism. New Monastic Communities can be defined as groups of people (at least some of whom have taken religious vows) living together permanently and possessing two main characteristics: (1) born in the wake of Vatican Council II, they are renewing monastic life by emphasising the most innovative and disruptive aspects they can find in the Council's theology; and (2) they do not belong to pre-existing orders or congregations—although they freely adapt their Rules of Life. New Monastic Communities developed and multiplied in the decades during which, in Western European countries and North America, there was a significant drop in the number of priests, brothers and sisters. Based on our empirical research in a new monastic community—the Fraternity of Jerusalem (a foundation in Poland)—we addressed the following: Why are New Monastic Communities thriving? Are they really counteracting the decline of monasticism? What characteristics distinguish them from traditional communities? We will show how they renew monastic life by emphasising and radicalising the most innovative and disruptive theological aspects identified in Vatican Council II.

Keywords: New Monastic Communities; Vatican Council II; monasticism

---

1. Introduction

Looking at the phenomenon of the Catholic religious life from the perspective of the last 300 years, one notices a sine wave tendency: after its collapse in the eighteenth century, there was a spectacular development in the nineteenth and twentieth centuries which stopped circa the mid-1960s when a reduction in the number of religious sisters, brothers and priests began. The eighteenth-century collapse was strictly related to the Enlightenment: its political consequences and the regional contexts in which it proceeded triggered the politics of dissolution of the monasteries and religious orders—a deliberate, state-driven politics of closure and appropriation of their fortunes. Hostie (1983) showed that between 1770 and 1850, the decrease may be counted in the hundreds of thousands: while in 1770 there were almost 300,000 members of male religious orders, by 1850 there were 200,000 fewer (Hostie 1983 after Finke and Wittberg 2000, p. 159). In Europe, the number of Franciscans dropped from 133,000 in 1815 to 39,000 in 1850; Dominicans decreased from 30,000–40,000 in 1780 to 5000 in 1844; in France, the number of Benedictine monasteries decreased from 2000 in 1789 to 20 in 1815 (Wittberg 1994, p. 38). In Poland, the general number of male monasteries dropped from 990 in 1772 to 188 in 1914 and the number of religious priests and brothers from 14,540 to 2252 in the same period (Derwich 2012). The slow increase began in the years after 1850, but these were new groups, founded after 1800 and not in previously established orders, who attracted new members (Finke and Wittberg 2000). In the nineteenth century (between 1800 and 1880), 400 new female religious communities were established in France, with 200,000 sisters, while in Ireland, their number increased rapidly from 1800 to 8000 (between 1800 and 1900), and in America, from more than 1300 to more than 40,000 (between 1850 and 1900) (Finke and Wittberg 2000, p. 160). Growth continued up to the middle of the 1960s, when the present "crisis" began. For instance, between 1974 and 2015, there was a general drop in the number of nuns from over 980,000 to 670,000 (−32 per cent); in the number of religious brothers from 70,500 to 54,000 (−23 per cent); and religious priests by 9 percent, from almost 147,000 to 134,000. At the same time, however, Catholic religious orders developed and grew in Africa, Asia and South America. Hence, even though the drop is clear in terms of quantity, it is not the general trend (Jewdokimow 2018).

In sociological terms, the reasons for the "crisis" in Europe and North America is usually explained by pointing to: (1) discrepancies between the form of religious life and the changing attitudes and needs of young Catholics (Greeley 1972); (2) social changes, which—leading to the secularisation of societies—reduced the attractiveness of the religious life, and at the same time created many new life opportunities, including professional ones, especially in economically developed countries, in particular, for women (Ebaugh 1977, 1993; Ebaugh et al. 1996; Finke and Stark 2000); and (3) reforms initiated by the Second Vatican Council (Dilanni 1993; Finke 1997; Finke and Stark 1992; Wittberg 1994). The significance of the Council is interpreted in sociological texts above all in the context of reducing the unique value of religious life in the eyes of both secular and religious people. The basis for this claim is derived from three post-conciliar documents: *Lumen Gentium*, *Gaudium et Spes* and *Perfectae Caritatis*. For example, Finke and Stark (2000) indicate that, as a result of these records, all Christians (not only consecrated persons) were defined as seeking sanctity (although this is actually a reminder of biblical records and it is a significant one), and religious life from now on should be directed *towards* the world, and not away from it by seeking enclosure. These losses—as these changes in the spirit of the theory of rational choice are defined—were not compensated by either a reduction in the cost of this demanding lifestyle or reward for them in the secular sphere (there was no increase in prestige, nor partial decline) (Finke and Stark 2000; Wittberg 1994). There are also indications of organisational changes related to the Council's provisions: limitation of collective activities for the growth of individual activities, which is treated as a factor that diminishes the sustainability of these communities (Finke and Stark 2000), as well as identity crises of religious priests (Sammon 2001).[1]

While discussing the challenges of monasticism today, one cannot omit these general tendencies and social changes. However, the weakness of these data is related to its institutional provenance. It should be emphasized that the above analysis refers to institutionally recognised and approved forms of consecrated life, which, according to the data, are in crisis because of the drop in the number of their members. However, does it indicate that monasticism and Catholic religious life in general are in crisis? As in the nineteenth century, today we observe the emergence of new religious forms, such as individual types of consecrated life, secular institutes, New Monastic Communities or other hybrid forms which absorb elements of traditions in religious life, attracting sincere individuals, yet they evade clear categorisation and institutional recognition due to which it is almost impossible to present their development quantitatively. We claim that focusing on these emerging forms may help us to understand how Catholic religious life in general, and monasticism in particular, seek to address both the "crisis" and the challenges of the contemporary world. Hence, even though we observe the massive drop in Catholic religious orders it is perhaps a mistake to interpret it as a general crisis of consecrated life. Rather, what we see is a stage of transformation. That transformation is triggered by both external and internal factors. External factors were reviewed above in the form of sociological hypothesis. Internal factors are related to institutional changes which affect all institutions. Analysing the history of

---

[1]   It should be emphasised that some of the theological interpretations of the Council with regard to its provisions and consequences also emphasise its negative influence on the condition of religious life. In 2005, Benedict XVI spoke about two hermeneutics (discontinuities and reforms) of the Second Vatican Council and constant discussion on this background. In addition, the reforms of religious life did not conclude with the Second Vatican Council, they are ongoing—the latest publication in this regard is *New wine in new wineskins. The consecrated life from the Second Vatican Council and its ongoing challenges since Vatican II. Guidelines.* (the publication is a result of the 2014 meeting of the Congregation for Institutes of Consecrated Life (2017) and Societies of Apostolic Life).

religious orders, Roger Finke and Patricia Wittberg conclude that these religious institutions undergo "the periodic cycles of revival, decline, and even extinction [. . .] and follow a life cycle that resembles that of a Protestant sect. The life of the movement begins in a high state of tension with the surrounding culture and seeks to make changes by restoring an old tradition or introducing a new one. Over time, however, the religious order frequently accommodates to the surrounding culture and the religious fervour of the founders becomes lost in highly routinized rituals" (Finke and Wittberg 2000, p. 166).

From the spectrum of new forms of consecrated life, within this article we focus on New Monastic Communities.[2] We claim that studying these entities allows us to address many relevant contemporary questions concerning general issues in religion, such as: How does religion transform itself in secular societies? How do religious institutions operate in a secular social context? How does culture intercept elements of the religious life and employ it for secular goals? This article is devoted to more limited, yet also vital questions. Based on our empirical research within one new monastic community—the Fraternity of Jerusalem (Poland)—we address the following questions: Why are New Monastic Communities thriving? Are they really counteracting the decline of monasticism? What characteristics distinguish them from traditional communities? More precisely, what are the breaking-off and continuity points? Do NMCs simply re-adjust traditional monasticism or do they transform it radically to the extent of (re)inventing it? Hence, we address here the questions of the future and challenges to Catholic monasticism.

1.1. Defining NMCs

New Monasticism has been interpreted by its protagonists as an answer to challenges of the future of Christian monasticism. New Monastic Communities can be defined as groups of people (at least some of whom have taken religious vows) living together permanently and possessing two main characteristics: (1) born in the wake of Vatican Council II, they are renewing monastic life by emphasising the most innovative and disruptive aspects they can deduct from the Council's theology; (2) they do not belong to pre-existing orders or congregations—although they freely adapt their Rules of Life; they are simultaneously attracted by the "old" monastic communities and exist in critical relation to them.

There are only a few studies concerning these communities (Hervieu-Léger 1986; Wittberg 1996; Landron 2004; Oviedo 2008) and they mainly focus on practical objectives, addressing such questions as: how should the ecclesiastical hierarchy behave towards NMCs, how bishops may recognise them canonically and how they can intervene to curtail certain eccentricities. This may result from the broader scarcity of sociological interest in monasticism and religious orders (Jonveaux et al. 2014; Jewdokimow 2018) which contrasts with historical and theological interest in the phenomenon of forms of consecrated life.

Studies show that NMCs are mainly concentrated in the United States and in Europe (predominantly in Italy, France and Spain) (Secondin 1991; Favale 2003; Rocca 2002, 2010), in the very regions where we notice a quantitative crisis of "old" forms of religious life. This reveals a general view that NMCs may be seen as a response to the crisis. These are, for instance, Bose (Italy), Figli di Dio (Italy), La Piccola Famiglia dell'Annunziata (Italy), Fraternitè monastique de Jerusalem (France), Fraternidad Maria Estrella de la Mañana (Spain), La Famiglia monastica di Betlemme, dell'Assunzione della Vergine Maria e di San Bruno (Italy), Ricostruttori nella preghiera (Italy) (Palmisano 2015, p. 14).[3]

---

2   It should be stressed that most NMCs are being recognised as (private or public) associations of the faithful and not as orders or institutions of consecrated life which results from the 1983 Canon Law regulations.

3   One shall also recall here Protestant and Ecumenical communities such as, for instance, Taizé, the Bruderhof, the Evangelical Sisterhood of Mary, Bonhoeffer's Finkewalde community in Germany, the Iona Community in Scotland, and the Community of Jesus in Cape Cod. All these communities have no relation to Vatican Council II, and as such, they do not meet our operational definition of NMCs (see in this article Section 1.1. Defining NMCs), and transcend the focus of our article which is Catholic monasticism. However, it also should be stressed that these communities have contributed to the phenomenon of the contemporary renewal of monasticism, and as such, should be recalled in the article on NMCs. It is an inspiring

Stefania Palmisano counted 50 NCMs in France, in Italy 45, and in Spain 10. However, due to the short lifespan these numbers should be frequently updated.

It should be stressed that the novelty of the term 'new monastic community' may be simplified because some monastic orders, established before Vatican II, renewed themselves in accordance with the Council's decrees, hence, they have been adaptive and innovative (these are: Benedictines, Cistercians, Trappists, and Camaldolians). Also, some of the NMCs which emerged after Vatican II are traditional in their modus operandi, meaning that they have reintroduced anterior liturgical forms, customs and traditions (for example, *La Famiglia monastica di Betlemme, dell'Assunzione della Vergine Maria e di San Bruno* (Italy)). However, after Vatican II, innovations introduced by classical monastic orders into their centuries-old existence did not challenge the inherent assumptions of monasticism while NMCs refer to this tradition freely, and thereby, challenge it.

We will demonstrate how they renew monastic life by emphasising and radicalising the most innovative and disruptive theological aspects which they identify in Vatican Council II, inter alia, monks and nuns living in the same complex; they restrict enclosure and limit collective prayer time in order to increase time available for labour, for evangelisation and voluntary social work, often outside the monastery; they are actively involved in ecumenical and inter-religious dialogue, and harbour barely concealed sympathy with oriental religions.

We will focus on the selected community—the Jerusalem Monastic Fraternity (JMF)—present its traits and discuss them in reference to the broader question of monasticism today. We focused on two communities established in Poland in 2010. We conducted interviews with five nuns and five brothers and performed participant observation during a lunch and recreational time in a female monastery. Interviews were transcribed and analysed in reference to research questions.

2. Findings

2.1. The History of The Jerusalem Monastic Fraternity and in Poland

In our study, we focused on two JMF monasteries located in Poland in the centre of Warsaw (they came to Poland in 2010, at the invitation of Cardinal Glemp). The two monasteries (male and female) are situated in one complex—from the street they appear to form one institution, but although the entrances and all other spaces are separate, they co-operate closely. In the male branch, there are 4 monks and, in the female, 11. There are three lay communities connected with the JMF in Warsaw: a community of families, an evangelical community and a community of Christian meditation. There is also a foundation (the Jerusalem Urbs Beata Foundation[4]), which is run by lay people. The foundation also manages a shop.[5]

The Jerusalem Monastic Fraternity was founded in 1975 in the Paris church of Saint–Gervais et Saint–Protais by a diocesan priest, Pierre–Marie Delfieux, with the support of the then Archbishop of Paris, Cardinal Marty. The desire to set-up a new kind of monasticism at the heart of the capital grew out of the young Delfieux's experience as a student chaplain at the Sorbonne during the years of contestation and matured while he was spending two years as a hermit in the Sahara Desert. Although interested in monastic life, he was critical of the form it had assumed over time, particularly medieval monasticism which he considered "rustic, cloistered and abbot-bound" and he agreed with Cardinal Marty that "Millennium monasteries"[6] should necessarily spring up within the walls of Paris.

Whereas the name "Jerusalem" appeared some time (1978) after the foundation—initially the community was called "Saint–Gervais"—the adjective "monastic" was present from the beginning

---

issue to investigate common points and differences of the contemporary process of returning to monasticism in different Christian denominations (for more on Protestant monasticism see for instance: Tennenhouse 2016; Eccles and Simon 2016; Montemaggi 2016).
4   See http://urbsbeata.pl/o-nas/.
5   See http://wspolnoty-jerozolimskie.pl.
6   This desire had already been expressed by Cardinal Marty during a 1972 Paris lecture (Cf. Marty 1979, pp. 43–47).

even though Delfieux immediately recognised a problem of definition when he questioned whether or not they were monks. Recognizing that only the future could answer that question, the problem was agreeing upon what "monk" meant. Monks should try to find a new way of living the truth of the Beatitudes in their time. According to Delfieux, the plan for this new life form would not be pastoral, sacramental, pedagogic or charitable but contemplative. In 1979, Cardinal Marty himself gave a monastic frame to the new community, placing it—as soon as its statutes have been approved—under the patronage of a traditional monastery.

Delfieux's choice of an urban setting led to specific organisational decisions: that of rented accommodation; salaried employment outside a cloister which had by now become metaphorical; special attention towards the liturgy understood not only as opus Dei but also as a public service which, as such, should at the same time manage to be attractive and "nourishing" for its participants. There followed the choice of a liturgical form which joined together creative aspects of active participation and a preference for places with artistic and architectural value which became excellent backgrounds for carrying out liturgical rites. Monks and nuns are divided not only by Canon Law, but also into two distinct institutions. They are usually both present in their various communities, sharing not only liturgical prayer by singing together in polyphony, but also doctrinal education and festivities.

2.2. Egalitarian Features—Mixitè

One of the traits of NMCs is challenging the strict division of male and female realms. In the case of JMF in Poland, there are two distinct, male and female, monasteries living in a very close symbiosis which may be called mixitè. It is not so developed as in some other NMCs where nuns and brothers live under one roof (as in Bose). Mixitè is one of the egalitarian characteristics of the JMF. For JMF, it means sharing liturgy, doctrinal instruction, singing lessons and festivities; they cooperate on a daily basis, for instance, in terms of economy; but lodging, community governance and vocational discernment between monks and nuns are separate and independent; they also remain distinct institutions in the eyes of Canon Law. While developing the Constitution, Delfieux indicated a preference for a configuration, whereby the male and female branches were part of the same institute. Although this option was vetoed by the Congregations for Institutes of Consecrated Life, JMF monks and nuns perceive one another as complementary and as belonging to the same family. According to the founder, the Church–historical reasons which caused an almost absolute separation between men and women was not evangelical but rather historical–cultural and sociological. The decision to associate monks and nuns is interpreted as a return to its origins,[7] taking on the value of exemplary witness.

Both nuns and monks from JMF understand this symbiosis in a broader context, as part of the critical process of changing the position of women within society—and with the reserve recognised by the Church—yet welcomed by the community.

"Surely this is a sign for the Church, because women, sisters, here are not subordinate but are quite autonomous. Sometimes because the community came from France, affirming its importance is necessary and I suppose that it has something of a feminist spirit, yet it is not feminism [...] often in France when we meet sisters, I get the idea that these women are shaped by French society where a woman holds her head high and does not wish to let a man rule her [...] So I suppose that this a sign not only for the world but also for the Church. I was very pleased when Pope Francis said a few years ago that a woman is not meant to be a servant. Also, the sisters have their own Superior, their training, their finances and are in no way subject to the brothers." (M2)

---

7 In this context, Delfieux quotes both passages from the Bible which testify that Jesus had a female entourage (Luke 8:1–2; 23, 69; 24, 10 and Mark 15:40–41) and examples of mixed monasteries in the past, such as Caesarea (fourth century) and Fontevrault (eleventh century).

"When we pray together, when we are together, then there is a fullness, the beauty of creation is shown even more [...] Pierre–Marie [Delfieux] asked for a testimony of chastity in this unclean world, that one should live in pure friendship [...] I have called it my own way to be like brothers and sisters, but you also have to look after it. If we do not fulfil this, we do not know each other, then there is no such communion, being close enough to be as brothers and sisters, and apart enough to be as brothers and sisters." (S1)

Interviewee S1 said that their approach towards a woman in the world derives from "human dignity" and not "feminist theology". According to her, shaping these kinds of relationships between men and women is relevant for the Church too. If priests are afraid of women, then this fear might manifest itself as ill-treatment or humiliation. This is the result of poor formation in seminaries.

In order to "be like brothers and sisters", meaning establishing an egalitarian community, nuns do not confess to brothers with whom they live because it would make their relationship asymmetrical and mixes up roles. According to S1, this gender pattern is not typical of Polish monastic culture:

"I remember my meeting with enclosed sisters, probably Carmelite. They said, so you have brothers. I replied that we are brothers and sisters together. So, you have fathers, your fathers to look after you. I replied, no. They have Carmelite fathers who are nearby, and they speak out and watch over them, they confess to them. I said we are brothers and sisters, they are not our fathers, and we do not confess to them, we do not confess to our brothers in principle, unless it is strictly necessary."

Mixitè illustrates the intention to build symmetrical, democratic relationships in the everyday life of the community. Another example of this being everyday duties such as cleaning, these jobs are shared equally in order to avoid overloading any one individual.

2.3. Openness Towards the World

Another trait of the JMF is openness towards the world. Of course, it is not specific for either Catholic religious orders or for monastic orders since Benedictines or Cistercians also engage in "in-the-world" activities. However, the JMF elaborated upon this connection innovatively. For the JMF, being open to the world is a multi-directional endeavour—it may be found in their relationship towards the city, work and in the structure of daily rhythms.

The Osmosis with the Contemporary Desert

Brothers and nuns repeat that the aim of their vocation is: "Being in osmosis with the contemporary world (here meaning the city), being accessible, and being a sign of God". According to interviewee M2, the Jerusalem Community aims at "liv[ing] in osmosis with the world, we are not separated from it by any enclosure". However, they direct themselves to the monastic tradition and to active forms of the religious life. Osmosis with the city takes place on many levels: living and working within it, and understanding themselves as individuals brought up in that city:

"The city looks in from every side, now there is silence, but [when] something is going on outside, or there is a demonstration in the street, something is happening. And it is our task to be monks in such a world, without abandoning it [...], the founder [claimed], we could theoretically be closed and separate from the world, but we have a form of life to share, being holy, living in harmony with God and at the same time seeking the deep connection with God which takes place in the heart thanks to silence and self-discipline." (M2)

Osmosis with the city is not only being practised by monks, but it is also embedded in the fabric of their monasteries. In Poland, the monastery is located in the city centre, next to a soccer stadium and on a very busy route. Noise is clearly audible in the monastery:

"We have a place, in Cologne, which is located in the tourist district and where there is a lot of activity, carnivals, and so forth. And the refectory, for example, where the reading room is with many windows, and in the evening it's just brothers in a goldfish bowl: people are walking down the street, and you can simply look inside.[8] It is the same in Paris, the same way where you come to the kitchen to cook dinner and the window is in the yard, and the courtyard is surrounded by a multi-storey tenement buildings, we are visible from the 10th floor. And this is a conscious choice, to be among people [...] In any case, the choice of this life, being accessible, its source is solidarity with them [people living in the city] and the desire to be close to them, to be available and to feel compassion for them." (M2)

Being centrally located means that the monks may be easily "accessible" and hence, they indicate the presence of God:

"So it seems to me that what is relevant about us is the fact that we do nothing, we do not give anything concrete, we do not produce anything, often we do not speak, but we choose life in the presence of God because He is so important to us [...] In fact, in such a large, modern city it is a difficult experience to come into contact with such an environment in which it is difficult to experience the spirit and go deeper." (M2)

The concept of the city is central to the theology of the Jerusalem Community. Of course, they are not the first religious order to locate its work in the city. From the 12th and 13th centuries onwards, monasteries were founded in the largest European cities by the Franciscans and Dominicans. Monasteries of different monastic orders have also been situated in cities, for example, the female Benedictines, Salesian Sisters or female Carmelites (Carmel), to mention but a few. According to M1, what distinguishes previous monks from the "new" ones is their attitude towards the city which they perceive as something not to be opposed, but within which one has to integrate.[9] For them, the city is the new desert where one may sacralise himself/herself. According to interviewee S1:

"Our unique attraction is actually life in big cities. This is an important element of our spirituality, big cities that are deserts, spiritual deserts. It has such a double positive and negative dimension in the sense that monks in the first centuries went to the desert, they searched for a place of loneliness, to seek God, to struggle with sin, to fight the devil, so here is our aspect of searching, the purification of the heart, our aim to be closer to God. The aspect of the desert as a place that does not give life, as a place without God [...]. So, this is the reality of the city, where a human created for communion, for love, for living in a brotherhood and for friendship, dies from loneliness." (S1)

Interviewee M1 highlights:

"The city is a spiritual desert because of the fact that the major stimuli in the city are work, play and entertainment. The spiritual dimension is weak here. And people leave the city and go towards nature, or perhaps into monasteries, right?" (M1)

According to S1, part-time work as a feature of the JFM should be reconsidered because it may be outdated being more attuned to the industrial era. The most recent general assembly of the JFM agreed that they have to look for new ways of demonstrating solidarity within the city. The interviewee S1 also claims that the practice of dividing time between working outside and living the life of a community of prayer inside is challenging and should be reconsidered because it is not easy to combine both in the present day.

---

8   For further information see: http://wspolnoty-jerozolimskie.pl. A brother to whom I talked (from the Cologne community) told me they do not feel as if they are being watched. See http://jerusalem.cef.fr/cologne-gross-sankt-martin/6310-gott-ist-in-der-stadt, a video created by monks and sisters from Cologne describing their life in the city.
9   However, one may recall here the urban monasticism from the fourth and fifth centuries.

The interviewee M1 underlines that the contemporary city is entirely different from the city of the 1960s and 1970s, and, therefore, one needs to find a way to connect with this new reality.

Then, [1960s/1970s] the reflection could have been really more direct, solidarity with those who go to work, live in rented flats and are city dwellers. Brothers doing part-time work [...] showed solidarity with the city and it was possible and greatly emphasised because everyone worked eight hours from 8:00 or from 7:00 to 15:00, normal working hours, so the brothers followed this pattern, but it has changed a lot. Today, the world of work and the world of the city have changed very much, and in this respect, we are looking for a new way to show solidarity with today's city." (M1)

2.4. Monks as Citizens and Workers

The specific spatial collocation of communities in the urban context is related to their other choices: of being not owners of property but renters, as well as the fact that monks and nuns tend to have an ordinary job outside the walls to which they are bound, as other workers all contribute to defining the identity of monks in the cities. The brothers and sisters work part-time to demonstrate their solidarity with lay people but also to combine contemplative and active elements of their life. However, work is less important than prayer and communal life.

Their work sense emerges from interviews with nuns: paying rent (where necessary), running accounts and setting aside a part for the poor, as well as sharing the fatigues of men and women working in the world. They tell us that part-time employment in communities can vary: some translate; others sell sacred objects, arts and crafts, cosmetics, honey, jams and marmalade in the monastery shop; some make icons; others are church secretaries. Nuns who are not so busy or who are studying deal with shopping, cooking and other domestic chores, such as being bursars. Such work should conform to the founder's criteria in the Fraternity Rule. Quoting Saint Basil, he points out: "This general rule may be established: choose the activities which safeguard our life in peace and tranquillity, which are not technically very difficult and do not lead to dangerous or unsuitable meetings" (Delfieux 2005, p. 36).[10]

There are four brothers in Warsaw and one novice (there are around 60 brothers worldwide). Now, only one brother works outside the monastery (in a Catholic institution), while others work within the monastery (three focus on church services and one—a hermit—as a translator). The sisters work in different professions but only in Catholic institutions. In the words of one of them:

"We work in various occupations according to what work can be found. Sometimes according to our studies, but we do not necessarily look in this direction, we have so many limitations, so if we can find any job, we are happy. We need to work only part-time and we cannot work on Mondays, because we have 'desert' days. And this form of work is becoming less and less popular." (S1)

The tension between contemplative and active elements is mirrored in the daily rhythm. A day is divided into two parts: the first part being work and active time; the second, communal, meditative time. On Monday, there is a day of the "desert" (no work and no communal praying). From interviews with the nuns, it further emerges that one of the severest difficulties of their monastic life—which they interpret as the most fatiguing form of ascesis—is the rhythm, the rigid timetable structure "fragmenting" their days and governing not only opus Dei but also their other daily activities (to avoid wasting time), giving them the sense of always being interrupted.

"You go to work, you come back, you have the rhythm of prayer, you have to do this, you have to do that ... How to manage it all? When you are young, you do not care about your health and you do too much which is against yourself ... " (S1)

---

[10] Translation of all quotations of Delfieux 2005 from Italian by Stefania Palmisano.

Another nun claims that because of this difficult composition of daily life a nun has to be mature to handle it:

> "So, if you want to combine these two areas, you have to be mature, then you will be able to do something outside in this Jerusalem which is the city, to work in the city, and then be able to come back and live here, inside." (S2)

The nuns also testify that while one gets used to this daily cadence, it is still a central aspect of their lives which they have to take into account: even if they are talking to somebody or reading, they have to stop and obey the call. Then there are other activities connected with daily life which intrude the nuns' lives, sometimes during prayer, lectio divina, or work (for example, when supplies do not arrive on time). In addition, nuns who are required to meet and talk to somebody may arrive late to the chapel for (individual) prayer, but they try to be punctual for the liturgy. They are not reprimanded by superiors if this happens infrequently, but this kind of "bother", i.e., "being disturbed by the world to the extent of finding oneself of the world", is a consequence of choosing to live in the city rather than retiring to the country. This last quotation comes from a monk whose order has monasteries in two European cities which are partly built of glass so that people can see them and acknowledge their existence. On Wednesday evenings after Chapter (an assembly of the whole community with males and females separated), ten minutes are devoted to "self-confession" where, after a hymn to the Holy Ghost, everybody (male and female) is free to talk about his/her omissions (e.g., being late, breakages, uncharitable thoughts and forgetfulness) and to ask for the community's forgiveness.

Living within the city is balanced with contemplative and communal (religious community) practices combined with prayer. This does not mean exclusion of people or seclusion from the world. In the JMF there is no papal enclosure. Monks and sisters work outside the monastery, which is also a challenge for them:

> "Our founder said that our monastery is a city. It does not mean that we go where we want, we do what we want. When we leave the monastery, we talk about it, we ask for permission. It is clear that I will not ask for permission to go to work, but if I have a certain path, I stick to it and I will not jump to the right, to the left, or take advantage of the fact that I went to work and I will do it, I will not walk around half of the city without telling anyone. Our lives require a lot of maturity, that you have to demand from yourself, to know why you came here. You can probably say that about every monastery, but the enclosure protects you." (S1)

2.5. Enclosure and Fuga Mundi

The traditional value of enclosure has been lost in the JMF. Although it does not appear, its meaning is radically transformed through a process of metaphorisation: from "mural" to "moral", i.e., from a place of radical separation from the world, a tangible expression of fuga mundi (flight from the world), a tool which permits safeguarding the self and contact with God. Even when the enclosure is partly mural, it becomes less a matter of space and more of time-management. The Constitution of the JMF states: "The monks/nuns adopt the reality of effective enclosure by living in a house reserved exclusively for them, particularly safeguarding the inviolability of their cells, every day ensuring periods of complete silence and perfect solitude and every week an entire 'desert' day in favour of a heart-to-heart with God alone." The Jerusalem Monastic Fraternity members consider traditional monastic enclosure as a means adopted in the past for reasons of historical–cultural contingencies. On this point, Delfieux writes: "Do not worry about that which is difficult to base explicitly on the text of the Gospels" (Delfieux 2005, p. 127).

2.6. Openness Towards Extra-Catholic Traditions

The last feature to be discussed is openness towards extra-Catholic traditions. The community is Catholic, with no members from other Christian denominations. Some Anglicans and Eastern Orthodox who were interested in the community converted to Catholicism in order to join it. The community's male and female branches are recognised today as institutes of consecrated life, which means that they must be Catholic. They take vows publicly in the Church. The intention for the future is to establish a federation of institutes, both male and the female, following the pattern of other communities (see the canonical recognition of the Beatitudes monastic community). Eastern influence, rather than Protestant, can be seen in the liturgy. The Catholic charismatic movement was stronger at the beginning because Delfieux's first spiritual brother came from that background, and still today, some brothers and sisters in certain communities share charismatic forms of prayer—but it is not present in Poland. The Warsaw community, however, offers hospitality to a charismatic prayer group which gathers in the chapel once a week.

The Jerusalem Monastic Fraternity combines broad social legitimation with canonical recognition as an institute of diocesan law. They came to this point step by step. The first stage was the elaboration of their statutes in 1979, consequently raised to a Pious Union. Later, after its recognition as an Association of the Faithful in 1984, both Constitutions ad experimentum were approved (the male branch in 1991 and the female in 1992) and finally the founding of the two Religious Institutes in 1996.

Having been recognised as two distinct institutes of consecrated life, both male and female communities are now working towards recognition as a federation.

2.7. Liturgy

The liturgy, like the Rule, is "composite": combined with elements drawn from the Western monastic tradition (reading the divine office and lectio divina) are new ones deriving from other Christian traditions in such a way that novices do not understand them fully. The liturgy is limited to three points during the day (Lauds in the morning, Sext at midday and Vespers before Mass in the evening) in order to allow the monks to work outside the community. Both monks and nuns attend these celebrations, singing in polyphony; they are separated before the presbytery but not distant from one another—they do not sit in stalls, but instead face the altar like the faithful.

One of the most noticeable aspects is the presence of Byzantine elements: icons, crosses, hymns, the daily incense ritual; the practice of metonymy,[11] lighting up the dome, icons, the altar and the menorah (the Jewish candelabra) with candles. Further characteristics are the use of various musical instruments at times which are usually dedicated to silence and more use of the body, originally inspired by Charismatic Catholicism by adopting different positions during prayer (mostly on foot, sometimes with arms raised and other times sitting on their heels) or movements (frequent processions, bowing, metonymy, interacting with the faithful).

According to interviewee M2, people today are developing a need for contemplative Christianity, related to prayer, silence and Eastern orthodox spirituality. It attracts not only young people, but also consecrated people.

"This need for another Christianity, as well as the different religious life that it expresses, among other things, not only that people can go there, young people, but that new communities, in any case Jerusalem, attract people who are already in the consecrated life and who come here from other communities or diocesan priests. There is also a characteristic feature that among us there are many who have a past in other forms of consecrated life, there is some difference and there is some novelty for which there is a demand, the model is not universal, it is not mass, but it is real. Also, there are among us former Benedictines, priests and sisters...as in France. The first group among Jerusalem communities, which was established in the 1970s, was composed of formers monks." (M2)

---

[11] Touching the ground by hand and then making the sign of the cross, repeating the sequence three times while singing a litany.

3. Discussion

Most NMCs were established after Vatican II and they are strictly related to the spirit of the Council: they have egalitarian characteristics (specifically male/female relationships and lay and religious people), openness towards extra-Catholic traditions and to the world. This results in many organisational innovations in comparison to classical monasticism such as: mixed male–female communal life and increase in status of women or broader individual autonomy. We recognised these aspects in the JMF under study. Sociologically speaking, NMCs represent many traits of advanced modernity such as: individualisation, gender sensitivity and self-fulfilment, to mention but a few. Modern, reflexive societies are strictly attached to the city. Monasticism emerged in the deserts, yet the version re-elaborated by the JMF has recognised this hyper-modern locus as the contemporary desert, and by doing so, aims to be present here in the same way as first monks were in their locations.

The JMF not only follows Vatican II principles, but it also adapts to the changing social environment in which they operate. They have understood the nature of contemporary work and aim to transform their working practices accordingly. We claim that the JMF are not only new, but they are also adaptable and attentive towards the contemporary world. By doing so they also re-connect with that world, treating it not as a threat but as a challenge and a natural environment.

Following social changes and actively looking to understand what the world requires from them, the community under study also seeks to adapt to the Polish context:

"This is a great joy for me, being among people who do not want to be separated, but who want to be open, to listen and to be what the world needs today […] We are not seeking to establish long-term forms but we are trying to listen and to understand what the world needs today and what we can do." (M2)

According to S1, all communities from the JMF have changed in their daily practices within the timespan of their existence. For example, sisters must have mobile phones with them while travelling by car in case of accident:

"Our rules are to serve life, and they are not to make us rigid or anachronistic." (S1)

Another adaptation is related to domestic tasks:

"To give an example, in France sisters do their own washing, but here there is no space, the laundry is in a tiny place, and there is nowhere to hang washing, so it is tumble-dried in a machine. For as long as I can remember, sheets were hung outside to dry. It has become more and more expensive; they are asking us to bring sheets to a monastery. I am preparing myself here and saying—we will be doing the washing ourselves—and then the General, she says 'No, not like in Paris', for her it was unthinkable that we would add further duties. I say, but who will pay for it? In our culture, it is a luxury and only hotels would do that, not sisters. Of course, we did not give it out anywhere, because she did not return to the subject. But during these last ten years she had not considered the issue from the Polish perspective."

Apart from practical, organisational differences, NMCs also differ from the ordo monasticum in terms of identity. They consider classical monastic orders to be outdated and believe that their means of differentiating themselves from the older orders convey a sense of the authenticity of their religious-life choices. New Monastic Communities remain in profound relationship to them—they purposefully choose elements from traditional monasticism which they reshuffle like bricolage.

Comparing old and New Monastic Communities is a promising field of study revealing various dynamics of tradition and adaptations to present social evolutions. Monastic life in Europe is not homogeneous, especially not in its relations with society, the institutional Church and the history of monasticism. New communities founded after the Council adopt a position of fracture from tradition, whereas old communities consider it as a pillar of their identity and their justification for existence. But joint evolutions of the new and the old are reducing the practical differences between them.

Variegated patterns can, therefore, be observed, constituting an unstable set which is open to evaluation according to external criteria. It would be interesting to explore the factors accounting for why new communities flourish in some societies (for example, Italy and France), and not in others (Austria), which welcomes new communities founded in other countries. Founding new communities is closely linked to a country's religious circumstances and older communities' contemporary position.

4. Conclusions

The NMCs seek to position themselves as a (re)invention of tradition, which is thought to mean a radical break with traditional monasticism. But the difference between new and old communities is not only a matter of degree: thus, this hiatus is barely noticeable if we simply compare the daily-life practices of the two, in efforts to find the instigators of the boldest changes. This attempt is destined to fail because traditional communities are today much closer, in practice, if not in theory, to the new communities than either of them would be willing to admit.

Moving on from the analysis above we shall now tackle the main question of this article: are NMCs (especially JMF) a response to challenges which monasticism faces today? In order to answer this question, it is worth pointing out that new and traditional monastic communities are not so very different as might appear at first. Three main reasons explain their tendential similarities:

1. In the wake of the Second Vatican Council, traditional monasteries changed profoundly in order to adapt to modernity, introducing important innovations which followed, in a similar vein, the orientations of the NMCs, thus reducing the practical differences between both of them. Monasticism—as we by now clearly understand—is not exempt from transformations assailing society as a whole. It is, therefore, no surprise that the individualistic impulses of advanced modernity have not stopped at the monastery gates.

2. Particular NMC innovations have proved to be the founding precepts of traditional communities outside Italy. While it is true that radical changes have been introduced by the Italian NMCs, those changes have been only tenuously adopted by most traditional Italian monasteries, yet traditional communities can be found in Europe where the style of life closely resembles that of the NMCs. Examination of contemporary European monasticism reveals marked differences in the organisation of community life, mainly explained by the variable of each individual country's social and religious history. To give but one example, abandoning enclosure in favour of work outside the monastery is considered typical of NMCs, and one of their primary innovations. But a study of traditional monasteries in Austria demonstrates that most of their work takes place outside the monastery, in schools or in parishes.[12] External work, far from being a novelty, has its roots in the eighteenth century when Emperor Joseph II, in line with the theories of the French economist Quesnay, promulgated a law closing religious communities which did not benefit society.

3. The largest and most prosperous NMCs are facing a process of institutional integration and operational routinisation which has the effect of eroding the innovative elements characteristic of their original flowering. As a consequence, they have ended up resembling traditional communities. The history of Bose is an example of this process. This community, born out of a radical return to the origins of monastic life (austerity, poverty, small in size, work outside the monastery, no habit, sober liturgy), experienced rapid social and economic development leading it gradually to abandon its original form for the traditional monastic model (buildings of monumental stature, work within the monastery, liturgical habit, polyphonic and, sometimes, Gregorian psalmody).

---

12   (Jonveaux 2014, pp. 71–86).

Despite these similarities, we argue that NMCs are, in reality, a response to challenges threatening monasticism today. Being aware of a vocational crisis, the community adapts to the contemporary world in many innovative respects. It does not negate the contemporary world, but instead seeks to understand it and follow it not only in its organisation but also in attitudes towards individuals.

This form of community is attractive to different groups. In terms of vocation, approximately 40 women have applied so far to join the female monastery (in the male section only three). Ten were accepted into the novitiate but only two took their final vows. Most of the applications were refused due to age (most of the applicants were over 35 years old, some over 45), and problems related to it, mostly with adapting to the cultural conditions in a monastery which expects subordination.

In 2017, the JMF performed a survey and distributed questionnaires to people attending Mass. Eighty respondents, lay people, declared that they came here, in the first place, because of the silence, the atmosphere of the church, the liturgy and worship. Consecrated people also participate in their liturgy and seminars attract people from Warsaw and beyond who "seek silence" and "humility" (M1).

To conclude, it is important to highlight that there is no sharp distinction between traditional and New Monasticism, with the first being static and obsolete, and the second active, in tune with transformation within the social context. We are witnessing an intersecting movement: while old communities are changing to become more like the new, the latter are becoming institutionalised and assuming the structure and patterns of the former. Well then, in the light of this tendential convergence, how can we explain the difference between them? The proposed answer in this paper has been that it is not a matter of degree but of changing perspectives. Goffman's metaphor of "frame" as "definition of the situation" helps to make this point clear (Goffman 1974). Working within a framework implies taking for granted (or at least sharing) the assumptions, rules and values of a given interaction context. Modifying the frame means calling it into question, problematising it or changing it. Monastic tradition may be interpreted as a frame to the extent that it institutes common sense with regard to how a monk's or a nun's life may be put into practice; a re-working intended to judge or modify its basic assumptions means changing the frame. Consequently, we argue that: (1) some NMCs are more similar to traditional monasticism than others and (2) "old" monasticism has also changed and attempted to keep up with modernity. Hochschild (2013) investigated interpretative variations based on a comparative study carried out in eight Benedictine monasteries in Germany, Austria and Hungary, developing the concept of "elastic tradition". According to these authors, the most evident differences among these monasteries are not only due to the leadership, constitutions and rules but also to the national differences regarding the role of the Catholic Church in the public sphere and in the theological debate as well as the novices and postulants' socio-cultural background.

Despite these similarities, we maintain that NMCs have triggered a paradigm shift which is particularly in tune with contemporary spiritual and religious research, which claim is supported by two research findings:

1. New Monastic Communities were born outside the Ordo monasticus. Whereas traditional communities introduce innovations which do not, however, invalidate monasticism's basic assumptions (which remain in the frame), NMCs question these assumptions (in which sense they are changing the frame) and they redefine the very identity of monasticism. Let us give some examples. No matter how hard Benedictine communities try to update the *Regula Benedicti*, they cannot abandon it; on the contrary, their loyalty is ensured by almost daily reading of a chapter. No matter how much they encourage collaboration between monks and nuns in neighbouring monasteries, they have no interest in initiating experiments of cohabitation "under the same roof". Ultimately, Benedictine monks wish to preserve tradition because they see in it the source of legitimacy of monasticism itself. Therefore, to integrate the changes which they make, they develop strategies of recomposition (for instance, as Jonveaux notes, they invent religious-type justification for professional and economic innovations). In any case, the changes—often imposed by the necessity of adapting to transformations of society or market imperatives—are registered in monasticism's chain of memories. Briefly, the principal divergence between old and new communities is their ideological position vis-à-vis tradition, which

marks a watershed: in old monasticism, the institution is the guarantor of tradition, instilling respect for its basic assumptions, whereas in New Monasticism, founders interpret tradition liberally, developing it creatively by modifying its basic assumptions.

2. The discomfort of ecclesiastical authorities tasked with validating NMCs' authenticity confirms the gap between old and New Monasticism. Bishops are reluctant to legitimise them because they subvert the traditional requisites of religious life; in other words, they "change the frame". Apart from the problems that bishops have to face in managing their dioceses, the mountain of work under which they are buried and the lack of directives with respect to new communities, it is the audacity and disruption of NMCs' innovations (mixité, ecumenism, temporary vows) which slow down and delay the recognition procedure. In essence, it is the variable principle determining their ambiguous legitimacy which is the radical novelty of NMCs.

Author Contributions: Conceptualization, S.P. and M.J.; Methodology, S.P. and M.J.; Investigation, S.P. and M.J.; Writing—Original Draft Preparation, S.P. and M.J.; Writing—Review & Editing, S.P. and M.J.

Funding: The article was financed with the resources from the National Science Centre (Poland), decision number: UMO-2016/21/B/HS6/01057.

Conflicts of Interest: The authors declare no conflict of interest.

References

Congregation for Institutes of Consecrated Life. 2017. *New Wine in New Wineskins. The Consecrated Life from the Second Vatican Council and Its Ongoing Challenges since Vatican II. Guidelines*. Rome: Libreria Editrice Vaticana.

Delfieux, Pierre-Marie. 2005. *Come monastero la città. Un nuovo volto del monachesimo*. Milano: Ancora.

Derwich, Marek. 2012. The main assumptions of the project Cultural heritage of dissolved monasteries on the territory of former Poland and in Silesia in 18th and 19th c.: Fate, significance, cataloguing. *Hereditas Monasteriorum* 1: 363–68.

Dilanni, Albert. 1993. Religious Vocations: A New Sign of the Times. *Review for Religious* 52: 745–63.

Ebaugh, Helen Rose Fuchs. 1977. *Out of the Cloister: A Study of Organizational Dilemmas*. Austin: University of Texas Press.

Ebaugh, Helen Rose Fuchs. 1993. *Women in the Vanishing Cloister: Organizational Decline in Catholic Religious Orders in the United States*. New Brunswick: Rutgers University Press.

Ebaugh, Helen Rose Fuchs, Jon Lorence, and Janet Saltzman Chafetz. 1996. The Growth and Decline of the Population of Catholic Nuns Cross-Nationally, 1960–1990: A Case of Secularization as Social Structural Change. *Journal for the Scientific Study of Religion* 35: 171–83. [CrossRef]

Eccles, Janet, and David Simon. 2016. The Community of the Resurrection: A Case Study in the (Re)Emergence/Evolution of Anglican/English Monasticism. In *Monasticism in Modern Times*. Edited by Isabelle Jonveaux and Stefania Palmisano. New York: Routledge, pp. 173–90.

Favale, Agostino. 2003. *Comunità nuove nella chiesa*. Padua: EDB.

Finke, Roger. 1997. An Orderly Return to Tradition: Explaining Membership Recruitment to Catholic Religious Orders. *Journal of the Scientific Study of Religion* 36: 218–30. [CrossRef]

Finke, Roger, and Rodney Stark. 1992. *The Churching of America, 1776–1990: Winners and Losers in our Religious Economy*. New Brunswick: Rutgers University Press.

Finke, Roger, and Rodney Stark. 2000. Catholic Religious Vocations: Decline and Revival. *Review of Religious Research* 42: 125–45.

Finke, Roger, and Patricia Wittberg. 2000. Organizational Revival From Within: Explaining Revivalism and Reform in the Roman Catholic Church. *Journal for the Scientific Study of Religion* 39: 154–70. [CrossRef]

Goffman, Erving. 1974. *Frame Analysis: An Essay on the Organization of Experience*. Cambridge: Harvard University Press.

Greeley, Andrew M. 1972. *The Catholic Priest in the United States: Sociological Investigations*. Washington: United States Catholic Conference.

Hervieu-Léger, Danièle. 1986. *Vers un nouveau christianisme? Introduction à la sociologie du christianisme occidental*. Paris: Éditions du Cerf.

Hochschild, Michael. 2013. Benediktiner zwischen Kontinuität und Wandel. ... einem internationalen Forschungsprojekt. *Erbe und Auftrag* 1: 23–45.

Hostie, Raymond. 1983. *The Life and Death of Religious Orders*. Washington: Center for Applied Research in the Apostolate.

Jewdokimow, Marcin. 2018. *Klasztor w perspektywie socjologicznej: W poszukiwaniu nowego ujęcia [A Monastery in a Sociological Perspective: Seeking for a New Approach]*. Warsaw: Wydawnictwo Naukowe UKSW.

Jonveaux, Isabelle. 2014. Redefinition of the Role of Monks in Modern Society: Economy as Monastic Opportunity. In *Sociology and Monasticism: Between Innovation and Tradition*. Edited by Isabelle Jonveaux, Enzo Pace and Stefania Palmisano. Leiden and Boston: Brill, pp. 71–86.

Jonveaux, Isabelle, Enzo Pace, and Stefania Palmisano, eds. 2014. *Sociology of Monasticism: Between Innovation and Tradition*. Annual Review of the Sociology of Religion Series No. 5. Leiden and Boston: Brill.

Landron, Olivier. 2004. *Les communautés nouvelles. Nouveaux visages du catholicisme français*. Paris: Éditions du Cerf.

Marty, François. 1979. *L'eveque dans la ville*. Paris: Éditions du Cerf, pp. 43–47.

Montemaggi, Francesca. 2016. *The Making of the Relational Christian Self of New Monastics in the UK, US, and Canada*. Edited by Isabelle Jonveaux and Stefania Palmisano. New York: Routledge, pp. 209–28.

Oviedo, Lluís T. 2008. Should we say that the Second Vatican Council has failed? *The Heythrop Journal* XLIX: 716–30.

Palmisano, Stefania. 2015. *Exploring New Monastic Communities. The Re-Invention of Tradition*. Aldershot: Ashgate.

Rocca, Giancarlo. 2002. Nuove forme di vita consacrata. *Vita Consacrata* 38: 563–75.

Rocca, Giancarlo. 2010. *Primo censimento delle nuove comunità*. Rome: Urbaniana University Press.

Sammon, Seán D. 2001. By Their Fruits You Shall Know Them: The Challenge of Renewal Among Men Religious in the USA Today. *Social Compass* 48: 209–28. [CrossRef]

Secondin, Bruno. 1991. *I nuovi protagonisti*. Milan: Paoline.

Tennenhouse, Laura F. 2016. New Monasticism as 'Reflexive Spirituality': A Case Study of the Simple Way. In *Monasticism in Modern Times*. Edited by Isabelle Jonveaux and Stefania Palmisano. New York: Routledge, pp. 154–72.

Wittberg, Patricia. 1994. *The Rise and Decline of Catholic Religious Orders*. Albany: State University of New York Press.

Wittberg, Patricia. 1996. *Pathways to Re-creating Religious Communities*. Costa Mesa: Paulist Press.

religions **MDPI**

Article

Forming "Mediators and Instruments of Grace": The Emerging Role of Monastics in Teaching Contemplative Ambiguity and Practice to the Laity

Paula Pryce

Department of Anthropology, University of British Columbia, Vancouver, BC V6T 1Z1, Canada; pdpryce@ubc.ca

Received: 5 June 2019; Accepted: 24 June 2019; Published: 27 June 2019

Abstract: Drawing from long-term ethnographic research with a global network of contemplative Christians, this paper discusses an emerging teaching role for North American monasteries as the numbers of avowed religious decline. Since the Trappist community of St. Joseph's Abbey in Spencer, Massachusetts, first developed the Christian meditation technique called Centering Prayer in the 1970s, monks and nuns have increasingly become teachers, models, and stabilizers of non-monastic practitioners who attempt to transform their ways of being and thinking towards monastic-inspired sensibilities. Their guidance includes the use of face-to-face, literary, and virtual means to teach methods of contemplative intersubjectivity and a commitment to lives based on service, hospitality, and humility, as well as on study and formalized rites. The paper focuses on non-monastics' strong attraction to monastic teachings on ambiguity as a source of creativity and wonder in uncertain times, as practiced through a combination of cataphatic and apophatic ritual, including Centering Prayer. The number of monastic postulants continues to falter, yet a much larger, "non-gathered" community of non-monastic oblates and neo-monastic contemplatives has grown increasingly reliant on monastics to help provide alternatives. The rising interdependence of monastics and non-monastics may become the basis of a transformation of Christian monasticism and a new concept of religious community.

Keywords: religious pluralism; religious ambiguity; contemplative Christianity; lay contemplatives; monasticism; spiritual formation; Centering Prayer

---

> Everything depends on maintaining and strengthening the communion we have with God in Christ. We bear fruit by remaining connected to Jesus, just as he bears fruit through his connection with the Father. We are not the originators of the divine grace that comforts and heals and saves; we are simply mediators and instruments of this grace.
>
> —Br. David Vryhof, SSJE[1]

Many lay people in my anthropological research on the global network of Centering Prayer had at one time given up on Christianity. They sometimes spent years following other religions, particularly those that emphasize unity with the divine. However, sometime into their inter-religious sojourns, these people stumbled upon ancient and current-day contemplative expressions of Christianity and thus began renewing a relationship with the religious traditions into which they were born. Contemplative

---

[1] This quote comes from the online platform, "Brother, Give us a Word", of the Cambridge, Massachusetts Episcopal monastery, The Society of Saint John the Evangelist (SSJE). Offered online or in email format, "Brother, Give Us a Word" is a daily lesson inspired by the fourth-century Desert Fathers' practice of mentoring by giving a single word on which novices could contemplate. See www.ssje.org.

Christianity,[2] an imperfect term I use to describe monastic-inspired, immanence-oriented forms of Christian ideals and practices, has become particularly attractive to a growing sector of spiritually devoted people who see human knowledge, and especially culturally specific religious knowledge, as inadequate in the face of a vast, largely unknowable universe. Rather than clinging to the parochial religious views they felt they had learned in childhood or abandoning religion altogether, these lay contemplatives have responded to the precarity and ambiguity of globalization with hospitable gestures of wonder and openness. The combination of monastic practice-oriented stability and the fluid, exploratory character of mystical ontology has become a resource for lay people who desire a connection with the divine, other humans, and all creation in the context of potentially unsettling religious, political, and cultural complexities of the contemporary pluralistic era. Albeit of a distinctive character, these people's desire for religious alternatives, including rigorous practices and sophisticated epistemologies, constitute one more example in a long history of American religious revivalism and enthusiasm (Roof 2001; Schmidt 2012; Schmidt and Promey 2012).

Some monastic communities have responded to this nascent contemplative Christian religious movement by offering formation adapted especially for lay people. Included are teachings on the value of humility in societies driven by achievement and acquisition, the discernment of a personal rule of life, and the practice of *kenosis* or self-emptying in Centering Prayer. Monastic instruction on ambiguity as an esteemed and necessary part of spiritual maturity goes further, however: silence, formalized rites, discipline, and service to others all work together to intentionally cultivate "unknowing" as a means to invite the divine into their midst. A lay desire for the nuanced and difficult lessons of Christian contemplation thus reveals a blossoming role for monks, nuns, and mendicants, even though their numbers continue to decrease. Especially in a globalized context in which they use digital media to teach beyond the physical walls of their cloisters, many avowed religious have become mentors on moral, philosophical, and phenomenological alternatives to a far-reaching network of lay contemplatives, drawing from ancient monastic disciplines to help their students become "mediators and instruments of ... grace" in an uncertain and rapidly changing world.

Beginning in 2009, my anthropological research of the vast global Centering Prayer network includes both monastic and non-monastic practitioners. Seeking to learn how this movement reaches across religious, social, and cultural boundaries, I have undertaken long-term, multi-sited participant observation research in monasteries, retreat centres, ashrams, zendos, and among numerous diverse religious organizations in the United States, Canada, the United Kingdom, Italy, Palestine/Israel, France, and South India. I have also learned from individual practitioners, who have written journals for me on their efforts to live as solitary contemplatives in otherwise ordinary communities, and I have followed the interactions, rituals, and teachings of online virtual communities. My book, *The Monk's Cell: Ritual and Knowledge in American Contemplative Christianity* (Pryce 2018), details my extensive ethnographic research, especially on the teaching relationships between the avowed religious and lay people in the American arm of The Centering Prayer network.

One American teacher of Centering Prayer has described her students as "broken-hearted Christians", lovers of the divine who say they could not abide the narrow-mindedness and banality they felt they had encountered in their childhood parishes (Bourgeault 2004).[3] Frequently university educated and of the middle and upper-middle classes, their increasing knowledge has prompted these

---

[2] My use of the term, "contemplative Christianity", is inadequate shorthand for a wide-ranging and diverse genre of Christianity that emphasizes divine immanence and connectedness, and focuses on enstatic practices, like silence, chant, *lectio divina*, and meditation. Many cloistered and semi-cloistered Christian monastic communities fall into this category. An increasing number of self-identified non-monastic Christians in the Western hemisphere find themselves feeling more connected to the contemplative aspects of other religions and have thus often drawn from the mystical texts and enstatic practices of both Christianity and other religions (Pryce 2018). This inter-religiosity is not unknown among monastics, as is clear from the writings of Merton (1965, 1968) and Thomas Keating's instigation of the annual Snowmass Conference, which has for decades brought together spiritual teachers from the world's "wisdom traditions" (Miles-Yepez 2006).

[3] Rev. Dr. Bourgeault (2008, 2016), a well-known non-monastic Episcopal priest, author, and retreat leader, was trained among the American Trappist monks at St. Benedict's Monastery in Snowmass, Colorado, who developed Centering Prayer,

seekers to steer away from easy answers and yet (despite some secularization theorists' predictions that such a demographic would reject religion (Berger 1967, 1999; Finke and Stark 2005), they continued to yearn for the divine. Such people often spend a great deal of time learning the practices and philosophies of religions like Buddhism, Sufism, Hinduism, and Judaism (Beneke 2006; Pryce 2018; Tipton 1982). Sometimes years later, they discovered that Christianity had its own enstatic, immanence-oriented traditions. By word of mouth and personal research, such as online searches, local lectures, and printed literature, some discovered, often to their astonishment, that Christianity also has a deep history of contemplative theologies and practices. Many individuals in my research told me that their childhood experiences gave them no inkling that some kinds of Christianity downplayed stringent doctrine and unyielding belief in favour of an emphasis on mystery and experiential communion through the aesthetics and practices of formal rites and intentional living, the *ora et labora* of monasticism. A Christianity of silence, wonder, and humility, they said, seemed to have enough openness and breadth to cultivate love for one's neighbour in an unfathomably diverse universe. Although they did not always re-join institutional churches in any formal way (Ammerman 2014; McGuire 2008; Tickle 2008), the people in my research slowly rekindled their relationship with Christianity, frequently with the guidance of monastic teachers.

Often emphasized in the American monastic communities in my research, Christian expressions of the unknowability of God have resonated profoundly with this expanding pluralistic movement of non-monastic Christian contemplatives. These people's inclination toward socio-religious boundary crossing and openness drew them especially toward certain ancient Christian motifs of the mystery and ambiguity of the divine. The writings of Hadewijch of Brabant, for example, have become increasingly popular among this group. The thirteenth-century Beguine mystic paid homage to the paradoxical "Abyss of Omnipotence" in which the unknowability of God "cannot be put into words, since it is unspeakable" (quoted in Petroff 1986, p. 197). A seeming mirror from the current era, Maggie, a woman from the American Northeast in my ethnographic research, described divine ineffability as "that unknown place beyond what is." A Midwesterner, Eleanor said something comparable: "Communion with God is an opening out into nothing. It really is *no thing*, something other than thing" (emphasis original). Contemplatives in my research have often described the deepest point of union with the divine as boundlessness and nothingness, which nevertheless confers what they have called "experiential knowledge."[4]

Boston College philosopher Richard Kearney (2010) has attempted to understand this contemporary outward-looking interest in ambiguity among people who seek to dwell at ease with sociocultural pluralism and religion. He coined the term, *anatheism*, for the lived theology of people, like those in my ethnographic research, who have abandoned the triumphalism of a Christian-centered universe in favour of an hermeneutical posture that seeks to replace defensive certitude with humility. Kearney's anatheism, or "god after god", recognizes certain people's need to adjust their views of the divine in a world of immeasurable diversity, especially a world in which so many people suffer. Anatheists, wrote Kearney, are those who recognize the limits of their own knowledge. Yet rather than rejecting God in so uncertain and expansive a universe, they emphasize the need to welcome God in the stranger, thus taking on hospitality and openness as the central rubric in their stance of unknowing. Their primary intention is not to define a doctrinal list of facts and rules about the divine, but to extend hospitality and service to others. However, truly welcoming the other—listening and attempting to understand—can result in the destabilization of one's conceptual foundations, including established notions of the divine. A sincere engagement has required people to be open enough to make doctrinal tenets secondary and to try to perceive the universe without

---

including Fr. Thomas Keating. Bourgeault's far-reaching global ministry provides a formidable example of how monastics have had a powerful influence on the formation of non-monastic contemplatives.

4   Uncited quotations derive from my ethnographic fieldnotes or from the journals of interlocutors who wrote reflections especially for my research.

preconception, which creates a world of increasing ambiguity. But in endeavouring to be open to a "stranger God" and to any stranger, wrote Kearney, they seek to create intimacy out of that ambiguity.

Like Kearney, Seligman and Weller (2012, p. 25) also see recent changes in religious observance, especially in ritual, as a response to the ambiguity born of the fast-paced globalization and virtual technologies of pluralistic societies. In their book, *Rethinking Pluralism: Ritual, Experience, and Ambiguity*, they note that repetition of ongoing, unending ritual cycles "allows us to live with ambiguity, not to remove it." Ritual is intrinsically relational, they wrote, emphasizing that ceremonial open-endedness itself is a gesture of hospitality. Seligman and Weller (2012, p. 98) said, "Accepting the world's discontinuities and ambiguities means that the world of building and refining relationships will never end. Ritual, at least in its relationship to the rest of experience, is never totally coherent and is never complete. Yet doing the work of ritual is one of the most important ways in which we live in such an inherently plural world." Indeed, ritual, especially the practice of silence, chant, and formalized liturgies with meanings that are not entirely clear, simultaneously offers constancy and fluidity. For people who shy away from the doctrinal certitude that conflicts with their desire to understand and accept human diversity, *cataphasis*, the active aspects of ritual, allow the stability of embodied action and repetition while at the same time opening immense space for reflection and interpretation, and even the cultivation of experiential ambiguity, or *apophasis*, which I will discuss further below (Pryce 2018, pp. 137–38; Louth 2012; cf. Luhrmann 2012, pp. 162–68).

Why Monasticism?

An orientation toward hospitality, service, and ritual is certainly not novel in Christianity, and is especially salient in Christian monasticism. To be sure, for many centuries Benedictine monasticism has formed itself around a rule of life based on a daily rhythm of prayer and work, as well as an imperative to greet the stranger as Christ in their midst (Benedict of Nursia 2011). Though perhaps seemingly ironic given the principle of monastic enclosure, the lived Benedictine tenets of hospitality, discipline, silence, and the formal rites of the Divine Office have become compelling for non-monastic contemplatives who are trying to embrace rather than reject a pluralistic world (e.g., Tomaine 2005). A contemporary re-orientation toward ritual and hospitality, now emerging out of people's desire for positive ways to address uncertainty and multiplicity, may explain a strengthening lay fascination with monasticism.

How have monastic communities responded to the upwelling? Some contemporary Christian monastics and mendicants have risen to the challenge by offering teachings on humility, hospitality, and a ritualized life which has recently become so attractive to a sector of the laity (e.g., Almquist 2008; Casey 2005; Chittister 2012; Funk 2001; Laird 2006; Rohr 2009; Smith 1989). While a teaching relationship between monastics and laity has a deep history (e.g., Baird 2006; McGinn 1994), rapid globalization and online communications have made convents and monasteries increasingly visible to people who may have previously had no contact or knowledge. Along with print media and the liturgies, workshops, and retreats they offer in their physical spaces, monastic communities have an increasing virtual presence. Through their own community websites and online platforms such as YouTube, they give lessons on monastic sensibilities, theologies, and practices which offer alternatives to more prevalent social norms.[5] An added benefit for those in cloistered life, online forums allow monastics to teach while preserving their seclusion. Further, monastics are in a strong position to get their message across. They often have considerable social and cultural capital such as institutional

---

[5] Just a few examples of websites of monastic communities and associated organizations include the Benedictine Sisters of Erie (www.eriebenedictines.org/, www.benetvision.org/, https://www.monasticway.org/, www.monasteriesoftheheart.org/), The Abbey of Regina Laudis (https://abbeyofreginalaudis.org/), The Center for Action and Contemplation (https://cac.org), The World Community for Christian Meditation (http://wccm.org/), Contemplative Outreach (www.contemplativeoutreach.org), the Anglican Benedictine Holy Cross Monastery (https://holycrossmonastery.com/), the Society of St. John the Evangelist (www.ssje.org), and the Monastery of Christ in the Desert (https://christdesert.org/). See Wagner (2012) for a study on virtual adaptations of religious practice and teaching.

authority, formal education, social connections, creative approaches to ritual and various media, and rhetorical, diplomatic, and technical communication skills. Whether through online resources, print media, or real-space interactions, the current scale of teaching that has emerged from convents, monasteries, and associated organizations is unprecedented.

Monastic and mendicant teachers thus have an integral role in the growing global socio-religious movement of lay contemplative Christianity. My decade-long ethnographic research with The Centering Prayer movement illustrates this phenomenon. Centering Prayer is a form of Christian meditation developed some forty years ago by American Trappist monks as an accessible contemplative practice for lay people. Fr. Thomas Keating, a Trappist monk and well-known author who died in 2018, had noticed a surge in the burning desire of spiritual seekers in the United States beginning in the 1960s. The abbot of St. Joseph's Abbey in Spencer, Massachusetts, from 1961–1981, he wondered why so many young people passed by his monastery to stay at a nearby Buddhist temple, or travelled to places like India "to satisfy their hunger for an authentic spiritual path." He was puzzled that they did not turn to their own Christian religious traditions, which he knew had a deep history of contemplative teachings and practices that sought to foster intimacy between humans and the divine. Similar to the "broken-hearted Christians" whom I encountered in my own research, Keating found that many of these seekers were former Roman Catholics or Protestant Christians who had become skeptical about their own religious traditions. He learned that "many of them were disaffected from the religion of their youth because of the legalistic and overmoralistic teaching that many had received in their local parishes and Catholic schools; they now felt spiritually enriched [not by Christianity but] by their experiences in Buddhism and Hinduism." At that time in 1970s and 1980s America, most of the people to whom he spoke outside of the monastic environment did not even know of the great contemplative Christian traditions that spanned church history (Keating 2002, personal communication; pp. 11–12, 14–15).

Fr. Thomas Keating, Fr. William Meninger (1997), and the late Fr. Pennington (1983) were remarkably successful in their efforts to spread contemplative Christian ideas, practices, and sensibilities beyond the walls of their monastery through their development and teaching of Centering Prayer. These three Trappist monks essentially adapted Centering Prayer from the notion of *kenosis* or "self-emptying" in Philippians 2:5–8, the monastic practice of *lectio divina*, and the methods and ideas in a fourteenth-century English mystical text, *The Cloud of Unknowing*, whose monastic author (Anonymous 1961) recommends a prayer practice of cultivating "a naked intent to God" through the use of a sacred word. Keating describes the main principles of Centering Prayer as "consenting to the divine" by letting go of any thought or sensation that causes one to bring the mind into focus. Slightly different from many other meditation techniques, the transformational quality of Centering Prayer rises from alertness, consent, and self-emptying, say teachers, rather than from attention on a mantra, breath, or image. Centering Prayer is thus less a discipline of concentrated focus than it is a repeated ritualized release of thought and sensation. Ambiguity and emptiness are the main drivers of the practice.

Despite some institutional hesitancy (e.g., Ratzinger 1989), Centering Prayer now enjoys a global reach that has expanded well beyond the confines of Roman Catholicism. With innumerable books, retreats, and teaching forums on the practice, as well as an online organization called Contemplative Outreach which, at the time I published *The Monk's Cell* (Pryce 2018, p. 296), was serving 120 international chapters in 39 countries, supporting over 800 prayer groups in the United States alone, teaching the methods of Centering Prayer to 15,000 newcomers annually, and sending out 40,000 digital monthly newsletters. In addition, Contemplative Outreach had thousands of followers on Twitter and on the Facebook pages of local chapters. Centering Prayer thus brilliantly demonstrates the potential of monastic communities' outreach to religious seekers who hunger for openness and ways to address the divine in uncertain times. Centering Prayer has become a resource to address pluralism and a world of shifting categories, helping to satisfy the growing non-monastic desire to foster creative ambiguity through ritualized practices. The expansion of its network shows well the kind of impact monastics can have on the formation of laity.

The Centering Prayer movement is but one of numerous pedagogical threads emanating from monastic communities, however. My research has investigated these teaching relationships through the online platforms of large associations like Contemplative Outreach and at smaller-scale endeavours, like the face-to-face liturgies, workshops, and retreats in religious communities with local non-monastic congregations. Whether they use live, print, or virtual media, the monks, nuns, and mendicants with whom I have worked have attempted to guide the laity with alternative ideals, practices, and sensibilities that prize communality and ambiguity over acquisitiveness and achievement. American monastic teachers in particular are forthright in their perspective that their country is strongly influenced by individualistic, status-centered cultural values that need to be understood, critiqued, and transformed. For example, well-known Benedictine nun, teacher, and author Chittister (2012, p. 116) described her view of prevalent American ideals in this way: "Get money, the culture demands. Or power. Or prestige, at least. Get the trappings of the good life, the rumor of the great life, the reputation of success, the culture says, and that will be enough. But", she then asserted, "it isn't." Joan Chittister and many other nuns, monks, and mendicants have spent considerable energy trying to teach the hospitable, open-minded alternatives that they feel Christian monasticism has to offer.

How do monastics support their students in re-visioning a way of being and thinking that is both hospitable and challenging to acquisitive- and achievement-oriented mores? Let me turn to the principle of monastic humility as an example, a key ideal in contemplative Christianity that is related to *kenosis* or self-emptying, the technique that underlies the practice of Centering Prayer. Monastic teachers have understood that, particularly in North America, humility is one of the most difficult monastic principles for non-monastics to learn and to sustain. An essay on the principle of humility from *Monastic Wisdom*, a monthly digital teaching of the Cambridge, Massachusetts Episcopal monastery, the Society of Saint John the Evangelist (SSJE), shows how monastics attempt to reform prevalent cultural perspectives. Set in an appealing, aesthetically minimalistic webpage, the article addressed a common perception of humility in North America. The author, Br. David Vryhof, SSJE, wrote,

> *humility has gotten 'bad press' in the modern era. Too often it has been associated with passivity, complacency, and unquestioning submission to those in authority. When we think of humility, we are likely to conjure up images of persons with low self-esteem; people with fawning, weak personalities; or people who are afraid to assert themselves. Modern Western culture is rightly suspicious of that kind of 'humility' because it denies our intrinsic worth as human beings.*[6]

In contrast to his assessment of common American cultural views, Br. David Vryhof sets out a different perspective by framing humility as a "truth that leads to freedom" and "a way of life that has been highly prized ... in Christianity", especially "in the Christian monastic tradition." Taking scriptural depictions of Jesus as his model, he relates the practice of humility to *kenosis*, the vulnerable self-offering that has drawn many non-monastics to contemplative Christianity. He wrote, "Consider the humility with which [Jesus] came to us, how he 'emptied himself, taking the form of a slave, being born in human likeness. And being found in human form, he humbled himself ... ' (Phil 2:7–8)." Br. David Vryhof thus encourages an understanding of humility as "a healthy balance between proper self-esteem—based on the knowledge that we are beloved children of God who are made in God's own image—and an honest awareness and acceptance of our limitations, weaknesses and faults." Clearly both hospitable and pluralistic in his tone, Br. David Vryhof reaches back to the writings of the Desert Fathers to describe humility as an ancient means of "finding one's place in right relation to God and

---

[6] Quotations from Br. David Vryhof's teachings on humility are from the Society of Saint John the Evangelist webpage, www.ssje.org/monasticwisdom/humility, accessed 25 March 2019.

neighbor, without being swayed by the need for attention or praise or honor or power." Humility, he wrote, prompts "living peacefully and gently with others. Its two chief characteristics were *a willingness to learn from others* ... and *a refusal to judge others*" (emphasis in original). Having thus worked to revise his readers' understandings of humility, Br. David Vryhof then gives suggestions on how to integrate humility into daily life, offering inspiring quotations, questions for reflection, a list of more extensive resources, and pragmatic, easy-to-do exercises to help ground his readers' new-found knowledge.

This online monastic teaching on humility from the Society of Saint John the Evangelist is a tiny example of the plethora of resources currently available from American convents and monasteries. Many monastic teachers understand that in a complex, mobile society like the United States with its dizzying array of potential lifeways, learning and developing alternative ideals, practices, perceptions, and sensibilities is a long-term and often arduous endeavour that requires concerted intention, agency, and discipline. The monastics in my research were well aware of how difficult the adoption of contemplative lifeways was for people dwelling outside of the stabilizing force of a communal religious life. Finding the means to anchor themselves could be especially elusive for well-educated lay people who critiqued doctrine, theology, historical representations, and the authority of religious institutions. Many of the monks and nuns in my research did not expect their students to become formal adherents or to set aside their questions. Instead, they honoured the quandaries associated with doubt, recognized the frailty of human knowledge (even among the intellectually learned), and emphasized divine mystery. These teachers urged a greater reliance on regular, disciplined practice than on either iron-clad adherence to doctrinal belief systems or the volatility of emotion-centered spirituality.

Given the steadying effects of regularity, rhythm, and repetition, monastic teachers have tried to persuade their students to develop and follow rules of life adapted for non-monastics, including a schedule of prayer and work and service to others. Keeping a rule outside of monastic communities is not that straightforward, however, especially when discipline is dependent on the will of individuals with little social structural support. Importantly, keeping a rule implies that a dedication to practice and service is more important than emotion. In an American context in which self-expression and sentiment are primary cultural modes (Hall and Lindholm 1999; Bellah et al. 1985), committing to a scheduled rhythm regardless of how one feels was a steep learning curve for non-monastics, and indeed, my research found that many struggled to follow through in the long term (Pryce 2018, pp. 52–53). We can see the predicament in the words of a man who had been trying to establish his life as a non-monastic contemplative. At a lay retreat in an American Midwestern Benedictine monastery, he said in despair, "I am not up to this. This spiritual work demands more of me than I can do. I just can't do it" (Bauman 2013). Roger, a man from the American Southwest, gave me a similar story: "I've been trying to keep a contemplative life for years. I really feel called to it! I keep tinkering, trying to get it right. But sometimes I find I just can't keep at it when everyone else around me is zoning out on their phones or whatever. It's so hard when you're the only one." Yet those who persisted learned that a disciplined (but realistic) schedule of practice was more dependable in helping one keep ideals than was a desire for emotional equilibrium or a euphoric sense of connectedness to the divine, which teachers believed could manifest as an unmitigated self-centered drive for spiritual experiences and status.

Let us return to the Society of Saint John the Evangelist for an illustration of monastic efforts to stabilize lay people through teachings on rules of life. The SSJE community has published a number of print and online resources that assist their non-monastic adherents in creating personal rules of life that are idealistic yet pragmatic enough to be realizable.[7] Their booklet *Living Intentionally* explains

---

[7] The Society of Saint John the Evangelist clearly has a commitment to helping non-monastics develop and adopt rules of life. In addition to *Living Intentionally*, this community has also made available print, online, and audio-recording versions of their monastic rule (SSJE 1997; https://www.ssje.org/worship/rule-of-life-resources/) and has published a smaller rule written specifically for their formal association of oblates, The Fellowship of Saint John (SSJE n.d.b; http://www.ssje.org/fsjrule/). Further, they have produced a number of other resources, including a video series called *A Framework for Freedom* and,

that, rather than being a restrictive list of uncompromising dictates, "rule" in the monastic context comes from the Latin *regula*, a word that suggests "a way of *regularizing* our lives so that we can stay on the path we have set out for ourselves. A rule is like a trellis which offers support and guidance for a plant, helping it to grown in a certain direction." The monks taught that the central purpose of a rule was "to live our lives for God with purpose and intention." It could be prescriptive, outlining daily practices and social responsibilities, and could also describe and identify the foundational principles and philosophies that underlie one's desire to live an intentional life. Particularly for those attempting to follow a contemplative life without the everyday support of a monastic community, SSJE members "strongly recommend [keeping a rule] simple, ... *realistic and achievable* ... Like any spiritual discipline, adopting a rule should help one to live more faithfully" rather than make life more difficult (SSJE n.d.a, emphasis in original).

An example of a lay person who chose to adopt a disciplined schedule of practice, a man named Andrew told me how monastic methods had become a tool to reinforce his intentions. Having learned some practical strategies from monastic teachers over the fifteen years he had been practicing Centering Prayer and other contemplative techniques, Andrew said during a period of instability when his marriage had broken up and he had moved far from family and friends for a new job, "For the aspects of my contemplative life that aren't going the way I want them to, I know the answer is to put them on my schedule and follow through with them. Not in an unbending way, but in a 'this is what I want and I'm going to give myself these gifts' way." Andrew's perspective was that monastic-style discipline had bolstered his voluntary choice to follow a contemplative lifestyle.

Perhaps paradoxically, monastic guidance on discipline through rhythm and repetition of work, prayer, and service offered non-monastic contemplatives a route to the creative ambiguity they so deeply craved. Ritualized forms, like Centering Prayer and intentional work, can provide a subjunctive framework that helps practitioners negotiate the indeterminate realities of both pluralized societies and an unknowable God. Seligman and Weller (2012, p. 93) described ritualized structures as "a unique human resource for dealing with ambiguity and the multivocal nature of all relationships—with beings human and divine." They added that ritual "presents a coherent and embracing way to live in a plural and hence also deeply ambiguous universe, one where order can never really be known, but still must be acted upon." In contrast to a dependence on the hard-edged belief and ephemeral emotion found in some manifestations of Christianity, regularized rites and a ritualization of everyday life provide a structure in which contemplatives can learn to address the uncertainty that particularly abounds in the shifting diversity of the contemporary world.

Learning to live with the sociocultural and religious precarity of globalization and pluralism was certainly not ritualization's only selling point for non-monastics, however. They have also used ritual to intentionally cultivate *apophasis* or "unknowing" as a path to intimacy with the divine and all creation. Contemplative Christians in my research, both monastics and their non-monastic students, used the shelter of repetitive cataphatic practices like Centering Prayer, the canonical hours, *lectio divina*, and intentional labour to foster union with the divine through the inner gestures of consent, *kenosis*, and self-emptying. As one teacher in my research described it, ritual is a "strong container" that allows a safe haven for apophatic exploration of an unknown universe. A regularized, stable practice, enacted regardless of sentiment, can craft potent, creative environments of experiential and intellectual ambiguity that foster a refinement of senses and an ability to hear and see in new ways.

Some of the lay practitioners in my ethnographic research learned well their lessons on unknowing. For instance, Elizabeth, an addictions counsellor from the Northeast region of the United States, described how her desire for intimacy with the divine had prompted her to patiently develop a

---

co-produced with the Center for the Ministry of Teaching at Virginia Theological Seminary, a community workshop program called *Growing a Rule of Life: Relationship with God, Self, Creation, and Others*, which includes a paper and online workbook and an online participation page (Framework for Freedom: http://www.ssje.org/framework%20for%20freedom/; Growing a Rule of Life: (https://www.ssje.org/growruleresources/).

Centering Prayer practice over a decade. She worked hard to follow monastic guidance on being faithful to a daily rhythm of two periods of meditation a day whether she felt any positive effects or not. Elizabeth said to me,

> I've learned that you can't do Centering Prayer because someone else says you should, or because you happen to feel like it, or because you want a good 'trip'. After all these years, I can see that sitting [and meditating] does something I might not be able to understand in the moment. It's a weird combination of doing something and doing nothing. I have to trust it ... Often enough, I find myself really letting go and entering that beautiful cave. I'm just sitting there and the universe opens up. I just keep practicing and sometimes nothing turns into something, or something turns into nothing, and I feel the flow of God.

Reflecting on the words of people like Elizabeth, we see that monastic communities have a clear and explicit role in mentoring formerly disillusioned lay people who have returned to Christianity after discovering its contemplative dimensions. Under the tutelage of their monastic teachers, lay contemplatives have begun to find steady ground in a volatile world. Monastics in my research used a variety of print and virtual media, as well as face-to-face encounters, to direct non-monastics towards a framework of practices and ideals that help temper the potential capriciousness of the contemplative arts. Their tools—like keeping a personal rule of life, subscribing to a daily rhythm of work and prayer, and acting in the service of others—were contemporary adaptations of historical Christian monastic disciplines, particularly those modelled on the fifteen-hundred-year-old Benedictine tradition. Curiously, many lay people felt that the firmness of monastic discipline, schedules, and formalized rites allows an intellectual and ontological liberty to explore beyond the limiting strictures of socio-religious world views. For anatheistic Christians who have a strong desire for the divine and an honest interest in connecting with people across cultural and religious barriers, the monastic pairing of cataphatic structure and apophatic freedom is deeply attractive. Christian non-monastics in my research were especially drawn to the uncertain meanings of monastic ritual, mystical texts, and silence, which seemed to reflect the ambiguity of both a pluralistic universe and the limits of human knowledge, while nevertheless providing enough stability to meander through a universe beyond imagining. By honouring and cultivating the unknown through ritual practice and alternative ideals, these Christian contemplatives invite an hospitable surrender and a connectedness with "the stranger", whether human or divine.

Funding: This research received funding from the Social Sciences and Humanities Research Council of Canada and The Louisville Institute.

Conflicts of Interest: The author declares no conflict of interest.

References

Almquist, Curtis G. 2008. *Unwrapping the Gifts: The Twelve Days of Christmas*. Lanham: Cowley.
Ammerman, Nancy Tatom. 2014. *Sacred Stories, Spiritual Tribes: Finding Religion in Everyday Life*. New York: Oxford University Press.
Anonymous. 1961. *The Cloud of Unknowing and Other Works*. Translated by Clifton Wolters. London: Penguin.
Baird, Joseph L. 2006. *The Personal Correspondence of Hildegard of Bingen*. Oxford: Oxford University Press.
Bauman, Ward. 2013. *Episcopal House of Prayer Newsletter*. Collegeville: Episcopal House of Prayer.
Bellah, Robert, Richard Madsen, William Sullivan, Ann Swidler, and Steve Tipton. 1985. *Habits of the Heart: Individualism and Commitment in American Life*. Berkeley: University of California Press.
Benedict of Nursia. 2011. *The Rule of Saint Benedict*. Translated and Edited by Bruce L. Venarde. Cambridge: Harvard University Press.
Beneke, Christopher J. 2006. *Beyond Toleration: The Religious Origins of American Pluralism*. New York: Oxford University Press.
Berger, Peter L. 1967. *The Sacred Canopy: Elements of a Sociological Theory of Religion*. New York: Anchor Books.
Berger, Peter L. 1999. *The Desecularization of the World: Resurgent Religion and World Politics*. Grand Rapids: Eerdmans.

Bourgeault, Cynthia. 2004. *Centering Prayer and Inner Awakening*. Cambridge: Cowley.

Bourgeault, Cynthia. 2008. *The Wisdom Jesus: Transforming Heart and Mind—A New Perspective on Christ and His Message*. Boston: Shambhala.

Bourgeault, Cynthia. 2016. *The Heart of Centering Prayer: Christian Nonduality in Theory and Practice*. Boston: Shambhala.

Casey, Michael. 2005. *Strangers in the City: Reflections on the Beliefs and Values of the Rule of St. Benedict*. Brewster: Paraclete Press.

Chittister, Joan. 2012. *Following the Path: The Search for a Life of Passion, Purpose, and Joy*. New York: Crown.

Finke, Roger, and Rodney Stark. 2005. *The Churching of America, 1776–2005: Winners and Losers in Our Religious Economy*. New Brunswick: Rutgers University Press.

Funk, M.M. 2001. *Tools Matter for Practicing the Spiritual Life*. New York: Continuum.

Hall, John A., and Charles Lindholm. 1999. *Is America Breaking Apart?* Princeton: Princeton University Press.

Kearney, Richard. 2010. *Anatheism: Returning to God after God*. New York: Columbia University Press.

Keating, Thomas. 2002. *Intimacy with God: An Introduction to Centering Prayer*. New York: Crossroads.

Laird, Martin. 2006. *Into the Silent Land: A Guide to the Christian Practice of Contemplation*. New York: Oxford University Press.

Louth, Andrew. 2012. Apophatic and Cataphatic Theology. In *The Cambridge Companion to Christian Mysticism*. Edited by Amy Hollywood and Patricia Z. Beckman. Cambridge: Cambridge University Press, pp. 137–46.

Luhrmann, Tanya M. 2012. *When God Talks Back: Understanding the American Evangelical Relationship with God*. New York: Alfred A. Knopf.

McGinn, Bernard. 1994. Meister Eckhart and the Beguines in the Context of Vernacular Theology. In *Meister Eckhart and the Beguine Mystics*. Edited by Bernard McGinn. New York: Continuum, pp. 1–14.

McGuire, Meredith. 2008. *Lived Religion: Faith and Practice in Everyday Life*. New York: Oxford University Press.

Meninger, William A. 1997. *The Loving Search for God: Contemplative Prayer and the Cloud of Unknowing*. New York: Continuum.

Merton, Thomas. 1965. *The Way of Chuang-Tzu*. New York: New Directions.

Merton, Thomas. 1968. *Zen and the Birds of Appetite*. New York: New Directions.

Miles-Yepez, Netanel, ed. 2006. *The Common Heart: An Experience of Interreligious Dialogue*. New York: Lantern Books.

Pennington, Basil. 1983. *A Place Apart: Monastic Prayer and Practice for Everyone*. Garden City: Doubleday.

Petroff, Elizabeth Avilda. 1986. *Medieval Women's Visionary Literature*. Oxford: Oxford University Press.

Pryce, Paula. 2018. *The Monk's Cell: Ritual and Knowledge in American Contemplative Christianity*. New York: Oxford University Press.

Ratzinger, Cardinal Joseph. 1989. *Letter to the Bishops of the Catholic Church on Some Aspects of Christian Meditation*. Congregation for the Doctrine of Faith. Rome: Vatican, October 15.

Rohr, Richard. 2009. *The Naked Now: Learning to See as the Mystics See*. New York: Crossroads.

Roof, Wade Clark. 2001. *Spiritual Marketplace: Baby Boomers and the Remaking of American Religion*. Princeton: Princeton University Press.

Schmidt, Leigh Eric. 2012. *Restless Souls: The Making of American Spirituality*. Berkeley: University of California Press.

Schmidt, Leigh Eric, and Sally M. Promey, eds. 2012. *American Religious Liberalism*. Bloomington: Indiana University Press.

Seligman, Adam B., and Robert P. Weller. 2012. *Rethinking Pluralism: Ritual, Experience, and Ambiguity*. New York: Oxford University Press.

Smith, Martin. 1989. *The Word is Very Near You: A Guide to Praying with Scripture*. Cambridge: Cowley.

SSJE (Society of Saint John the Evangelist). 1997. *The Rule of the Society of Saint John the Evangelist*. Lanham: Cowley.

SSJE. n.d.a. *Living Intentionally: A Workbook for Creating a Personal Rule of Life*. Cambridge: Society of Saint John the Evangelist.

SSJE. n.d.b. *The Rule of the Fellowship of Saint John*. Cambridge: Society of Saint John the Evangelist.

Tickle, Phyllis. 2008. *The Great Emergence: How Christianity Is Changing and Why It Matters*. Grand Rapids: Baker Books.

Tipton, Steven M. 1982. *Getting Saved from the Sixties: Moral Meaning in Conversion and Cultural Change*. Berkeley: University of California Press.

Tomaine, Jane. 2005. *St. Benedict's Toolbox: The Nuts and Bolts of Everyday Benedictine Living.* Harrisbury: Morehouse.

Wagner, Rachel. 2012. *Godwired: Religion, Ritual, and Virtual Reality.* New York: Routledge.

religions MDPI

Article

The Beguine Option: A Persistent Past and a Promising Future of Christian Monasticism

Evan B. Howard

Department of Ministry, Fuller Theological Seminary 62421 Rabbit Trail, Montrose, CO 81403, USA; evanhoward@fuller.edu

Received: 1 June 2019; Accepted: 3 August 2019; Published: 21 August 2019

Abstract: Since Herbert Grundmann's 1935 *Religious Movements in the Middle Ages*, interest in the Beguines has grown significantly. Yet we have struggled whether to call Beguines "religious" or not. My conviction is that the Beguines are one manifestation of an impulse found throughout Christian history to live a form of life that resembles Christian monasticism without founding institutions of religious life. It is this range of less institutional yet seriously committed forms of life that I am here calling the "Beguine Option." In my essay, I will sketch this "Beguine Option" in its varied expressions through Christian history. Having presented something of the persistent past of the Beguine Option, I will then present an introduction to forms of life exhibited in many of the expressions of what some have called "new monasticism" today, highlighting the similarities between movements in the past and new monastic movements in the present. Finally, I will suggest that the Christian Church would do well to foster the development of such communities in the future as I believe these forms of life hold much promise for manifesting and advancing the kingdom of God in our midst in a postmodern world.

Keywords: monasticism; Beguine; spiritual formation; intentional community; spirituality; religious life

1. Introduction

What might the future of monasticism look like? I start with three examples: two from the present and one from the past. My first example is Jessica and Weston who, along with their son Simeon, own a home in Minneapolis, Minnesota in a neighborhood of amazing diversity and some pretty serious need. Weston is a carpenter and makes some of his income building things. But they also raise a little support through a Christian non-profit so they can devote time to art therapy, God-discussions while doing woodwork with neighbors, and other creative ideas. They live near friends who share a common Christian vision and they pray with them regularly. Some neighbors are associated with the same non-profit, an organization which asks that they make a serious effort to blend contemplative, prophetic and missional currents of Christianity in their life and work. Both Weston and Jess meet with spiritual directors who provide support and accountability. Sometimes they struggle to see just where they fit in all of this but they are willing to play with it.

My second example is not an individual, but a group—The Church of the Sojourners in San Francisco. This community started in the 1980s with a few families who wanted to share more deeply the life of Acts 2. Singles and families have various jobs but pool most of their money together into a common fund which pays for their shared housing, utilities, transportation and other common expenses. They worship together on Sundays and eat together frequently. Important decisions are made in common. They often absorb into their community a few people who we might call higher need. They share a covenant of commitment to Christian values and while not requiring involvement in any particular "outreach program," this community has manifest, for many years, the presence of Christ in their neighborhood.

My final example (from the past) is Marie d'Oignies, the woman some identify as the "first Beguine" (see especially King and Feiss 1993; Mulder-Bakker 2006). Marie grew up in the town of Nivelles in the diocese of Liège near Brussels in Belgium. From her childhood, she was attracted to simplicity and refused the fine clothes her parents offered her. Her parents arranged that she would be married at age fourteen to John, the son of another wealthy local family. After her marriage, she began to practice the ascetical life more seriously. John also came to a deeper relationship with God and they moved to nearby Willambroux and practiced a semi-monastic life together: fasting and spending their time in prayers, physical labour, and works of charity. She and John participated with an informal community near a group of lepers. John disappears from the story but we hear of Marie's popularity growing exponentially. She moved once again in 1207 to a cell in Oignies to avoid attention. There she maintained her practice of prayer and provided spiritual counsel. She died in 1213 and her example stimulated a host of women's communities.

In 2017, Rod Dreher, senior editor at *The American Conservative*, published *The Benedict Option: A Strategy for Christians in a Post-Christian Nation*. This book, which became a much discussed best-seller, advertises itself as "a guide for Christians under siege today" (Dreher 2018, back cover). "Recognizing the toxins of modern secularism, as well as the fragmentation caused by relativism," Dreher urges, "Benedict Option Christians look to Scripture and to Benedict's Rule for ways to cultivate practices and communities" (Dreher 2018, p. 18). Dreher's vision is to facilitate a visible expression of philosopher Alasdair MacIntyre's call for a "new Benedict": a figure who symbolizes the foundation of religious communities whose lives together nurture the development of virtue (MacIntyre 1981). Dreher's call to a "Benedict Option" is not the first proposal for alternative communities of virtue. Indeed, the phrase "new monasticism," as used in the past fifteen years, was coined from a similar desire to respond to MacIntyre's call for a "new Benedict" (Wilson 2010; House 2005). I applaud these proposals for creative communities of virtue. I wonder about the link to *Benedict*.

I have been visiting both "new monastic" communities and more traditional congregations of religious life for over thirty-five years. As I visit these communities and read their own self-evaluations, I am struck with a conviction regarding both traditional religious life and "new monasticism" that while formal "monastic" entities (institutes of religious life—for my use of monastic and other terminology, see Howard 2008, 2013), are vital and will remain for perpetuity, a promising future for religious life in the next decades may be discovered in less institutional forms of life. Those who live these forms of life may not make solemn vows. Their communities may not be recognized by a formal ecclesiastical body. Yet their values, their rhythm of activities, and their sense of community and identity all bear sufficient resemblance to recognized religious institutes that it is appropriate to identify these forms of life as a semi-religious movement. Kaspar Elm identifies such expressions as *vitae regularis sine regula*, a "regular" or religious life without a formal rule (Elm 2016).

One example of this kind of less-institutional expression of devotion in history is the varied communities of women (and men) known in Europe especially in the thirteenth and fourteenth centuries often identified as "beguines" (the communities of men were called "beghards"). Both contemporaries and scholars universally interpret them as "semi-religious" (McDonnell 1969; Simons 2001; Dean 2008; Swan 2014). Indeed, they are often identified as a type of semi-religious life (Elm 2016, pp. 286–87). Thus, while there have been a number of less-institutional expressions of lay devotion in Christian history, the beguines, in all their ambiguity, function nicely as a counter-symbol to the institutional image of Benedict. Furthermore, just as Dreher and others have turned to the context of Benedict for parallels to this present age, so I think we can identify instructive parallels between the contexts of beguine experiments and contemporary search for appropriate religious life, indeed, perhaps moreso. For these reasons, I will refer to expressions which seek to live an ordered life of devotion yet without formal institutional affiliation or structure (intentional but not as institutional) as "The Beguine Option."

My aim in this essay is thus to propose a fresh mythological support for the ideological reframing of religious virtuosity as expressed in Catholic religious life and Protestant new monastic expressions today (Wittberg 1994). Wittberg argues that the ideological frame of traditional Catholic religious life has collapsed and that "the most commonly suggested replacement" "was unable to be realized on a communal basis" (Wittberg 1994, p. 240). At this same moment, Protestants are experimenting with religious life, open to ideological suggestions (House 2005; Graham Cray and Kennedy 2010). There are currently groups founding twenty-first century "beguine" communities today (Dean 2008, Raber 2009). Thus first, I see indications that less-institutional, ecumenical experiments in semi-religious life could be profitable in the decades to come (at least), and second that the image of a new *Beguine* Option may just have the mythological strength to support this fresh ideological frame.

I would like to suggest, in the present article, that this Beguine Option—expressions which seek less institutional forms of whole-hearted devotion—can be identified throughout the history of Christianity. Furthermore, this Beguine Option describes (with some points of divergence that I will develop later) a wide range of contemporary experiments in religious life, experiments which I believe are uniquely suited to meet the needs of a postmodern generation. In what follows, I will first present a description of beguine life in the in the thirteenth and fourteenth centuries as summarized from the diverse communities identified with the name. I will then turn back to identify similar expressions found throughout Christian history, demonstrating the *persistent past* of the Beguine Option. Moving from the past to the present, I will next describe a variety of contemporary semi-religious expressions, noting the significant similarities and differences from the Beguine Option as already described. Finally, I will place my discussion in dialogue with other reflections on the future of monasticism, suggesting that some kind of Beguine Option has unique promise for living and spreading the Gospel of Christ in a postmodern generation.

2. The Medieval Beguines

Describing beguine life is complicated by a number of factors (Dean 2008). Scholars struggle to identify the meaning of the term "beguine" itself (McDonnell 1969, pp. 430–38; Simons 2001, pp. 24–32, pp. 121–23; Miller 2007). The term was used both as attribution of praise and as a term of derision, with the consequence that historians today examining uses of the term must be careful identifying the links between terms and communities (Böhringer et al. 2014; More 2018). "Beguine" also was just one of a number of terms used to describe similar informal women's communities throughout Europe (Dean 2008; Swan 2014, p. 12). Furthermore, some women who eventually joined more institutional orders (for example, Cistercians or Third Order mendicant orders) still pursued values and practices associated with their non-institutional counterparts (Lester 2011; More 2018). Fourth, sources for the documentation of beguine life are hard to find and "house rules and statutes have been neglected in the literature" (Böhringer et al. 2014, p. 224; see de Vries 2016). Finally, beguine communities were independent and practices varied between groups. Thus, any summary of "beguine life" must be seen only as a rough composite drawn from the most common practices that can be identified from the sources available.

One searches for a single "founder" of the beguine movement in vain. It is best to see the rise of beguine communities (however they may have been named) as responses to changes in the medieval world, changes that parallel developments in the post-modern world today. Europe was experiencing something of a renewal following what has been termed "the twelfth-century renaissance" (Benson et al. 1982). Cities and roads were being developed. Universities were gaining strength. A new economy based on coinage was emerging. At the same time, new vehicles of production and consumption were developing: forest clearing, cloth merchants, fairs or festivals, credit instruments and more. Some call it the emergence of a "profit economy," an economy that gave birth to new rich and new poor alike (Little 1978; Wood 2002; Ekelund et al. 2015). The new rich were the merchants, who were able to link producers and processes of production with consumers. Some religious movements—such as Francis of Assisi and his earliest followers—responded to these developments with an outright rejection of money and the socio-political stratification associated with these developments (Flood 2001; Flood 2010; Vauchez 2012). Some beguines, however, explored these developments as opportunities for community independence, for example through involvement in the cloth industry (Simons 2001, pp. 8–10; Miller 2014a, pp. 59–80). The Gregorian reforms and land acquisitions brought new power to the Church. The world of monasticism had become something of a smorgasbord of competing options, each religious order claiming to be the clearest expression of the apostolic life. At the same time, pious laity were finding new avenues of devotion as some sought the apostolic life as hermits or as traveling preachers, while others formed confraternities of mutual support (Vauchez 1993; Melville 2016, pp. 89–124). Ecclesiastical opinion of these new avenues varied. The communities of devout women we call beguines (or other kindred terms) were formed in the midst of this shifting range of possibilities.

The situation for women was exceptionally complex (Bynum 1987). Alison More writes, "Both men and women sought perfection in the world; however, the social and secular forms of devotion that emerged were more problematic for women and their male contemporaries. In particular the lay piety performed by men was often incorporated into guilds, confraternities, or other structures that were seen as having a distinct secular role. In contrast, there was no acceptable outlet for some to carry out public devotion" (More 2018, p. 4; also Dean 2008). On the one hand, women's monastic houses or double monasteries of men and women were being established in greater numbers than ever before (some by women—see, for example, Lester 2011). There was also the option—particularly in the later twelfth through fourteenth centuries—of joining various "third orders," particularly in association with a recognized mendicant group. Indeed, narratives of devout women periodically highlighted (or overstated, or invented) associations with recognized orders in order to protect women whose way of life was perhaps more independent and less institutional than some might approve (More 2018). But a third option was to explore a less institutional route, founding informal communities of like-minded devout. The environment was ready for women who wanted to make a life for themselves in pursuit of Christ to try something new. It is from this milieu that the beguines emerged.

The process of founding a beguine community varied greatly (for examples, see Simons 2001, 36–48; Miller 2014a; research is also summarized in Swan 2014, pp. 23–48). At times, someone was able to procure a home (or a sympathetic person would endow the home) and sisters would move in and set up a community. Sometimes, a group of devout women (or men—beghards) would cluster around a "holy person" and a community would form, either living in their own homes and meeting in common or finding a place of common residence. At times, a group would follow a preacher who would then help establish this following into an intentional community of semi-religious devout. Some communities developed a close relationship with a local church while others were fiercely independent. Thus, the housing arrangements of beguines varied according to the size and wealth of the community. Beguines could live in private homes or in a communal dormitory. The layout of a communal estate itself varied. Some beguinages had no chapel of their own and the residences were not necessarily "planned" for the beguinage. These were called "convent" beguinages. Other "court" beguinages were developed with a main central church and a courtyard around which the residences were arranged (Simons 2001, pp. 48–60).

Other elements were important in founding a beguine community. If the members were to live within a common house, they needed to secure potential sources of income. While a few, such as the community gathered around Ida of Nivelles, practiced begging, most beguines either supported themselves and the community through independent resources or through manual labor. Another factor involved was the identification of a common vision, often a longing to live in the mix of active and contemplative lives, where the pursuit of God in prayer and an active life through charity, manual labor, and teaching were blended in different ways within each community (Simons 2001, pp. 61–90; Miller 2014a, pp. 35–80; research also summarized in Swan 2014, pp. 71–83). Vision is, in turn, connected to motive. Different people might find beguine membership attractive for different reasons. Tanya Stabler Miller writes:

> Wealthier women might join a beguinage in pursuit of apostolic ideals. They also might find
> the beguine life a more flexible, and thus more appealing alternative to the cloister, where

they would be cut off from family, friends, and associates. At the same time, beguinages offered women of middling and lower socioeconomic status a safe haven in which to worship and work (Miller 2014a, p. 36).

One more element in the foundation—or at least the preservation—of a beguine community was permission. Permission was needed by many people for many things: permission to preach or encourage one another, to celebrate mass together, to form a business, to dress in ways that looked like a nun, to waive one's obligations in military or legal services (involving the use of oaths), and more. For this reason, it was advantageous to have associations with people in high places who might plead your cause. Perhaps the most celebrated examples of this are Jacques de Vitry who advocated for the beguines of the Liège region before Innocent III in 1216 (for various assessments, see Sandor 1988; Neel 1989; Wright 2012) and King Louis IX of France who founded and supported the royal beguinage in Paris (see Miller 2014a, pp. 14–34).

As I mentioned above, a summary of the "life of a Beguine" can only be a composite drawn from a variety of sources. Some works present the life of a single beguinage and others draw from the records of a range of communities. My aim here is simply to present a broad summary, drawing from a couple of studies (de Vries 2016; Miller 2014a, pp. 37–41; research also summarized in Swan 2014) to demonstrate that beguines perceived themselves as attempting to lead a "religious" life—an intentional form of life centered around Christian devotion—while avoiding the institutional connections.

Evidence for regular common meetings abound in the literature, though what meetings were common in what communities varied. Common meetings often included mass, community prayers, gatherings to conduct the business of the community, and selected meals (Miller 2014a, pp. 105–7). These are the normal kinds of common gatherings one expects to find in monastic environments. Historian Jennifer Deane underscored the importance of their times of prayer, recounting that, "beguines were petitioned or even required in statutes to pray for their benefactors, and in some communities the daily prayer cycle was structured along lines similar to monastic schedules" (Dean 2008).

In many houses, times of work were both common and times of prayer. One can perceive the blend of prayer and work in this account of the Beguinage of Saint Elizabeth in Ghent:

> On work days they hold to the practice of rising early in the morning and coming together in the church, each going to her own place, which she has specially assigned to her, so that the absence of anyone may thereby be more easily noticed. After they have heard the Mass and said their prayers there, they return to their houses, working all day in silence, in which thing they are considered very useful to the whole country. And while working thus, they do not cease from prayer, for in each convent the two women who are best suited for this recite clearly the psalm "Miserere" and other psalms which they know, and the "Ave Maria," one singing one verse, the other the next, and the rest silently with them, or diligently listen to those who are reciting. Late at night, after Vespers, they go into the church, devoting themselves to prayers and meditations, until the signal is given and they go to bed. On Sundays and holy days, with masses and sermons, prayers and meditations, they devote themselves to the Lord's service in all things; nor may anyone leave the Beguinage on these days without special permission from the principal mistress. (Amt 2010, p. 214)

The quote above reflects a beguinage at which their primary work is performed within the walls of the convent itself. Yet quite often beguines went out to serve in hospitals, leprosariums, schools or other similar places. Indeed, activity, whether in employment or in service, was a distinctive character of beguine forms of life. Yet even as they left their domicile, care was taken through specific rules to preserve an element of monastic "separation" from the world and to guard the reputation of the women who served outside the beguinage (de Vries 2016).

Though beguines did not generally renounce their possessions nor make formal vows of poverty (indeed, some beguines were shrewd merchants: managing estates, administering segments of the textile industry, and granting loans), they heartily embraced a life of simplicity (de Vitry 1998, pp. 81–82;

Simons 2001, pp. 62–68; More 2018, pp. 22–24). The *Règle of Perfect Lovers*, a late thirteenth-century devotional treatise designed to describe beguine virtue, includes poverty as one of the four pillars of beguine life (along with purity, humility, and love. Miller 2014a, p. 113). After Pope Nicholas's decree *Supra montem* in 1289 which established a more formal "Franciscan" third order, informal beguines were often directed (or forced) to join this expression, where they could still hold property, yet make commitments to simplicity (More 2018, pp. 37–38). Similarly, with regard to chastity, beguines did not take formal vows of chastity—and were free to leave their beguinage in order to get married—yet the virtue of chastity was highly praised among the beguines and their admirers (de Vitry 1998, p. 52; Miller 2014a, p. 16).

Prospective members would join a community through a combination of availability, existing relationships, and formal application. Women might be permitted to join for a trial period of one year, after which there was a welcoming ceremony. Beguines generally did not make vows of stability and so were free to leave to get married or for other reasons, though it appears that house commitments generally lasted. While ministry activities and church attendance required that beguines would leave the beguinage on occasion, the kinds and amount of allowable travel was regulated (de Vries 2016; Miller 2014a, p. 38), although the beguines in Paris maintained a lively network with patrons, spiritual advisors, and theologians of the region (Miller 2014a, p. 40).

The clothing of a beguine was designed by each beguinage, often sewn by their own members with their own cloth, strictly avoiding decorative embellishments. The regulations at Ghent declared that "none may have anything which is unusual or suspect in its shape, sewing, or belting, or in the way of nightcaps, hoods, gloves, mitts, straps, purses and knives" (Amt 2010, p. 215). Miller describes their dress as "humble garb evocative of habits" (Miller 2014a, p. 1). The community itself was generally led by a *magistra* or mistress, chosen by the community. The magistra supervised the affairs of the community and could also serve as the in-house spiritual director. Most beguinages lived according to a rule of life and yet this rule was not an officially recognized document but was "the living tradition of a particular beguine community that had been formulated by the women themselves" (Swan 2014, p. 59), much as customaries functioned in earlier monastic communities. Thus, without formal habit, abbess, or approved Rule of life, the beguines dressed and ruled themselves much as a monastic community.

As one can imagine, not everything was harmonious and pure in beguinages. It is likely that some (though certainly not all) of the accusations of sexual impropriety by women who were not cloistered actually happened (Swan 2014, pp. 64–65). Hadewijch, beguine visionary and mystical writer, was likely evicted from her beguinage (Hart 1980, p. 4). There is evidence that beguinages, just as with traditional convents, developed means by which members were corrected and conflict was resolved (Amt 2010, p. 215).

As we have seen, though the women in beguinages established a common life of devotion together, based on commonly held values, they did not make formal vows. Historian Gert Melville describes this element as characteristic of beguine life: "The movement belonged to women who wanted to live a life of poverty, penance, humility, chastity, and deeply interior piety but who had no intention of professing vows, observing a traditional rule, or retreating from the world into a monastery" (Melville 2016, p. 193). The 'rules' established by the headmistress of the beguinage in 's-Hertogenbosch stipulated that beguines should be obedient to their headmistress (see de Vries 2016, p. 137), but this is not to be equated with the vow of obedience in traditional monastic settings. Intentional, but not as institutional: this is characteristic of beguine life. We have seen this above with reference to nearly every area of life: clothing, housing, work, leadership, and on and on. The beguines sought to live a fully devout life and yet also chose to do so in conscious distance from the formal mechanisms of religious life. *Vita regularis sine regula* (Elm 2016).

And it is really their devout life that is most important. Jennifer Deane warns the interpreter of beguine life of being fixated on what the beguine is *not* (not married, not nun, and so on. Dean 2008). Robert of Sorbon, in the mid-thirteenth century, urged the students at the new college he was establishing in Paris, to look to beguines as models. Miller writes, "Robert associated the label 'beguine' with a specific set of behaviours compatible with his goals for his college: a community of secular clerics committed to living a religious life defined by what one *did* rather than by a particular habit or rule" (Miller 2014b, p. 142). When we turn our attention from what the beguine was not toward what they *were*—how they spent their lives—we discover the value of this choice of life in their context. For the beguine, life was a life of community self-government, of economic participation in the market, of a blend of contemplative mysticism and apostolic service to those in need (Simons 2001, pp. 61–90), and of educational development (Miller 2014a, pp. 103–25), a form of life that was extremely difficult for women of that time to realize.

Furthermore, in spite of the many ecclesiastical tensions surrounding beguine life, the beguines succeeded as a movement. Walter Simons reports the foundation of two hundred beguinages before 1320, supporting several thousand beguines (Simons 2001, p. 109). He explains this success by the blend of the contemplative and active offered through the beguine form of life. I would suggest that the offering of this blend was possible in medieval culture uniquely (and perhaps iconically) through the intentional, but not institutional way modeled by the beguines. Walter Simons claims as much in his overview of Christians "on the margins of religious life: hermits and recluses, penitents and tertiaries, beguines and beghards." After noting the unique feature of beguine/beghard movement as consisting almost entirely of women, he concludes his review of the various medieval marginal expressions by citing Jacques de Vitry who proclaimed that:

> We do not consider religious only those who renounce the world and go over to a religious life, but we can also call regulars all the faithful of Christ who serve the Lord under the evangelical rule and who live in an orderly way under the one highest and supreme Abbot. (Simons 2014, p. 323)

Similarly, Gert Melville concludes, "the Beguine way of life remained powerful enough, because of both its strength in numbers and the depth of its faith, to continue to present an alternative path to the monastery's traditional purpose: preparing the way for the individual soul's journey back to God" (Melville 2016, p. 195). I concur with de Vitry and Melville. Furthermore, I find this way of life to be a worthy model for the future of religious life today. It is the forms of life resembling these late medieval devout women that I am calling the Beguine Option.

3. A History of the Beguine Option—The Persistent Past

Devout Christians who desired to live in common, but not necessarily to be enclosed in a cloister; believers who wished for local permission to pursue their way of life, but did not need to go the route of formal papal recognition; sisters and brothers who made sincere promises to live a life of simplicity, purity and mutual submission, but who were not prepared to renounce all property and make formal public vows, Christians who wanted to live as religious, but did not require a developed Rule of Life—this intentional but somewhat less institutional Beguine Option has a long history in the Christian Church, a history worth remembering. My survey of this material will be both sweeping and yet selective. My aim here is simply to demonstrate that the Beguine Option is not an isolated phenomenon in history. Similar forms of life have appeared in various times and places throughout Christian history.

3.1. The Patristic Period

Indeed, current scholarship regarding the pre-history of Christian monasticism is revising the simple "Antony—founder of anchorite institution; Pachomius—founder of cenobite institution" model of monastic origins in light of evidence pointing toward early informal local collections of ascetics or *apotaktikoi* who led a life of strict religious practice, served local villages, but did not establish formal institutions (see Judge 1977; Goehring 1999; Harmless 2004, pp. 417–23). We also find Christians, very early, like Justina (d. 268) who "began monastic observance in her home, cut her hair in the common style of monastics, and observed the seven daily periods of prayer" (Swan 2001, p. 112; see also p. 123). The domestic ascetic movement, a movement which itself was probably connected with that of widows and virgins (Clark 1986; Elm 1994), was influential in the foundation of monasticism throughout the Roman Empire (Palladius 1964, pp. 142–43; Silvas 2005, pp. 75–83; Theodoret of Cyrrhus 1985, pp. 186–89; Magnani 2018).

Palladius' fifth century *Lausiac History* documents a wide range of forms of life identified with the term "monk" or "monastic life" (e.g., Palladius 1964, pp. 49–51). In the early Christian east, a common expression of religious life was the wandering ascetic, following Jesus's own pattern of itinerant ministry. Robert Murray, in his article on "The Features of the Earliest Christian Asceticism," writes of these early examples of devout life, "Certainly the wandering ascetics of the Syriac-speaking Near East resisted all institutionalization" (Murray 1975, p. 70). Rather than understanding the origins of Christian monasticism in terms of a few founders who established recognized institutions, it is probably best to see writers like Athanasius and Jerome drawing attention to certain forms of life in the midst of many others, certain forms which then became the dominant symbols (and approved institutions) of Christian monasticism (Harmless 2004, pp. 417–58). At the council of Chalcedon, the ecclesial hierarchy deemed it necessary to require monasteries to be placed under the direct supervision of the local bishop and "only the bishop's express authority could allow new foundations" (Melville 2016, p. 10). The ruling was not enforced and informal expressions appeared throughout Christendom. Perhaps the importance of this regulation was that officials would periodically appeal to it when they wished to curb particular expressions.

3.2. The Medieval Period

As we move into the medieval period, I will only provide examples from the Christian West, as the developments in Coptic and Byzantine monasticism are complex, my knowledge here is limited, and the sources are less available (see Morris 1995; Hatlie 2007; Vivian 2002). We find a description of domestic ascetic expressions in Patrick of Ireland's writings. Westley Follett writes:

> In his *Confessio* Patrick marvels at the conversion of people who had only recently worshiped idols and that the sons of the Irish and the daughters of their kings had become 'monks and virgins of Christ'. While it is doubtful that we should understand these as cenobitic monks and nuns in a Pachomian or Benedictine sense, there is no question from Patrick's remarks in the *Confessio* and his *Epistola ad milites Corotici* that the promotion of the religious life, and particularly its commitment to celibacy, was a central feature of his ministry to the Irish. It seems likely that Patrick's virgins remained at home with their unbelieving families rather than forming a separate Christian community. (Follett 2006, p. 28)

Our understanding of Celtic monasticism has matured. We no longer see Celtic "monasteries" in light of contemporary models, but rather in terms of the settlements early Celtic religious life resembled. Part of the discussion around the nature of Celtic monasticism is the identification of the *manaig*. *Manaig* have been considered as tenants of monastic properties, yet they were also persons or family groups who lived within range of the monastic enclosure and shared some of the benefits of the community life and rhythm, and were also obliged to keep some of the ritual and monastic practice. We see something similar in the early *minsters* of England. Sarah Foot writes, "The household of a widow living in quiet seclusion with her unmarried daughters might be thought of as a *monasterium*, just as was a new community created by the royal grant of a portion of land to an aspiring abbot and a group of like-minded men." (Foot 2006, p. 5).

Following the example of Frankish queen Radegundis (Melville 2016, p. 16), many monasteries were founded by nobles such that Marilyn Dunn describes Frankish monasticism of the seventh century as a situation "where monasteries directed by family groups became centres of aristocratic power as well as religious cult" (Dunn 2003, p. 158; for the Columbanian tradition, see especially Fox 2014). This kind of expression is not that different from the life of Macrina and Basil in fourth century

Cappadocia. The synods of Aachen (816–819) attempted, with mixed success, to unify all monastic communities within the Benedictine rule and to encourage priests to become more "monastic" through commitments to common residence and a common rhythm of prayer (Melville 2016, pp. 40–42). Yet even as the Benedictine flowering reached its peak in the years of Clunaic dominance, many hermits would find their way near the monastery to live a loosely institutional but highly intentional life of devotion (Leyser 1984, p. 19).

In the eleventh century, we hear of the Hirsau reform movement through which many lay people "gathered together to live the 'common life in the form of the primitive Church'" Pope Urban II gave permission for this movement in a bull of 1091. Converts renounced life in the world, living together without entering a religious house, but rather dwelling in pious communities (Grundmann 1995, p. 223). Similarly, in 1122 Norbert of Xanten urged his convert Theobald of Champagne not to join the Praemonstratensians, but rather to marry and live a religious life in the world. Thus, Norbert and Theobald formed the *Fratres et Sorores ad Succurrendum*, a third order which "anticipated by a century the Franciscan Tertiaries" (Davison 1927, p. 91).

All of these expressions bear similarity to—and can serve as early historical examples of—the Beguine Option I descried above. Now we are up to the period of time when the beguines themselves emerged. As mentioned in the section on the beguines, the twelfth century was a period of lay flowering. Lay preachers proclaimed the faith in the town squares. Confraternities of laity formed together and committed to regular times of support, common service activities and even standards of holy living (see Vauchez 1993, pp. 107–27 and Thompson 2005, pp. 69–102). Ultimately, in 1221 the Brothers and Sisters of Penance received official recognition through a *Memoriale propositi*. Another example of a similar expression at this time is the Humiliati. Frances Andrews, author of the first English-language major study of this group, summarizes the earliest references to the Humiliati as describing "both groups of clerics living in community and lay men and women devoted to the religious life in small ad hoc associations promoting the catholic faith" (Andrews 1999, p. 2; see also Brasher 2003; Brasher 2017). Condemned as heretics in 1184, they appealed to Rome and were ultimately accepted in 1201 in part through the creation of a Third Order of married Christians eager to pursue the devout life and even to encourage their neighbors through preaching. After recounting the story of the Humiliati and their acceptance, Gert Melville proclaims, "The church had blazed a new trail. It had begun to occupy a new social space, with the help of the forces that that same space had produced" (Melville 2016, p. 200).

The trail that was blazed by the approval of the Humiliati was widened into a road—and later transformed into a highway—through the incorporation of the community of Francis of Assisi and other mendicants (on Francis see Moorman 1988; Thompson 2012; Vauchez 2012; removed for peer-review, chapter 2; on Domincans see Hinnebusch 1966; for other mendicants see Andrews 2006). Francis chose to leave Assisi and the merchant option he had available. Nor did he join any of the local monasteries. At the start of his ministry, Francis of Assisi chose to live as a lay penitent, living and serving lepers, much as Marie d'Oignies and her husband did in Liège in these very years. In time, the little brothers of Assisi received approval from Rome not only as a community of penitents but also as an international agency of gospel proclamation (as did other mendicant orders during this period). The Order of Friars Minor, even within the final decade of Francis's life, struggled to navigate the uneasy tensions between radical abandonment to God, apostolic service, voluntary poverty, and faithfulness to the church. Over the course of the thirteenth century—and not without its share of internal conflict (Burr 2001)—the Franciscans institutionalized in three orders as a mission arm of the Roman church (on the institutionalization of the second order see Knox 2000; More 2018). The third order, along with the third orders of other mendicant orders served as officially recognized religious institutes with whom lay devout who desired or needed might choose to affiliate.

Other informal intentional groups, such as the Poor Catholics, also received a measure of approval in this same window of time. Nonetheless, the thirteenth and fourteenth centuries were not only periods of high interest in the semi-religious life but also mixed approvals of the same. It is fruitless here to document the changing fortunes of those who sought to live a *vita regularis sine regula* (Elm 2016; see Grundmann 1995). André Vauchez describes the fate of the penitential confraternities as follows:

> The number of penitents, both isolated or in communities, remained large until the end of the Middle Ages. But beginning with the early fourteenth century, the papacy tried to channel this kind of religious life, which was popular with both laymen and laywomen, in the direction of greater regularity. The confraternities of penitents were absorbed by third orders, which recruited their own members primarily among women, and which themselves often evolved toward claustral forms of life, ending up as semi-monastic congregations. In this way the originality of this typically medieval movement was progressively lost—though the movement was to be reborn in new forms in the sixteenth and seventeenth centuries. (Vauchez 1993, p. 127; yet also see More 2018)

One final example may serve to fill out our sampling of the Beguine Option through the middle ages. John Van Engen writes of the Sisters and Brothers of the Common Life:

> Beginning in the 1380s, in market towns along the IJsel River (east-central Netherlands) and in the country of Holland, groups of women and men formed households organized as communes and a lifestyle centered on devotion. They lived on city streets alongside urban neighbors, managed properties and rents in common, and prepared textiles or books for local markets–all the while refusing to profess vows as religious or to acquire spouses and property as lay citizens. (Van Engen 2008, loc 99)

The Sisters and Brothers of the Common Life thrived in the fourteenth and fifteenth centuries, in part due to their legal expertise in navigating canonical privileges. Today we are familiar with this group because one of their number, Thomas à Kempis, penned the influential *Imitation of Christ*. Some of these modern devout, as they were also called, formerly joined or formed houses of canons regular, most notably the canons of Windesheim. Yet many other devout remained in households ordered through informally written "ways" or "customaries" (Van Engen 1988, pp. 155–86). Kaspar Elm describes the self-conscious awareness of the modern devout precisely as a semi-religious expression:

> The early Christian hermits of Egypt, Syria and Palestine, Elijah and Elisha, the prophets of the Old Testament and the pious Essenes were for them not merely the prototypes of monks and monasticism, but creators of free societates that lived sine regula, sine statutis obedientialibus, sine habitu aut ceremoniis regularibus. ... What monks, canons, and mendicants, and indeed the military orders had long claimed for themselves—to live according to the model of the Apostles and to return to the early church—semi-religious now claimed as well, and with an exclusivity similar to that of other orders and their branches. (Elm 2016, p. 308).

3.3. The Modern Period

In the modern period, the Western Church divided and the options for semi-religious life in time became more available to all the divisions. Indeed, it is not really fair to talk about "intentional yet less institutional" options, because after 1540 or so, the institutions themselves begin to change, enabling opportunities that were not available in the medieval period.

Approval of the Society of Jesus (the Jesuits) as a religious order did not come easy (Meissner 1992, 178–181). After much discussion, the band of Ignatius of Loyola's followers submitted their proposal for approval which was received, at first. Contrary voices complicated matters in the finalization process, however. Some were concerned about the Jesuit abolition of recitation of the divine office in choir. But more central to the final judge was the creation of a new religious order itself. After much prayer (and perhaps a little human persuasion), the Society of Jesus was finally confirmed on 27 September 1540. This was a significant development in that (1) the Vatican approved the creation of a new order, and more significantly that (2) this order was designed—perhaps even more than the Dominicans—as a vehicle for apostolic ministry.

Because they were a dispersed, missionary society many of the features of traditional monastic life had to be revised or abandoned. Jesuits could or should not be called back from their ministries to join in the communal recitation of the divine office or attend chapter meetings (Taft 1993, pp. 301–2). The requirements associated with these were released. Often, they would form houses within which a team of missionaries would be based. Those who were present might gather regularly for meals and prayer. Daily private self-examination and regular confession and reception of the sacrament was expected. But this was an army at war. And because of this, adjustments were made. As one of their early leaders proclaimed: "We are not monks; the world is our house!"

The next step came thirty-five years later. The Roman church had issued a clarion call for evangelism and purity of life through the council of Trent (1545–1563), and Philip Neri (1515–1595) embodied the spirit of that call superbly. He spent his time as a layman and as a tutor, ministering among those without education, without resources, or those in the prostitution industry. He helped found the Confraternity of the Most Holy Trinity of Pilgrims and Convalescents to minister to the needs of poor pilgrims. He initiated regular gatherings for preaching, song, and discussion and pioneered many creative means of communicating the Christian faith. In time, he was ordained and it seemed fit for him to organize a community of secular priests in order to provide mutual support in the work. This was the beginning of the "Congregation of the Oratory of St. Philip Neri (or Oratorians. see Moss 1957, pp. 166–67; http://www.newadvent.org/cathen/11272a.htm)." This community, though with pontifical approval, chose not to make solemn vows to a large order, but rather to offer simple commitments to membership within local, self-governing houses or Oratories. A Rule of Life was drawn up for the Oratorians seventeen years after Neri's death as a collection of the custom of Neri and his followers. Philip Neri is commonly thought of as the "father" of the Societies of Apostolic Life, religious groups that do not make formal religious vows, may own property but usually live in some arrangement of a supportive community. Societies of Apostolic Life are usually organized around particular tasks or mission goals.

The third step was made through the combined work of Vincent de Paul and Louise de Marillac. Vincent de Paul helped start the Confraternities of Charity around 1621, which volunteered to care for sick, beggars, victims of war and others in similar straits. The ministries of these charities grew as both volunteers and generous gifts multiplied. But they needed administration and a common vision. Together, Vincent de Paul and Louise de Marillac were the parents of the Daughters of Charity. Louise de Marillac began to visit the various ministries in 1629. She studied their activities, corrected abuses, and revived their zeal. There were a number of younger women serving the charities and she held these girls in her heart. She was burdened for their spiritual formation. Thus, in 1633 de Paul and Marillac formed the Daughters of Charity, gaining formal approval for their life and Rule in 1645. Here is how the second paragraph of this rule begins:

> They should consider that although they do not belong to a religious order, that state not being compatible with the duties of their vocation, yet as they are much more exposed to the world than nuns—their monastery being generally no other than the abode of the sick; their cell a hired room; their chapel, the parish church; their cloister, the public streets or the wards of hospitals—they are obliged on this account to lead as virtuous a life as if they were professed in a religious order; to conduct themselves wherever they mingle with the world with as much recollection, purity of heart and body, detachment from creatures; and to give as much edification as nuns in the seclusion of their monasteries. (Ryan and Rybolt 1995, p. 169)

Notice: this group openly states that they are *not* nuns. They do not belong to a religious order. And yet they have a Rule of Life. And yet they have a religious *vocation*. And yet they are officially recognized by the Catholic church. This rule describes their life of poverty, chastity, and obedience: not defined as a formal monastic order, but as appropriate to women who work in the world in a common ministry together day in and day out (annual simple vows). The rule describes the love they are to express toward the sick poor and the virtues they are to exhibit in their relationships with one another. The rule specifies a set of common spiritual practices that each sister is obligated to maintain: self-examination and confession, regular assemblies for discussion, regular times of worship. Indeed, specifications are made for brief but sincere acts of devotion: hearing some devotional book read for a quarter of an hour, kneeling in silence for a moment and then reciting a prayer, setting aside brief times for meditation. What you see when you read this document is a "daily office" conducted at the workplace and wherever possible.

In founding their community in such a manner (and getting approval for this foundation), the Daughters of Charity changed the shape of the history of religious life. To quote Louise Sullivan in her introduction to the life and works of Louise de Marillac, "The form of consecrated life begun by Vincent and Louise with the Daughters of Charity has become the norm for most religious congregations. Though cloistered orders are alive and well, most religious women today live their lives in active apostolic communities" (Sullivan 1995, p. 50). I cannot emphasize how significant this is. This is a formal approval for a form of life that the beguines had been exploring three hundred years prior. Yes, there are a few nuns who pray in cloisters, but the vast majority of consecrated women today are now living lives of active service in the world, walking that tightrope of active service and trying to maintain a sincere and disciplined life of devotion and community. Diarmuid O'Murchu tells the story of a number of "paradigmatic foundresses" in his *Religious Life in the 21st Century*, many of which followed in the path of the Daughters of Charity and bear close resemblance to the Beguine Option which was—by fits and starts—increasingly permitted within the Roman Catholic community. The Daughters of Charity became the most imitated and adapted form of religious life in its time and is still today the model for many, many religious congregations, Catholic and Protestant alike.

This brings us to consider those whose ties with Rome were severed during the sixteenth century. As with other topics in this essay, I can only provide a few samples of the convoluted history of the relationship of "Protestantism" with "monasticism" (see Biot 1963; Peters 2014).

While Martin Luther and his followers dissolved the institution of monasticism within the German Protestant region, Luther himself left a window of respect open for intentional Christian communities particularly for the purpose of education (see Luther 1961, pp. 446–47). This was the window that Augustus Herman Francke (1663–1727) opened in his founding of many schools in Halle. Francke was a Pietist, a Lutheran who emphasized spiritual renewal (Erb 1983). One of the students in his school in Halle was Nicolaus Ludwig, Count Zinzendorf (1700–1760; for Zinzendorf and the Moravians see Langton 1956; Lewis 1962). In 1722, Zinzendorf offered asylum to a group of persecuted Christians on his personal estate. Soon, other religious refugees of one sort and another came to find a home. But keeping the peace among a wide range of religious refugees was not easy and things grew tense in the settlement. Zinzendorf invested himself in prayer and visitation, interviewing the members one-by-one and facilitating small group interaction as well. On 13 August 1727, they experienced a deep spiritual awakening—a true breakthrough. They drew up a covenant describing how they might continue to live together and support the Lord's work, called "The Brotherly Union and Agreement at Herrnhut" (Zinzendorf 1983, pp. 325–30). This document describes their celebration of special days of worship. It encourages but does not demand regular confession. It restricts the interaction between single persons of different sexes. It urges the community members to model virtues of the Christian life. Arrangements are made to care for the sick and to correct the erring or intransigent. There are further instructions for the "watchers," encouraging them to sing a hymn at the change of the hours of the night. In actual fact, this community instituted a round-the-clock rotation of prayer that lasted one hundred years. A wide range of mission expressions emerged from the Moravian movement. The Moravians also experienced their own tensions within the Lutheran authorities. Living in common yet not cloistered; an agreement yet no solemn vows; a combination of prayer and mission. Within the Lutheran church, two centuries after the Protestant Reformation, one can identify the emergence of what I am calling a Beguine Option, an option that has inspired others in the centuries that followed (Winter 1994; Grieg 2004).

Anabaptists did not accept the Lutheran arrangement. They thought that reform included a change in Church–State relations and a reform of the shape of the church itself. Anabaptists found themselves collecting together in independent communities. In time, some communities documented their way of discipleship together in *Ordnungen*, an order describing community practices and behavior that were normative for a given community (see https://gameo.org/index.php?title=Congregational_ Orders_and_Church_Disciplines_(Gemeindeordnungen)). Essentially, the *Ordnungen* were rules for the life of a community living together without cloister, committed to the sharing of possessions (see Walpot 1994) without a vow of poverty. Some historians of Anabaptism see significant connections between the modern devout and the values of the Anabaptist communities (Davis 1974). Needless to say, Anabaptist forms of life have survived and are active in Mennonite, Amish, Bruderhof and other communities today.

In 1536, Henry VIII of England began what is known as "the dissolution of the monasteries." Over the next six years, hundreds of convents, friaries, houses of canons and the like were disbanded. Their assets became the property of the State, and the State made new arrangements for the thousands of religious who had previously lived in these estates. Thus, there was almost no monasticism life in England for three hundred years. I say "almost" because there were a few "Beguine-ish" exceptions. Mary Ferrar, in 1625, acquired some property in Huntingdonshire complete with an abandoned chapel. Family began to collect there and they formed a little community, complete with regular recitation of the prayers through the day and service to local children in need. The vision of the "Little Gidding" community was renewed in a community in England between 1970 and the 1990s (see Van de Weyer 1988), and their charism is currently kept alive by a new Community of Christ the Sower (http://www.stmarymagdalenes.org/christthesower.htm). The community was established for people who were not vowed religious, but rather for folks who work in the world. Members make commitments of simplicity but take no vows of poverty.

Greg Peters, in his *Reforming the Monastery: Protestant Theologies of Religious Life*, identifies a 1659 plan for an community inspired by the Carthusian order; an Anglican dean around 1668 who gave spiritual direction to twelve women "living monastically" in a convent in London; a 1707 reference to a community of women in Bath and Wells, who established an Anglican sisterhood of the Little Gidding type; and many other expressions of a longing for the renewal of some type of "Anglican" monastic life. Peters concludes his chapter on the Anglican tradition with a thorough retelling of the story of the rebirth of religious life in the context of the Oxford movement, and describes the foundation of a Sisterhood under the oversight of parish priests and which combined both contemplative and charitable dimensions (see Peters 2014, pp. 53–90).

Needless to say, many more examples can be named (see also Biot 1963; Bloesch 1964; Bloesch 1974). Bonhoffer's underground experimental seminary Finkenwalde was an exploration in semi-monastic life. George McLeod's pioneering efforts with the Iona community in Scotland combined both Christian community life and restorative manual labor. I think it is fair to say, as we follow the developments of modernity, that the religious institutions of this period increasingly made room for forms of religious life which desired to live in common without being cloistered, to live in simplicity without renouncing all property, to live pure lives without expecting members to be celibate, to receive ecclesial permission and support without becoming smothered by accountability, and to explore the combination of an intentionally devout life and occupation in the world. As we shall observe in the next section, I see a flowering of just such expressions emerging today.

4. Contemporary Expressions of the Beguine Option: A Pervasive Present

I began this essay with two contemporary examples of the "intentional yet less institutional" forms of life that I am here calling the Beguine Option. In section two, I described this option in greater detail, presenting a summary portrait of beguine life in the late middle ages. Then, in section three, I have traced the "persistent past" of these forms of life, providing sufficient examples to demonstrate that Christians have often explored semi-religious ways of life through which they embody whole-hearted devotion.

Having already provided a couple of contemporary examples—and there being hundreds of other examples I could give (for sample lists, see https://www.nurturingcommunities.org/communities; https://christiancommunity.org.uk/about-us/links-to-other-christian-communities/ and https://en.wikipedia.org/wiki/Society_of_apostolic_life)—it seems best to summarize the contemporary scene not by giving further examples of individual communities, but rather to summarize the work of a few relevant networks of intentional Christian expressions that bear resemblance to our Beguine Option. As we shall see in the final section, the word "network" is important as we consider what a postmodern "intentional yet not as institutional" monasticism might look like.

The Community of the Beatitudes (https://beatitudes.org/en/) was originally founded in 1973 as "The Lion of Judah and the Immolated Lamb" by the French couple Gerard and Josette Croissant and a couple of friends. They were acknowledged as an association of the faithful by diocesan right in 1985. They changed their name to Community of the Beatitudes and were received as an international association of the faithful by pontifical right (approval by the Vatican and not merely local permission) in 2002. They have long been a member of the Catholic Fraternity of Charismatic Covenant Communities and Fellowships. After some controversy and a few cases of moral failure, the Holy See intervened in 2010 and were reorganized as an "Ecclesial Family of Consecrated Life" under the Congregation for Institutes of Consecrated Life and Societies of Apostolic Life. By this time, the community of the Beatitudes numbered over seventy houses worldwide. The distinctive charism of the Community of the Beatitudes is that they welcome faithful from all states of life: married people with children, single people, consecrated lay people who live in chastity, priests, and permanent deacons whether single or married. Married and celibate singles live together in a common estate, though in designated dwellings. Associates with lesser degrees of commitment also share life together with those who make full commitment. The communities celebrate common worship, common meals, common decision-making processes, and shared service in areas of need. The Community of the Beatitudes is simply one example of the many "new communities"—clearly not individual communities, but networks of communities—established in the Roman Catholic church after the Second Vatican council.

The Fresh Expressions movement (http://freshexpressions.org.uk/) was born in 2004 as a collaboration between the Church of England and the British Methodist Church. The inspiration for the movement was some exploration into what a "mission shaped church" might look like. People began to think about the need for a mixed economy of church forms. Bishop Steven Croft, one of the early leaders, identified "a Fresh Expression is a form of church for our changing culture established primarily for the benefit if people who are not yet members of any church." A number of experiments were established and new partners have been added (the Salvation Army, the United Reformed Church, the Church of Scotland and the Baptist Union of Great Britain). Studies conducted between 2012 and 2016 showed 1109 Fresh Expressions of Church identified in 21 UK Dioceses with 50,600 attending. These statistics were just for the Church of England.

My reason for mentioning this movement is that some of the "Fresh Expressions" are monastic-like in structure and life. Indeed, in 2010 some of the leaders of the Fresh Expressions movement published a little book titled *New Monasticism as Fresh Expression of Church*. In the Introductory chapter, bishop Graham Cray, another of the pioneers of the movement, shares why he thinks New Monasticism is important to Fresh Expressions (Cray 2010). He argues that new monastic expressions (1) address the need and challenge of discipleship, (2) help Christian entrepreneurs sustain the long haul in planting church among the non-churched majority, (3) maintain the link between mission and discipleship, and (4) contribute to a 'deeper' ecclesiology. Contributors to the rest of the book share many stories of their own communities, some of which include both married and singles, living in common without being cloistered, rhythms of prayer joined with times of regular employment, commitments to simplicity without vows of absolute poverty. It is striking to see the similarities between the early beguine movement (which never really spread into England) and the monastic "fresh expressions."

The Nurturing Communities Network (https://www.nurturingcommunities.org/) is "an informal and growing network of Christ-centered intentional communities that strive to bear witness more fully to God's kingdom here on earth." (https://www.nurturingcommunities.org/vision/). Its roots go back to the flowering of Christian communities in North America during the 60s and 70s (see Jackson and Jackson 2009; Jackson 1978; Janzen 1996). Anabaptist and charismatic elements both combined as various communities found relationship and support for one another. A few forged a semi-formal alliance in Shalom Mission Communities, who provided "visitations" and helpful guidance for one another when needed (see http://www.shalommissioncommunities.org/).

In 2009, as new Christian communities were popping up all over, Jonathan Wilson-Hartgrove, then director of the School for Conversion had a conversation with David Janzen, well respected leader in the intentional Christian community scene. They both admitted the need for pastoral guidance of young communities and Janzen chose to help. David Janzen and friends began visiting communities, providing encouragement and ties between kindred spirits. This work became labeled the Nurturing Communities Project. Some of the wisdom of this work is now contained in Janzen's *The Intentional Christian Community Handbook for Idealists, Hypocrites, and Wannabe Disciples of Jesus* (Janzen 2013). Another element that developed was a series of gatherings for leaders or community folks. Regional gatherings of communities are now common.

There are probably somewhere between 50 and 100 active communities all together in this network. Nearly all are Protestant communities, with a few members of Catholic Worker houses represented at the gatherings and a strong Anabaptist element present. Intentional Christian community is the common element between the various expressions. While most of these groups do not maintain a developed office of prayer, it is interesting to note that nearly all of these communities have some pattern of common prayer or worship, often daily. Most community members are employed in regular jobs, though some work part time and spend other time volunteering. As with the early beguines, the practice of active service is important to these new communities. Various means of arranging housing, sharing of income and possessions, decision-making and other elements characterize the forms of life of these communities. The large majority of members are married or single, yet there are a handful who have made commitments to celibacy. Few have developed any kind of formal Rule of Life. Yet this is a healthy and growing network of intentional yet not necessarily institutional religious life.

The Missional Wisdom Foundation "stands are the fulcrum between spiritual tradition and innovation" (https://www.missionalwisdom.com/about/). The Missional Wisdom Foundation emerged out of the nexus of declining Methodist churches in the US, planting creative intentional communities, and theological reflection on mission and monasticism. Elaine Heath, then professor of evangelism at Perkins seminary, along with Scott Kisker, began in the 2000s to connect ideas from their Methodist heritage with insights from the history of monasticism and what was becoming known as "new monasticism." they helped foster the planting of a few intentional communities linking college students, neighborhoods, and a Methodist-based rule of life. Some of this story is recounted in Elaine Heath and Scott Kisker's book *Longing for Spring*, which specifically mentions the beguines as an historical model for consideration (see Heath and Kisker 2010). Interest in this work developed, and by 2011 Elaine Heath and friends established the Academy for Missional Wisdom. They began to train people to form "micro-communities" of faith, which Heath and Larry Duggins documented in their *Missional. Monastic. Mainline: A Guide to Starting Missional Micro-Communities in Historically Mainline Traditions* (Heath and Duggins 2014). Their work has further developed into providing resources, planting communities, teaching classes and pioneering a "dispersed community" of members located in various places linked through a common rule of life (https://www.missionalwisdom.com/rule-of-life) and regular pattern of support and encouragement. There are about ten active communities currently connected with Missional Wisdom and more cohorts developing all the time.

The four networks I have outlined above (Community of the Beatitudes, Fresh Expressions, Nurturing Communities Network, Missional Wisdom Foundation) provide a sampling of the forms of life emerging on the edges of the Christian Church today. These networks represent the Roman Catholic, Anglican, Anabaptist, Mainline, traditions and more. Most of these networks, though emerging from within one tradition, are openly ecumenical. And I could add more names to this list: a collection of "new friars" around the world (Bessenecker 2006, 2010), the Community of St. Anselm located at Lambeth Palace in London which provides a monastic immersion to people aged 20–35 (https://www.stanselm.org.uk/), Ravens Bread (http://www.ravensbreadministries.com/) which links together many who are lovers of solitude (new hermits?), the Order of Sustainable Faith which is forming both residential and dispersed expressions of semi-monastic life connected with the Association of Vineyard Churches (https://www.sustainablefaith.com/theorder).

My point in all of this is first to help us look at the "present" of monasticism. Looking at religious life from the perspective of these emerging networks, it is perhaps best not to speak of a demise of religious life in the twenty-first century, but rather of the early stages of a new birth of religious life. People are hungry to live an intentional—and even somewhat communal—life of devotion to God. But my second accompanying point is to note the resemblance of these new expressions to what I have traced through history as the Beguine Option. The new communities are not making solemn vows. Seldom do they abandon all property before joining, though most make some commitment to simplicity. They try to blend the active and the contemplative (though I still think that many are weak on the contemplative—more on this later). They have guidelines with varied degrees of rule-like specificity. They are largely self-governing though with valuable relationships with kindred spirits. Many of these groups are connected with networks of support and accountability such that moral failures or community conflicts can be addressed. In sum, the expressions of intentional Christian living emerging from the ground up seem to me to look much more like the beguines than the Benedictines.

5. The Beguine Option: A Promising Future for Religious Life Today

Having examined the persistent past and the pervasive present of the Beguine Option, it remains for us to explore the promising future of the Beguine Option. Needless to say, a full review and evaluation of the literature regarding the future of religious life, even within the Roman Catholic community, is impossible here (see for example, Schneiders 2000, 2001, 2013; Flanagan 2014; Pope 2014; Schreiter 2015; O'Murchu 2016; Maya 2018). It is sufficient to say that there is a significant reconsideration going on within the Roman Catholic community. Interpretation of the vision—and application of interpretations of the vision—of Vatican II play an important role in the reconsideration. To what degree is religious life simply part of a holiness hierarchy? To what degree are active religious a service arm of the episcopacy? How do religious balance separation from the world and authentic world engagement? How does religious life function as a prophetic witness to the Church and the world? How do we nourish hope in the midst of apparent decline? These questions and more characterize the discussions regarding the future of religious life within Roman Catholic circles. As I review this material, I am struck by the interest in forging ecumenical relationships, the interest in viewing religious life less from the perspective of institutional categories and more from dynamic functions, the openness to new and creative options.

There is very little reflection on the future of religious life from "Protestant" viewpoints, primarily because there is so little religious life in these circles. Yet some are responding to what they see as a hopeful rise of intentional Christian communities and even a new monasticism, imagining what this might (or "should") look like. Donald Bloesch advocates for a monasticism that is evangelical, a small-scale model of the church, is mixed with both men and women, acts as an agent of reconciliation between churches, is involved in outreach, is in conflict with the dominant values of the culture, and functions as an eschatological sign of the coming kingdom of God (Bloesch 1974, pp. 108–13). The contributors to *School(s) for Conversion: 12 Marks of a New Monasticism* list twelve "marks" of the monasticism they envision including "Sharing Economic Resources with Fellow Community Members and the Needy Among Us," "Humble Submission to Christ's Body, the Church," "Support for Celibate Singles Alongside Monogamous Married Couples and their Children," and Care for the Plot of God's Earth Given to Is Along with Support of Our Local Economies" (House 2005). More recently, Greg Peters, in his *The Monkhood of All Believers: The Monastic Foundation of Christian Spirituality*, issues a restatement from the Protestant community for the universal call to holiness symbolized in our baptismal vows as a groundwork of spiritual growth pursued through ascetical practice by all believers, some of whom will find that vocation best embodied in formal religious life and others not (Peters 2018). Once again, as in Roman Catholic circles, the trend is to see potential in a devout life that is clearly intentional, yet not as institutional as traditional monasticism.

We must, of course, realize that we are at the cusp of a new era. Just as the Ancient world gave way to the medieval and the medieval gave way to the modern, so we are now in the transition between the modern and "something else." Just what that something else is, we don't know. We call the transition *postmodern*. The fact of the matter is that our institutions themselves are undergoing significant change; patterns of family, work and employment, housing, education, and church are simply not what they were seventy years ago (see Borgmann 1992; Castells 2009; Castells 2010; Castells 2011). What this means is that even trying to think of what religious life might look like *within* an institutional framework might be an exercise in futility. When Marie d'Oignies and Francis of Assisi began their experiments of life among the poor, having rejected the option of joining any of the nearby monasteries, many of their contemporaries (and perhaps Marie and Francis themselves!) regarded their form of life as non-monastic, but rather "something else." Yet it was the future of religious life. I suspect we should be prepared for something similar in our own era.

Yet whatever the future of monasticism looks like, I believe that some kind of Beguine Option has promise. Not that I entirely reject a Benedict Option (Dreher 2018). As I mentioned at the start of this essay, Alasdair MacIntyre and others have made a call for a "new Benedict." This call has inspired fresh reflections (Wilson 2010; Okholm 2007; Stock et al. 2007) and some valuable relationships (The Nurturing Communities folk met for a season at St. Johns Benedictine monastery in Collegeville where great mutual conversations were fostered). All well and good. But Benedict was a synthesizer and, in his *Rule*, brought a unifying coherence out of a vast variety of experiments, expressions and rules which preceded him. Frankly, I do not think we are ready for that kind of synthesis or unifying coherence. I am of the conviction that we are in need of just that vast variety of experiments, expressions, and rules so that down the line some new Benedict may arise an discern how the experiments can be best synthesized for the era ahead. But right now we are simply not ready. It is not that there is no place for a fresh recovery of the Benedictine charism. A Benedict Option is a worthy experiment. But my suspicion is that a Beguine option has a lot more promise in a postmodern era.

When, in 2007, I was just turning my attention from the field of Christian spirituality more generally toward monastic studies more particularly, I presented a paper to discuss among a few colleagues who called ourselves Evangelical Scholars in Christian Spirituality. I titled it "A Call to Order(s): Evangelical Monasticism in a Postmodern World—Preliminary Considerations (cf. https://spiritualityshoppe.org/a-call-to-orders-evangelical-monasticism-in-a-postmodern-world/). In this essay, I was exploring monasticism from the point of view of Protestant evangelicalism. What might monasticism in a postmodern age within this ecclesial community look like? I still think that a few of the suggestions I made in that paper are worth restating here along with a few more. As will become clear, I think that these suggestions paint a portrait of religious life which bears similarity to what I have been describing as the Beguine Option. Hence my conviction that the Beguine Option has a promising future for Christian monasticism.

First, I think that the very presence of some kind of religious life, whether more or less institutional, is itself a postmodern statement, and this would be exceptionally so in a Protestant environment which itself emerged with the modern era. The development of monasteries would be a frank admission that discipleship is much more than information transfer. Christian discipleship in a monastic setting is formation into a life and a form of life. The development of the university was characteristic of the shift from medieval to modern (Leclercq 1982). I suspect a renewal of some kind of monastic life could navigate the shift from the modern to the postmodern, just as Benedict and the Beguines helped navigate the shifts between the ancient and the medieval and between early and late medieval.

Second, I can imagine new explorers of religious life reexamining our goals and aims. After Vatican II, Roman Catholic religious began perceiving religious life less as some kind of "holiness factory" or as a functional arm of the church. Now the prophetic function is more commonly mentioned. Protestants have barely begun to consider what the aims, functions and meaning of religious life might be. All this will require a new "theologizing" of religious life (and I suspect this will be required for all traditions): examining history to discover the concerns and the questions that have driven the ups and downs of monastic history, interpreting the Scriptures and theological categories afresh to address these concerns and questions in light of the best strategies we can employ, evaluating and re-inventing practices and "the practice" of religious life for a new setting. I think that the beguines, even more than Benedict, left the door open for discovering the purpose of the religious life in the process. And while this kind of openness does not easily communicate a clear ideological frame, I think it provides what is necessary to do the work of ideological frame alignment (Wittberg 1994).

Third, I suspect that the most promising overarching community form for the future of monasticism will not be "institutions" as we think of them, but rather *networks* (or perhaps it might be better to say that many postmodern institutions will look more like networks). If the model for the modern age was the machine, I think a key model for postmodern transition is the network (Barabási 2014; Campbell and Garner 2016; Castells 2015). What this means is that our structures of leadership, our mobilization of resources and ministries, our use of property and much more will be decided more in view of links between people than by formal affiliations (see also Howard 2018, pp. 164–67). *Hubs*, like the Missional Wisdom Foundation, the Leadership Conference of Women Religious, the Nurturing Communities Network will all serve as connecting points between the various *nodes*, such as individual communities or interested persons. Once again, the image of a Beguine Option more accurately communicates this loose connection of networks within or outside or on the margin of institutions. Even the boundary marker of beguine habits expressed distinction without institutional identification, similar to other beguines yet independent to one another.

Mention of the structures of "leadership" brings us to a fourth suspicion. I suspect, with others, that Religious life must return to its origins as a movement of the laity, with leadership emerging from earned authority rather than through organizational position. The institutional elitism of the Roman Catholic Church is already being dismantled through highly publicized scandals. At the same time, the reticence of non-Catholics toward elitism will be tempered by a longing to be mentored by people who are seen to "live well." From either side, I see a growing interest in *ammas* and *abbas* and intentional communities who through lives of integrity demonstrate what impact a consecrated life could have. It is not just a matter of moving from heirarchy to a more democratic approach to leadership, but rather a growing respect for those who lead from life. Though good Benedictine models of collaborative leadership can be found, I suspect that the Beguine option presents more palatable ideology support for the kind of religious life needed in this next season.

This is not to imagine that some kind of new monasticism will be any purer or more harmonious that that of a previous age. Sexual scandals, for example, have arisen in all ages. What I hope we learn in a postmodern age is how better to deal with them. Conflicts and divisions have marred the Christian community since Acts 5–6 and I suspect that it will be no different in the future of Christian religious life. I only hope that we are able, in the midst of a postmodern monasticism, to learn wisdom regarding how better to navigate these matters.

Fifth, I continue to think that religious life is somehow caught up in identity, and that this sense of being "different" (than the world, than lay culture) will find unique expression(s) in the future of monasticism. Margaret Miles speaks of monasticism as creating a "counter-culture"; Walter Capps speaks of a "monastic impulse"; Sandra Schneiders speaks of a fundamental "God quest" undertaken by the consecrated celibate; Diarmuid O'Murchu talks about constructing a "monastic archetype"; (Miles 2000; Capps 1983; Schneiders 2013; O'Murchu 2016). I think all of these are poking at the issue of identity. A phrase that I have thrown around in the past few years: *late modern society has produced many collections, but few real communities; many individuals, but few real solitaries.* My hope is that new forms of religious life can move beyond the late modern morass of identity (and the current postmodern confusion) into something freshly Christlike. This comes from the mutual exploration—and the somewhat consensual adoption of—practices, values, and beliefs that undergird a community's sense of who they are vis-à-vis the surrounding world. Here again, I find the Beguine Option to be a compelling model for religious life in the future. If any group knows what it means to be both caught and committed within the ambiguities of self-understanding and the pains of others' misunderstandings, it is the beguines.

Finally—and more recently—I have had this hunch that a new postmodern monasticism must be accompanied by a new postmodern mysticism. It is fascinating to me that many beguines were pioneers of the new mysticism of their own day. Some became well-known mystical writers, such as Mechtild of Magdeburg, Hadewijch, and Beatrijs of Nazareth (see McGinn 1998). I hear people like Bernadette Flanagan writing about solitude and the contemplative in her exploration of women and new monasticism or Elaine Heath talking about "the mystic way of evangelism" (Flanagan 2014; Heath 2017). Another of the 12 marks of a "new monasticism" is "Commitment to a Disciplined Contemplative Life" (House 2005). At the same time, I am keenly aware of the struggle of millennials to navigate their own faith experience. Some people have complained to me that they think new monastic communities are weak on the contemplative. Part of this is due to their own sense of the need for action. But I also think there is more. A new mysticism is needed to support the drive to new intentionally *Christian* forms of life. My suspicion is that this new mysticism will require significant permission for a variety of experience, ambiguity, and darkness. But, as I mentioned, I am only beginning to think about this. In any case, the creative mystical pioneering of the beguines can give us courage today to explore our own relationship with God in new experiences and with new language in the context of our new settings of religious life.

Thus, when I look at all of these six suggestions—presence, reexamination of goals, networks, laity and earned authority, identity, mysticism—I find the Beguine Option (intentional yet less institutional) to have significant potential in the context of a transitional, postmodern, Christianity. This Beguine Option has a persistent past, a pervasive present, and, in light of all we have seen in this final section, I think it has a promising future as well.

Funding: This research received no external funding.

Conflicts of Interest: The author declares no conflict of interest.

References

Amt, Emilie Amt. 2010. *Women's Lives in Medieval Europe: A Sourcebook*. London: Routledge.

Andrews, Frances. 1999. *The Early Humiliati*. Cambridge: Cambridge University Press.

Andrews, Frances. 2006. *The Other Friars: The Carmelite, Augustinian, Sack and Pied Friars in the Middle Ages*. Woodbridge: The Boydell Press.

Barabási, Albert Láazló. 2014. *Linked: How Everything Is Connected to Everything Else and What It Means for Business, Science, and Everything Else*. New York: Basic Books.

Benson, Robert L., Giles Constable, Carol Dana Lanham, and Charles Homer Haskins, eds. 1982. *Renaissance and Renewal in the Twelfth Century*. Cambridge: Harvard University Press.

Bessenecker, Scott. 2006. *The New Friars: The Emerging Movement Serving the World's Poor*. Downers Grove: InterVarsity Press.

Bessenecker, Scott, ed. 2010. *Living Mission: The Vision and Voices of New Friars*. Downer's Grove: InterVarsity Press.

Biot, François. 1963. *The Rise of Protestant Monasticism*. Baltimore: Helicon.

Bloesch, Donald G. 1964. *Centers of Christian Renewal*. Philadelphia: United Church Press.

Bloesch, Donald G. 1974. *Wellsprings of Renewal: Promise in Christian Communal Life*. Grand Rapids: William B. Eerdmans Publishing Company.

Böhringer, Letha, Jennifer Kolpacoff Deane, and Hildo van Engen, eds. 2014. *Labels and Libels: Naming Beguines in Northern Medieval Europe*. Turnhout Belgium: Brepols Publishers.

Borgmann, Albert. 1992. *Crossing the Postmodern Divide*. Chicago: University of Chicago Press.

Brasher, Sally Mayall. 2003. *Women of the Humiliati: A Lay Religious Order in Medieval Civic Life.* Studies in Medieval History and Culture. New York: Routledge.

Brasher, Sally. 2017. Toward a Revised View of Medieval Women and the Vita Apostolica: The Humiliati and the Beguines Compared. *Magistra* 11: 1–14.

Burr, David. 2001. *The Spiritual Franciscans: From Protet to Persecution in the Century after Saint Francis.* University Park: The Pennsylvania University Press.

Bynum, Caroline Walker. 1987. Religious Women in the Later Middle Ages. In *Christian Spirituality: High Middle Ages and Reformation.* World Spirituality: An Encyclopedic History of the Religious Quest. New York: Crossroad, pp. 121–39.

Campbell, Heidi, and Stephen Garner. 2016. *Networked Theology: Negotiating Faith in a Digital Culture.* Grand Rapids: BakerAcademic.

Capps, Walter. 1983. *The Monastic Impulse.* New York: Crossroad.

Castells, Manuel. 2009. *The Power of Identity.* The Information Age: Economy, Society, and Culture 2. West Sussex: Wiley-Blackwell.

Castells, Manuel. 2010. *The End of Millennium.* The Information Age: Economy, Society, and Culture 3. West Sussex: Wiley-Blackwell.

Castells, Manuel. 2011. The Rise of the Network Society. In *The Information Age: Economy, Society, and Culture 1,* 2nd ed. West Sussex: Wiley-Blackwell.

Castells, Manuel. 2015. *Networks of Outrage and Hope: Social Movements in the Internet Age,* 2nd ed. Cambridge: Polity Press.

Clark, Elizabeth A. 1986. *Ascetic Piety and Women's Faith: Essays on Late Ancient Christianity.* Studies in Women and Religion 20. Lewiston: The Edwin Mellen Press.

Graham Cray, Ian Mobsby, and Aaron Kennedy. 2010. *Ancient Faith, Future Mission: New Monasticism as Fresh Expressions of Church.* Norwich: Canterbury Press.

Cray, Graham. 2010. Why is New Monasticism Important to Fresh Expressions? In *Ancient Faith, Future Mission: New Monasticism as Fresh Expressions of Church.* Edited by Graham Cray, Ian Mobsby and Aaron Kennedy. Norwich: Canterbury Press, pp. 1–11.

Davis, Kenneth Roland. 1974. *Anabaptism and Asceticism: A Study in Intellectual Origins.* Studies in Anabaptist and Mennonite History 16. Scottdale: Herald Press.

Davison, Ellen Scott. 1927. *Forerunners of Saint Francis and Other Studies.* Boston: Houghton Mifflin Company.

Dean, Jennifer. 2008. "Beguines" Reconsidered: Historiographical Problems and New Directions. In Monastic Matrix, Commentaria 3461. Available online: https://monasticmatrix.osu.edu/commentaria/beguines-reconsidered-historiographical-problems-and-new-directions (accessed on 16 August 2019).

de Vitry, Jacques. 1998. The Life of Marie d'Oignies. In *Two Lives of Marie D'Oignies.* Toronto: Peregrina Publishing.

de Vries, Jennifer E. 2016. The Proper Beguine's Interaction with the Outside World: Some Beguine Rules from the Late Medieval Low Contries. In *Shaping Stability: The Normation and Formation of Religious Life in the Late Middle Ages.* Edited by Krijn Pansters and Abraham Plunkett-Latimer. Disciplina Monastica 11 Turnhout. Belgium: Brepols Publishers, pp. 137–50.

Dreher, Rod. 2018. *The Benedict Option: A Strategy for Christians in a Post-Christian Nation.* New York: Sentinel.

Dunn, Marilyn Dunn. 2003. The Emergence of Monasticism: From the Desert Fathers to the Early Middle Ages. Malden: Blackwell Publishing.

Ekelund, Robert B., Jr., Robert F. Hébert, and Robert D. Tollison. 2015. The Political Economy of the Medieval Church. In *The Oxford Handbook of the Economics of Religion.* Oxford: Oxford University Press.

Elm, Susanna. 1994. *'Virgins of God': The Making of Asceticism in Late Antiquity.* Oxford Classical Monographs. Oxford: Clarendon Press.

Elm, Kaspar. 2016. Vita Regularis sine Regula. The Meaning, Legal Status and Self-Understanding of Late-Medieval and Early-Modern Semi-Religious Life. In *Religious Life Between Jerusalem, the Desert, and the World: Selected Essays by Kaspar Elm.* Translated by James D. Mixon. Studies in the History of Christian Traditions 180. Leiden: Brill, pp. 277–316.

Erb, Peter. 1983. *Pietists: Selected Writings.* Classics of Western Spirituality. New York: Paulist Press.

Flanagan, Bernadette. 2014. *Embracing Solitude: Women and New Monasticism.* Eugene: Cascade Books.

Flood, David. 2001. Franciscans at Work. *Franciscan Studies* 59: 21–62. [CrossRef]

Flood, David. 2010. *The Daily Labor of the Early Franciscans.* St. Bonaventure: The Franciscan Institute.

Follett, Westley. 2006. *Celi De in Ireland: Monastic Writing and Identity in the Early Middle Ages*. Woodbridge: Boydell Press.

Foot, Sarah. 2006. *Monastic Life in Anglo-Saxon England c. 600–900*. Cambridge: Cambridge University Press.

Fox, Yaniv. 2014. *Power and Religion in Merovingian Gaul: Columbanian Monasticism and the Frankish Elites*. Cambridge: Cambridge University Press.

Pope, Francis. 2014. Apostolic Letter of His Holiness Pope Francis to All Consecrated People on the Occasion of the Year of Consecrated Life. Available online: http://w2.vatican.va/content/francesco/en/apost_letters/documents/papa-francesco_lettera-ap_20141121_lettera-consacrati.html (accessed on 5 August 2019).

Goehring, James E. 1999. *Ascetics, Society, and the Desert: Studies in Early Egyptian Monasticism*. Studies in Antiquity and Christianity. Harrisburg: Trinity Press Intrenational.

Grieg, Pete. 2004. *The Vision and the Vow: Rediscovering Life and Grace*. Orlando: Relevant Books.

Grundmann, Herbert. 1995. *Religious Movements in the Middle Ages*. Translated by Steven Rowan. Notre Dame: University of Notre Dame Press. First published 1935 and expanded in 1955/1961.

Harmless, William. 2004. *Desert Christians: An Introduction to the Literature of Early Monasticism*. Oxford: Oxford University Press.

Hart, Mother Columba. 1980. Introduction. In *Hadewijch: The Complete Works*. Classics of Western Spirituality. New York: Paulist Press.

Hatlie, Peter. 2007. *The Monks and Monasteries of Constantinople, ca. 350–850*. Cambridge: Cambridge University Press.

Heath, Elaine A. 2017. *The Mystic Way of Evangelism: A Contemplative Vision for Christian Outreach*, 2nd ed. Grand Rapids: Baker Academic.

Heath, Elaine A., and Scott T. Kisker. 2010. *Longing for Spring: A New vision for Wesleyan Community*. New Monastic Library 5. Eugene: Cascade Books.

Heath, Elaine A., and Larry Duggins. 2014. *Missional. Monastic. Mainline: A Guide to Starting Missional Micro-Communities in Historically Mainline Traditions*. Eugene: Cascade Books.

Hinnebusch, William A. 1966. *The History of the Dominican Order: Origins and Growth to 1500*. Staten Island: Alba House, vol. 1.

Howard, Evan B. 2008. What Do We Call It? Monasticism and the Vocabulary of Religious Life. Available online: https://spiritualityshoppe.org/what-do-we-call-it/ (accessed on 16 August 2019).

Howard, Evan B. 2013. What is Monasticism? A Few Reflections. Available online: https://spiritualityshoppe.org/what-is-monasticism-a-few-reflections/ (accessed on 16 August 2019).

Howard, Evan B. 2018. *A Guide to Crhistian Spiritual Formation: How Scripture, Spirit, Community, and Mission Shape Our Souls*. Grand Rapids: BakerAcademic.

Jackson, Dave, and Neta Jackson. 2009. *Living Together in a World Falling Apart: The Classic "Handbook on Christian Community" with Updated Reflections*. Evanston: Castle Rock Creative, Inc. First published 1974.

Jackson, Dave. 1978. *Coming Together: All Those Communities and What They're Up To*. Minneapolis: Bethany Fellowship.

Janzen, David. 1996. *Fire, Salt, and Peace: Intentional Christian Communities Alive in North America*. Evanston: Shalom Mission Communities.

Janzen, David. 2013. *The Intentional Christian Community Handbook for Idealists, Hypocrites, and Wannabe Disciples of Jesus*. Brewster: Paraclete Press.

Judge, Edwin A. 1977. The Earliest Use of Monachos for 'Monk' (*p. Coll. Youtie 77*). *Jarbuch für Antike und Christentum* 20: 72–89.

King, Margot H., and Hugh Feiss. 1993. *The Two Lives of Marie d'Oignies*. Toronto: Peregrina Publishing.

Knox, Lezlie. 2000. Audacious Nuns: Institutionalizing the Franciscan Order of Saint Clare. *Church History* 69: 41–62. [CrossRef]

Langton, Edward. 1956. *History of the Moravian Church: The Story of the First International Protestant Church*. London: George Allen and Unwin, Ltd.

Leclercq, Jean. 1982. *The Love of Learning and the Desire for God: A Study in Monastic Culture*. Translated by Catherine Misrahi. Reprint. New York: Fordham University Press. First published 1961.

Lester, Anne E. 2011. *Creating Cistercian Nuns: The Women's Religious Movement and Its Reform in Thirteenth-Century Champagne*. Ithaca: Cornell University Press.

Lewis, Arthur James. 1962. *Zinzendorf: The Ecumenical Pioneer: A Study in the Moravian Contribution to Christian Mission and Unity*. London: SCM Press.

Leyser, Henrietta. 1984. *Hemits and the New Monasticism: A Study of Religious Communities in Western Europe 1000–1150*. New York: Palgrave Macmillan.

Little, Lester K. 1978. *Religious Poverty and the Profit Economy in Medieval Europe*. Ithaca: Cornell University Press.

Luther, Martin. 1961. Appeal to the Ruling Class of German Nationality as to the Amelioration of the State of Christendom. In *Martin Luther: Selections from His Writings*. Edited by John Dillenberger. New York: Anchor Books.

MacIntyre, Alasdair. 1981. *After Virtue: A Study in Moral Theory*. Notre Dame: University of Notre Dame Press.

Magnani, Eliana. 2018. La vie consacrée des femmes et l'ascétisme domestique. Normes, liturgies, pratiques (fin ive-début xiie siècle). *Revue Mabillon: Revue Internationale d' Histoire et de Littèrature Religieuses* 29: 5–25. [CrossRef]

Maya, Teresa. 2018. Comunión "En Salida": An Apostolic Call for our time in Religious Life. LCWR Presidential Address August 2018. Available online: https://lcwr.org/sites/default/files/.../presidential_address_-_teresa_maya_ccvi.pdf (accessed on 5 August 2019).

McDonnell, Ernest W. 1969. *The Beguines and Beghards in Medieval Culture with Special Emphasis on the Belgian Scene*. New York: Octago Books.

McGinn, Bernard. 1998. *The Flowering of Mysticism: Men and Women in the New Mysticism, Vol. 3 of The Presence of God: A History of Western Christian Mysticism.*. New York: The Crossroad Publishing Company.

Meissner, William W. 1992. *Ignatius of Loyola: The Psychology of a Saint*. New Haven: Yale University Press.

Melville, Gert. 2016. *The World of Medieval Monasticism: Its History and Forms of Life*. Translated by James D. Mixson. Cistercian Studies Series 263; Collegeville: Liturgical Press. First published 2012.

Miles, Margaret. 2000. *Fullness of Life: Historical Foundations for a New Asceticism*. Eugene: Wipf and Stock.

Miller, Tanya Stabler. 2007. What's in a Name? Clerical Representations of Parisian Beguines (1200–1328). *Journal of Medieval History* 33: 60–86. [CrossRef]

Miller, Tanya Stabler. 2014a. *The Beguines of Medieval Paris*. Philadelphia: University of Pennsylvania Press, Kindle.

Miller, Tanya Stabler. 2014b. Labelling Lay Religiosity in Thirteenth-Century Paris. In *Labels and Libels: Naming Beguines in Northern Medieval Europe*. Edited by Letha Böhringer, Jennifer Kolpacoff Deane and Hildo van Engen. Turnhout, Belgium: Brepols Publishers, pp. 135–50.

Moorman, John R. H. 1988. *A History of the Franciscan Order: From Its Origins to the Year 1517*. Chicago: Franciscan Herald Press.

More, Alison. 2018. *Fictive Orders and Feminine Religious Identities, 1200–1600*. Oxford: Oxford University Press, Published to Oxford Scholarship Online: April 2018.

Morris, Rosemary. 1995. *Monks and Laymen in Byzantium 843–1148*. Cambridge: Cambridge University Press.

Moss, Doley C. 1957. *Of Cell and Cloister: Catholic Religious Orders through the Ages*. Milwaukee: The Bruce Publishing Company.

Mulder-Bakker, Anneke, ed. 2006. Mary of Oignies: Mother of Salvation. In *Medieval Women: Texts and Contexts*. Turnhout: Brepols.

Murray, Robert. 1975. The Features of the Earliest Christian Asceticism. In *Christian Spirituality: Essays in Honour of Gordon Rupp*. Edited by Peter Brooks. London: SCM Press, pp. 63–78.

Neel, Carol. 1989. The Origins of the Beguines. *Working Together in the Middle Ages: Perspectives on Women's Communities Signs* 14: 321–41. [CrossRef]

Okholm, Dennis. 2007. *Monk Habits for Everyday People: Benedictine Spirituality for Protestants*. Grand Rapids: Brazos Press.

O'Murchu, Diarmuid. 2016. *Religious Life in the 21st Century: The Prospect of Refounding*. Maryknoll: Orbis Books.

Palladius. 1964. *The Lausiac History*. Translated by Robert T. Meyer. Ancient Christian Writers 34. New York: Paulist Press.

Peters, Greg. 2014. *Reforming the Monastery: Protestant Theologies of Religious Life*. New Monastic Library: Resources for Radical Discipleship 12. Eugene: Cascade Books.

Peters, Greg. 2018. *The Monkhood of All Believers: The Monastic Foundation of Christian Spirituality*. Grand Rapids: Baker Academic.

Raber, Jean Hughes. 2009. Simple Lives: A New Beginning for the Beguines? Commonweal 05/22. Available online: https://www.commonwealmagazine.org/simple-lives (accessed on 16 August 2019).

House, Rutba, ed. 2005. *School(s) for Conversion: 12 Marks of a New Monasticism.* Eugene: Cascade Press.

Ryan, Frances, and John E. Rybolt, eds. 1995. *Vincent de Paul and Louise de Marillac: Rules, Conferences, and Writings.* Classics of Western Spirituality. New York: Paulist Press.

Sandor, Monica. 1988. Jacques de Vitry and The Spirituality of the Mulieres Sanctae. *Vox Benedictina: A Journal of Translations from Monastic Sources* 5: 277–87.

Schneiders, Sandra M. 2000. *Finding the Treasure: Locating Catholic Religious Life in a New Ecclesial and Cultural Context.* Religious Life in a New Millennium 1. New York: Paulist Press.

Schneiders, Sandra M. 2001. *Selling All: Commitment, Consecrated Celibacy, and Community in Catholic Religious Life.* Religious Life in a New Millennium 2. New York: Paulist Press.

Schneiders, Sandra M. 2013. *Buying the Field: Catholic Religious Life in Mission to the World.* Religious Life in a New Millennium 3. New York: Paulist Press.

Schreiter, C. Robert. 2015. Reimagining Consecrated Life in a Changing World. In New Theology Review 28/1. Available online: newtheologyreview.com/index.php/ntr/article/view/1137/1962 (accessed on 16 August 2019).

Silvas, Anna M. 2005. *The Ascetikon of Basil the Great.* Oxford: Oxford University Press.

Simons, Walter. 2001. *Cities of Ladies: Beguine Communities in the Medieval Low Countries 1200–1565.* Philadelphia: University of Pennsylvania Press.

Simons, Walter. 2014. On the margins of religious life: hermits and recluses, penitents and tertiaries, beguines and beghards. In *The Cambridge History of Christianity.* Edited by Miri Rubin and Walter Simons. Cambridge: Cambridge University Press, pp. 309–23.

Stock, Jon, Tim Otto, and Jonathan Wilson-Hartgrove. 2007. *Inhabiting the Church: Biblical Wisdom for a New Monasticism.* Eugene: Casade Books.

Sullivan, Louise. 1995. Louise de Marillac: A Spiritual Portrait. In *Vincent de Paul and Louise de Marillac: Rules, Conferences, and Writings.* Edited by Frances Ryan and John E. Rybolt. Classics of Western Spirituality. New York: Paulist Press, pp. 39–64.

Swan, Laura. 2001. *The Forgotten Desert Mothers: Sayings, Lives, and Stories of Early Christian Women.* New York: Paulist Press.

Swan, Laura. 2014. *The Wisdom of the Beguines: The Forgotten Story of a Medieval Women's Movement.* Katonah: BlueBridge Books.

Taft, Robert. 1993. *The Liturgy of the Hours in East and West: The Origins of the Divine Office and Its Meaning for Today,* 2nd revised ed. Collegeville: The Liturgical Press.

Theodoret of Cyrrhus. 1985. *A History of the Monks of Syria.* Translated by R. M. Price. Kalamazoo: Cistercian Publications.

Thompson, Augustine. 2005. *Cities of God: The Religion of the Italian Communes 1125–1325.* University Park: The Pennsylvania State University Press.

Thompson, Augustine. 2012. *Francis of Assisi: A New Biography.* Ithaca: Cornell University Press.

Van de Weyer, Robert. 1988. *The Little Gidding Way: Christian Community for Ordinary People.* London: Darton, Longman, and Todd.

John H. Van Engen, trans. 1988, *Devotio Moderna: Basic Writings.* Classics of Western Spirituality. New York: Paulist Press.

Van Engen, John H. 2008. *Sisters and Brothers of the Common Life: The Devotio Moderna and the World of the Later Middle Ages.* Philadelphia: University of Pennsylvania Press.

Vauchez, André. 1993. *The Laity in the Middle Ages: Religious Beliefs and Devotional Practices.* Translated by Margery J. Schneider. Notre Dame: University of Notre Dame Press. First published 1987.

Vauchez, André. 2012. *Francis of Assisi: The Life and Afterlife of a Medieval Saint.* Translated by Michael F. Cusato. New Haven: Yale University Press.

Vivian, Tim. 2002. The Coptic Orthodox Church. In *Coptic Monasteries: Egypt's Monastic Art and Architecture.* Edited by Gawdat Gabra. Cairo: The American University in Cairo Press, pp. 10–33.

Walpot, Peter. 1994. True Yieldedness and the Christian Community of Goods. In *Early Anabaptist Spirituality.* Classics of Western Spirituality. Edited by Daniel Liechty. New York: Paulist Press, pp. 138–99. First published 1577.

Wilson, Jonathan R. 2010. *Living Faithfully in a Fragmented World: From After Virtue to New Monasticism,* 2nd ed. Eugene: Cascade Books. First published 1997.

Winter, Ralph D. 1994. William Carey's Major Novelty. *Missiology: An International Review* 22: 203–22. [CrossRef]

Wittberg, Patricia. 1994. *The Rise and Decline of Catholic Religious Orders: A Social Movement Perspective*. Albany: The State University of New York Press.

Wright, Benjamin. 2012. Women, Heresy, and Crusade: Toward a Context for Jacques de Vitry's Relationship to the Early Beguines. In *A Mirror for Medieval and Early Modern Studies*. Chicago: The Newberry Library, pp. 149–58.

Wood, Diana. 2002. *Medieval Economic Thought. Cambridge Medieval Textbooks*. Cambridge: Cambridge University Press.

Zinzendorf, Nicolas Ludwig Count von. 1983. Brotherly Union and Agreement at Hernhutt. In *Pietists: Selected Writings*. Classics of Western Spirituality. Translated by Peter Erb. New York: Paulist Press, pp. 325–30. First published 1727.

religions

MDPI

Article

The 'Greening' of Christian Monasticism and the Future of Monastic Landscapes in North America

Jason M. Brown

Department of Humanities, Faculty of Environment, Simon Fraser University, Vancouver, BC V6B 5K3, Canada; jason.minton.brown@gmail.com

Received: 12 June 2019; Accepted: 11 July 2019; Published: 16 July 2019

Abstract: Christian monasticism has an ancient land-based foundation. The desert fathers and later reform movements appealed to the land for sustenance, spiritual metaphor, and as a marker of authentic monastic identity. Contemporary Roman Catholic monastics with this history in mind, have actively engaged environmental discourse in ways that draw from their respective monastic lineages, a process sociologist Stephen Ellingson calls 'bridging'. Though this study is of limited scope, this bridging between monastic lineages and environmental discourse could cautiously be identified with the broader phenomenon of the 'greening' of Christianity. Looking to the future, while the footprint of North American monastic communities is quite small, and their numbers are slowly declining, a variety of conservation-minded management schemes implemented since the 1990s by some communities suggests that the impact will remain for many decades to come.

Keywords: religion and ecology; spiritual ecology; greening of religion; environmental humanities; monasticism; history of monasticism; landscape

1. Introduction

When the monks of Our Lady of Guadalupe Abbey arrived at their new home in Carlton, Oregon, in 1955, they found a landscape quite different from the one their scout had purchased. All that remained of the lush Douglas fir forests were stumps and the previous owner had quite literally cut and run. Over the next several decades the monks slowly replanted the steep hillsides of their 1300-acre sanctuary nestled in the foothills of the Coastal Range. Today, the monastery boasts an 800-acre working forest with dozens of acres of restored Oregon White Oak savanna, one of the most rare and endangered ecosystems in Oregon.

The monks of Guadalupe Abbey's understanding of the land has also undergone transformation since their arrival. In the 1990s, under pressure from environmentally conscious members of their community, they hired a consulting forester who helped the monks envision and transition their forestry operation from a tree farm that maximized timber growth, to an ecosystem management approach that mimicked a natural forest while also providing timber revenue. Guadalupe Abbey is a unique place, but their turn toward more ecological approaches to stewardship and land management has been repeated many times over in the North American monastic landscape.

While there was once a time when monks sought a more complete *fuga mundi*—fleeing from the world—The Second Vatican Council (1962–1965) brought sweeping changes to Roman Catholic clerical and liturgical life. Many monastic communities have, as a result, gradually opened to the wider world, including the insights and convictions of what would become the environmental movement. There has been since the 1970s, but mostly since the 1990s, a slow but significant 'greening' of many religious institutions, who have incorporated the insights of environmental discourse on their own terms (Ellingson 2016). In this essay, I will argue that contemporary Catholic monastic communities in North America have consciously 'bridged', to use Bruce Ellingson's term, contemporary environmental discourse with their own monastic lineages. This trend can be cautiously identified as part of a wider 'greening' of Christianity, which has taken place over the last several decades. This bridging has resulted in more ecologically sustainable management practices and land tenure arrangements. So, while monasticism is generally in decline in North America, the unique monastic landscapes that these communities have lovingly cared for over many decades will persist long into the future.

While this study is not exhaustive, it is based on significant ethnographic research among contemporary monastic communities in the American West and Southwest. This essay also draws from publicly available scholarly and journalistic sources in order to show a wider diversity of perspectives in the North American context. Of course, women's monastic communities are also engaging these themes, but my work looks primarily at men's communities.[1] The ethnographic case study in this essay is drawn from my firsthand ethnographic work and is based on semi-structured walking interviews with over 50 monastics.[2]

2. The Land Based Context for Monasticism

The purpose of the monastic life is to seek God. However, in seeking God, monastic communities have often sought some measure of separation from the busy social world. In fleeing to remote natural settings, monastics sought to be alone with God like Jesus of Nazareth who often prayed in the desert. This is not to say that historical monasticism is inherently environmentally conscious as we might think of it today, but simply to point out that monastic spirituality and institutional identity are deeply land-based.

The first wave of Christian monasticism gained momentum in the 4th century CE. Behind the more well-known Saint Anthony the Great (251–356 CE), an early Desert Father, were thousands of men and women who flocked to the Syrian and Egyptian deserts to live the life of contemplative silence. The desert was a spiritual ecology that taught the monks how to pray through its vast expanses and its harsh and dangerous conditions. Saint Jerome (347–420), an early Desert Father and translator remarked that 'the desert loves to strip bare', and this is precisely what these early monastics were trying to do spiritually. Biblical scholar Belden Lane writes that, "In desert and mountain wilderness, people discover liminal places suggesting thresholds between where they have been and where they are going" (Lane 1998). The desert was sensed as a space on the margins between this world and the next and represented a kind of spiritual battlefield.

As monasticism was institutionalized by the Roman Catholic Church and spread into Europe, monastic orders and communities continued to be founded in rural or semi-wilderness areas, both out of a desire to hold the world at a distance, and as an homage to their desert fore-parents. Saint Benedict in Italy and later reform movements such as the Cistercians[3] often sought remote rural settings for their monastic communities.

Monastic cloisters often included spaces for vegetable gardens, domesticated animals, orchards, a cemetery, workshops, and accommodations for guests and pilgrims. However, no single cloister could be wholly self-sufficient. As historian Christopher Brooke has documented, the monastery cellarer, charged with keeping the monastery well stocked with supplies, often had to source items such as wheat, beans, milk, butter, cheese, fish, wool, pig skin for parchment, timber, and stone for building from the surrounding countryside. Monasteries also needed access to vineyards for wine, orchards for fruit, flowers for the altar, and beeswax for candles. The monastic community was a highly

---

[1] See (McFarland Taylor 2009). As Sara McFarland Taylor points out, women's monastic communities are deeply engaged in bridging environmental discourse with their own monastic lineages. In fact, she points out that in some cases, they are going a step further by engaging in what Ellingson and McFarland Taylor call 'bricolage', the intentional mixing and combining of two distinct traditions in the creation of a third, or hybrid, tradition.

[2] This essay is a revised version of a chapter in my PhD dissertation, published in 2017 at the University of British Columbia.

[3] A variant of the Cistercians are now called Trappists, from the French community located in Trappé, France, now belonging to the Order of Cistercians of the Strict Observance (OCSO).

disciplined, hierarchical institution—a major social and political actor whose land-base was embedded within the feudal or manorial tenure systems that pervaded Europe during that period (Brooke 2003).[4]

Monastic communities were also imagined as liminal spaces between heaven and earth with the cloister garden at its center harkening back to the Garden of Eden. The cloister took on the tension between body and soul, earth and heaven, and the biblical land-based motifs of the paradise-garden and the desert-wilderness that are the setting of the messianic hopes for the Israelites. Historian of monastic architecture Megan Cassidy-Welch has written of monastic sacred space, noting that, "within the cloister, spaces of theological abstraction have been anchored to the earth" (Cassidy-Welch 2001, p. 69). The cloister garden for example was a kind of axis mundi representing the idealized Garden of Eden in and among the desert wilderness of the world.

There was also a recurring sense in monastic reforms that in order to get back to the purity of the monastic movement, a community should seek out remote outposts that test the limits of comfort and safety. Historian Ellen Arnold's study of a Carolingian-era Benedictine monastery complex called Stavelot-Malmedy shows just how important land was to the livelihoods and spiritual narratives of this monastic community. Stavelot-Malmedy was located in the forested Ardennes region of Belgium and thrived between the 7th and 9th centuries. Saint Remaclus (?–671) founded the monastery in 650 CE with a group of fellow monks. In their written history, Stavelot-Malmedy is set in a rugged wilderness. With land donated by Sigibert III, the monastic charter says, "In our forest called the Ardennes, in an empty space of solitude" the forest was a place "in which a throng of wild animals springs forth" that was "confined by mountains," "impeded by swamp", and whose local population was "not fully established", and "bound up in idolatry" (Arnold 2012, p. 34). As Arnold shows in her study, the Ardennes had in fact been cultivated and occupied for many hundreds of years prior and was not excessively far removed from major transit corridors. The monastic founders' suggestion that the area was wild and dangerous appealed to their monastic heritage of fleeing the world for the desert wilds and thus tended to exaggerate the remoteness, sparseness of the population, and presence of danger. She writes:

> Throughout the centuries, monks of the Ardennes developed the idea of the forest as a wild and dangerous landscape because it tied them to their religious heritage. But they had established their monasteries in a landscape that had long been full of people, and they were active participants in the regions social and agricultural structures. Thus, the monks not only had to define themselves in relation to the wild; they also had to define themselves in relation to local people and the domesticated landscape. To do this, they told stories of how the power of the saints and of God allowed the monks to transform the wilderness into a beautiful and controllable landscape. They then in turn, used this calm and pastoral view of the forest to represent rebirth, tranquility, and the fertility of both land and soul (Arnold 2012, p. 28).

Land was not just an integral part of their livelihoods but bound up with the monastic sense of self, history, and spirituality within a medieval agrarian view of place and landscape.

While medieval monasteries enjoyed a very large land base in Europe, the Protestant Reformation, beginning in the 16th century, and the French Revolution in the 18th century reduced Benedictine and Cistercian landholdings considerably, especially in England and France. These upheavals coincided with the broader dissolution of the feudal land systems throughout much of Europe (Horn 1973; Rippinger OSB 1990; Peters 2015). While monasticism did undergo a modest revival in the 19th century, it would never again reach the extent and influence it had during the feudal/manorial age and prior to the advent of the Mendicant orders of the late 12th and early 13th centuries. Debates about monasticism's environmental impact on feudal landscapes are ongoing (Bartlett 1993; Oram 2008;

---

[4]   While there is no official estimate of the historical extent of monastic landholdings, some have guessed that monastic tenure encompassed at least 50% of some regions throughout Europe (Josep-Maria Mallarach, pers. Comm).

Alberth 2012; Arnold 2012), but what is clear is that land provided a context both for monastic subsistence and spirituality.

As Mallarach and Papayannis (2007), Mallarach et al. (2012), and Mallarach et al. (2014) point out, a number of historical monasteries and hermitages in Europe have become the basis for protected areas. Moreover, many monasteries still in operation have adopted ecologically minded management practices and outlooks (Mallarach et al. 2014). For example, the Camaldoli Hermitage, which founded in 1024 by Romuald (951–1025). When Romuald arrived, he set his monks to planting trees to ensure a steady supply of wood. With a larger monastery at the base of the mountain and a cluster of hermitages up higher, Camaldoli has become an exemplary case of successful pre-modern forestry practices. It even served to inform the modern codification of the Italian Forestry Code during the 19th century (Pungetti et al. 2012). Today, the Hermitage, which is still in use, is the one of the longest continuously occupied monasteries in Europe. After World War II, it became part of the Casentine National Park, which encompasses 36,000 hectares, and is one of the largest national parks in Europe (Pungetti et al. 2012).

3. The Greening of Religion Controversy

In 1967, historian of technology Lynn White, Jr. levelled a controversial critique of Christianity's role in the environmental crisis (White 1967). White was certainly not the first to criticize Christianity or point out its penchant for ecological harm, but the publication of his piece in the journal *Science* gave the piece enough exposure to create a broader conversation among Western academics. White, himself a Presbyterian, claimed that through the biblical injunction to dominate the earth found in Genesis chapter one, Western Christianity had become "the most anthropocentric religion the world has ever seen," and Western technology and science thus had followed suit (White 1967, p. 1205).

Since White's article, there have been a great many attempts to respond to White's thesis, especially among Christians. The fields of religion and ecology, religion and nature, and spiritual ecology have sought to address the diverse ways in which religion contributes to environmental problems and solutions and to encourage a kind of 're-enchantment' of the natural world (Sponsel 2012; Vaughan Lee 2013). During the late 1990s and 2000s, then professors at Harvard, Mary Evelyn Tucker and John Grim organized a series of conferences on world religions and ecology, which included hundreds of scholars and practitioners from the world religions. The proceedings from that series were later published as a series called *Religions of the World and Ecology* and summarized in their recent book *Ecology and Religion* (Grim and Tucker 2014).

Sociologist Stephen Ellingson has shown that despite White and others early criticisms, the religions were late to the environmental movement. This is partly because they often chose to engage in what Ellingson calls "bridging" between religious and environmental values and discourse (Ellingson 2016). This means that religious environmental organizations, churches, or religious orders are engaging their religious traditions in light of environmental problems and finding ways to talk about them in their own idiom. Ellingson notes that while Christianity may have been late to the environmental movement, there are now almost 100 religious environmental organizations in existence today (Ellingson 2016). This is not to say that all self-identified Christians have become models of ecological sustainability, but that the language of environmentalism is finding expression in Christian categories and framings such as stewardship, sacramentalism and prophetic justice.

Before I discuss the contours of monastic environmental bridging, it is important to briefly point out that not all scholars agree that there has even been any significant greening of religion in general and Christianity in particular. While there has certainly been a surge of conversations surrounding the environment in Christian circles, some scholars suggest that we have not yet seen a measurable shift in pro-environmental *behaviors* among religious people and particularly Christians in the United States (Clements et al. 2014; Taylor et al. 2016). Religion and nature scholar Bron Taylor even goes a step further in a recent essay, claiming that Christianity is more likely to be a hindrance to the environmental movement than a partner (Taylor 2019). Luckily, in this essay, I am not seeking to adjudicate once and for all the phenomenon of greening among all self-identified Christians or even all monastic institutions. However, I do feel confident speaking of a general shift among North American Catholic men's monastic communities toward more ecologically minded theology *and* land management practices, which I will now address.

4. Monasticism and Environmental Discourse

Beginning in the 1960s, but especially during the 1990s, monastic communities in North America have actively engaged with environmental discourse that call for minimizing pollution, protecting wilderness, and managing agricultural lands sustainably. Trappist monk and writer Thomas Merton is something of the unofficial nature writer of the contemporary monastic tradition. Merton was a gifted poet and writer, and his writings ushered in a surge of post-WWII monastic vocations. Before his death in 1967, Merton joined the Wilderness Society and saw a strong connection between the monastic desire to seek God within and the setting of monasteries among wild and rural landscapes. When he entered Gethsemani Abbey in 1941, Merton fell in love with the hilly wooded landscape. In 1967, Merton was even permitted to move full time into a small hermitage on the Abbey property, the first of his order to do so. At the heritage, Merton wrote beautiful poetry, weather reports, and spiritual prose that masterfully described his wooded surroundings. He also began to re-imagine the role for monks in the budding environmental movement through his brief correspondences with environmental writer Rachel Carson. He wrote:

> If the monk is a man whose whole life is built around a deeply religious appreciation of his call to wilderness and paradise, and thereby to a special kind of kinship with God's creatures in the new creation . . . then we might suggest that the monk, of all people, should be concerned with staying in the 'wilderness' and helping to keep it a true 'wilderness and paradise.' The monk should be anxious to preserve the wilderness in order to share it with those who need to come out from the cities and remember what it is like to be under trees and to climb mountains.

(Merton 1967, p. 89)

This last phrase is very much reminiscent of 19th century conservationist John Muir, who saw wilderness not as a spiritual battlefield, but a paradise, a sanctuary. What Merton is doing here is carrying forward the biblical and monastic motifs of the wilderness and the garden, the eschatological hope of the monk to return to his true nature before the fall. However, by embracing the logic of the American environmental movement, rather than converting the wilderness into a paradise through agricultural work as his monastic ancestors sought, wilderness is envisioned *as* paradise, a move also made by Henry David Thoreau in his essay *Walden* (Brown 2017).

This bridging work between monastic history and spirituality on the one hand and the environmental movement on the other trickled down into monastic communities throughout North America. Coinciding with Merton's later writings and the Vatican II council, the monastic movement in North America sought to rediscover its spiritual roots. Unsurprisingly, this also meant rediscovering monasticism's relationship to land. Benedictine historian Joel Rippinger OSB writes that the post-Vatican II-era monastic renewal was:

> accompanied by the Benedictine equivalent of the experiments in communal and rustic 'return to nature' that were so much a part of the American counterculture of the time, and the results of this were the closure of many community buildings and a monastic diaspora of some who wanted to live in smaller communities in cabins or rustic retreats (Rippinger OSB 1990, p. 176).

Just as the many monastic movements before them had done, and just as strands of America's back-to-the-land movement were trying out, many monastic communities attempted to return to a simpler way of living, often with an emphasis on being close to the land.

One community that exemplified this movement was Christ in the Desert Abbey located in Abiquiu, New Mexico. The community was founded by three monks from Mount Savior Benedictine Abbey in upstate New York. The monks were inspired by the 1960s move toward greater simplicity, and a more solitary land-based, desert monasticism (Graña 2006). The monastery now boasts a completely self-reliant solar panel array, which is one of the largest in New Mexico, straw bale-insulated green buildings, water conservation infrastructure, and large vegetable gardens. Similar to many monastic communities who have an internet presence, their website embeds the contemporary value of ecological sustainability within the Benedictine vocation of contemplative prayer: "The Benedictine charism, notable for simplicity, humility, stability, and hospitality, is especially well suited to sustainable stewardship of the natural environment."[5]

In the 1980s, Terrance Kardong OSB, a Benedictine monk, published an article entitled "Monks and the Land", which celebrates the Benedictine land-based heritage and laments the rise of industrial farming and its contribution to the decline in monastic land-based industries and general stewardship practices. He also suggested that there are few monasteries left in the US that are fully managing their own land or doing so sustainably. Citing the agrarian writer Wendell Berry, Kardong called for a return to the traditional land-based Benedictine values of stability, work, and stewardship, just as reformers before him have done. He admonished, "A monastery is not nowhere but somewhere. We must take good care of that somewhere. To be a monk is not to practice an ethereal spirituality that treats place as irrelevant" (Kardong 1983, p. 144). Drawing on his monastic roots, Kardong sounds a warning that Benedictine monasticism has strayed too far from its land-based foundations and needs an agrarian revival, which in many ways paved the way for many of the changes that took place in the 1990s.

Since the 1990s, many Trappist monasteries have also engaged with the contemporary environmental movement, both theologically and practically. One celebrated case involves a community of Trappist monks who actively sought out consultation in order to improve their land management practices in line with contemporary environmental discourse: Holy Cross Trappist Abbey, located in Clarke County, Virginia. In 2007, they sought the help of students and faculty at the University of Michigan's Natural Resource Management program to conduct a thorough assessment of the community's practices. The team published a report, which includes a detailed environmental assessment of the 1200-acre property (Buckner et al. 2010).

The study begins in familiar territory, by citing foundational Benedictine values that harmonize with contemporary environmental discourse around stewardship, care, and connection to place. For example, this quotation from the 2005 Cistercian Constitution Section 27A "The brothers are to be concerned about conservation of the environment and to manage natural resources prudently" is seen as ample support for engaging in environmentally friendly management and practices. The introduction cites the Benedictine ethos of 'Work and Prayer', and the Cistercian admonition to be 'lovers of the place' as further moral impetus to be better stewards of the land.

The study presents a detailed assessment of the 'sustainability' of eight domains: land use, energy, water, solid waste, toxics, economies, food, and buildings. Their conclusions suggested that while the monks love their land, the monastery was far from a model of ecological sustainability. They found that monoculture farming practices were degrading local water and soil quality, that cattle grazing was increasing soil erosion, and that invasive plants were threatening local biodiversity. They found a poor native-habitat-to-developed-spaces ratio and an undeveloped trail system. Energy production was inefficient, and CO_2 emissions were higher than local averages. They used more water but generated less waste than the average North American. In addition, the monastery used over 100 harmful chemicals and had asbestos and lead paint in structures and mold growing in several places. The baking

---

[5]   Christ in the Desert Monastery. Available Online: https://christdesert.org/about/sustainable-stewardship/ (accessed on 12 June 2019).

of fruitcakes, one of their livelihood enterprises, generated significant carbon emissions, and their food was sourced through corporate, non-organic distributors. The community had a lot of work to do.

Since the report, the community has set to work on both ensuring that the community remains on the land and that their management practices are in greater harmony with the principles of ecological sustainability. The community was recently featured in *National Geographic* for their efforts, which included establishing an 80-acre green cemetery, where natural burials occur, and ashes can be spread. While they have not returned to farming the land themselves, due to dwindling vocations, one of their tenants has begun farming 200 acres organically, and they have fenced off streams where cattle used to graze to reduce contamination and erosion (Bruno 2017). The community has also created a 'conservation easement' with a local land trust, which ensures the property will remain intact and undeveloped in perpetuity. Conservation easements, an increasingly popular tool in private conservation efforts, are essentially legally binding agreements wherein a third party purchases the rights to develop the property in perpetuity. The third party outlines what is allowable and not allowable on the land based on conservation and restoration priorities and is tasked with monitoring the easements in perpetuity. As we will see, this strategy promises to have a lasting impact on the future of monastic landscapes.

Another noteworthy 'bridging' event occurred in 2008 at the Abbey of Our Lady of Gethsemani, Thomas Merton's monastery. The Abbey held a conference titled 'Monasticism and the Environment' (Mitchell and Skudlarek 2010). This wide-ranging interfaith conference in which Buddhist and Catholic monks participated, argued for a shift toward a "green" monasticism, whether Buddhist or Catholic, through theological and spiritual interpretation of their respective traditions and wiser use of resources and land bases. The talks each addressed some aspect of bridging between monasticism and environmental discourse, pointing to the Benedictine work ethic, the sacramental theology of Catholicism, or the examples of saints, such as Saint Francis of Assisi.

5. An Ethnographic Case Study in Land-Based Monasticism

In April of 2016, I spent approximately 10 days at Our Lady of Guadalupe Trappist Abbey as an ethnographic researcher. The Abbey is a Trappist monastery that was founded in 1955 by monks from Pecos, New Mexico, who had abandoned the site, because it was difficult to farm. The monastery is located is a small valley between two ridges that run north and south in the semi-arid western foothills of the Oregon Coastal Range. It is surrounded by rural properties on all sides, an increasing amount of which are devoted to wine grapes. The property is home to mule deer, bobcats, and many migratory and resident birds, and the large retreatant pond shelters carp and bullfrogs.

Once they arrived, the monks continued growing grain in the bottomlands and raised sheep and cattle on the hillsides until the farm closed in the mid-1960s due to shifts in agricultural policy that made small farming untenable. They eventually sold their livestock and leased their farmland to a local farmer, putting all of their energy into other industries, such as a carpentry shop, which manufactured church pews and other furniture, and a book bindery that sourced clients from local universities. In the 1980s, the Abbey added a fruitcake bakery and, in the 1990s, a wine storage and labeling facility. The approximately 300 acres of leased farmland grew a variety of commodities such as grass seed until 2016, when the monks decided to start a contract with a leasee, who has planted the land with hazelnut—a common commodity crop in Western Oregon.

Starting in 1967 with a Christmas tree operation, the monks began actively managing about 880 acres for timber production, planting mostly Douglas fir, but also experimenting with Ponderosa pine (*Pinus ponderosa*), Knobcone pine (*Pinus attenuata*), hybrid poplar (*Sp. populus*), and Leland cypress (*Cupressus leylandii*). In the 1980s, active harvesting was begun by a small crew of monks. The small monastic forestry crew planted, thinned, pruned, and harvested the trees themselves in small block cuts and replanted them in tightly spaced monocrop tree plantations. Plantings were not concerned with privileging native species, and management was designed to maximize the production of timber resources.

The monks of Guadalupe inherited a classically Trappist agrarian theology, which imagined human beings working cooperation with God to improve the earth through cultivation. They were proud stewards of the land and saw the forest as a kind of 'tree-farm' for the production of products and revenue. As the monks grew older and vocations continued to shrink throughout the 1970s, they began to reach out for help with managing their land. One landmark came in the late 1980s, when a heavy-handed clear cut near a favored picnic area angered several of the monks who were beginning to advocate a more environmental approach that was consistent with their monastic values and the need to generate some revenue from the forest. It was decided to discern a new forest management strategy and to hire a professional forester to manage the forest with the help of a small monastery forestry crew. In 1995, this forester conducted an inventory of the property and developed a management plan that would balance spiritual values and ecological health with the need to generate revenue.

Since 1995, under the monks' direction, the manager has transitioned the property to an ecosystem-based management approach, obtaining Forest Stewardship Council (FSC) certification, a third-party certification that ensures that ecological principles are used in management and harvest. In practice, this means there has been a decrease in patch cut size to no more than two acres and the increased use of commercial thinning as a harvesting technique, in order to diversify the forests' age and structural diversity. Harvest areas leave more standing dead trees and wildlife trees and more downed trees for woody debris and has focused on clearing areas around shaded white oak and madrone trees to increase native tree species diversity and more bird habitat.

In 2010, they also began aggressively managing for invasive species such as False Broom (*Brachypodium sylvaticum*), Scots Broom (*Cytisus scoparius*), and English Hawthorn (*Crataegus laevigata*) and have designated a small 80-acre section of forest as a future old growth forest area set aside from thinning and commercial harvest.

The forest manager was also instrumental in enrolling the property into a conservation easement program funded by the Bonneville Power Administration, a hydroelectric dam company that has been legally obligated to purchase conservation easements for habitat restoration in and around the Columbia River because of the land it flooded by building their dams. After a lengthy process and assessment, the monastery entered into an agreement to keep the property undeveloped and to continue to manage the forest sustainably.

In addition, the easement qualified the monastery for additional funds that were used to restore areas of Oregon White Oak (*Quercus garryana*) savanna on the property. According to the Oregon Conservation Strategy, Oregon White Oak savanna is an endangered ecosystem, with less than 5% of its historical range remaining. In the past, the white oak was left to be overgrown or cleared to make way for more Douglas fir and sold as firewood.

The climate of the area before European settlement was adapted to White Oak, and Kalapuyan Peoples used fire to clear the area of trees to maintain open hunting grounds. Without fire, the Douglas fir trees outgrow the White oaks, eventually shading them out completely. By harvesting all the trees except the White oaks, a stand replacing fire is mimicked, and the oaks return to health and vigor, reproducing naturally.

From its early agrarian roots through its industrial tree farm planting to its contemporary context as an ecological working forest, Our Lady of Guadalupe has undergone significant changes in its approach to land and forest management. For example, as we walked by a particularly straight row of Douglas fir trees, a Brother related to me a memory of the former forest manager monk:

> Father Romaine, when he was with us, he was one of the main planters and he walked by here once and said, 'this is what some people contemptuously call a tree farm', at which he took great umbrage at because *he* thought it was a forest. But if you look at it compared to the other parts of the forest it *is* kind of a tree farm.

The monk I was speaking with, who had been raised with a strong environmental consciousness, felt that there was, in fact, a difference between a naturally generated forest and an intensive geometric, monoculture plantation. For Father Romaine, however, steeped in the agrarian approach to forestry, where trees were essentially crops, the distinction was belittling of the work he had done to reestablish the forest from the degraded state it was in when they arrived in the 1950s.

The monastery now sees itself as a kind of sanctuary to monks and visitors alike. This is because one condition of the conservation easement allows public access for quiet recreational hiking. In fact, the monastery is now one of the largest intact forest areas in Yamhill County, Oregon, which is primarily agricultural and has very few protected areas. This fact was seen as part of the monastery's ministry to the wider world. As another monk related:

> To me the only purpose of a monastery is to be a sanctuary. And certainly there's been times
> in history where there's been even more need, but for us today I think there's an intense need
> for sanctuary and that's what we have to offer.

Embedded in Western Oregon, which embodies a strong tension between environmentalists and loggers, the monastery has been influenced by elements of both. While it is rooted in the Trappist agrarian sensibility, the community has since enthusiastically adopted a program of ecological restoration, invasive species removal, and forest certification. The paradigm of forest management is "ecological forestry", with an emphasis on restoring native species and endangered ecosystems and increasing the forest's structural and age diversity—a major shift from its former days as a production-oriented tree farm. And while Trappists are known for their hard work, they now primarily see the forest as a sanctuary rather than a crop.

6. The Future of Monastic Landscapes

According to the *Center for Applied Research in the Apostolate*, in 1970, there were approximately 41,886 male members of Catholic religious communities. By 2015, that number had dropped to 17,791—that is a loss of over 500 per year (Palacios et al. 2015). It is increasingly common that the average age at a men's monastery will be in the 70s or even 80s.

However, while vocations to monastic communities are, generally speaking, declining, interest in monastic and contemplative spirituality is being explored, rediscovered, and repurposed by an ever growing and wider variety of spiritual, social, political, and environmental movements. In the spiritual realm especially, retreats and monastic spirituality are increasingly common at monasteries in North America. Thus, between the declining numbers of monks making lifelong vows to their communities and the increasing interest in their landscapes as spiritual refuges, it is not certain what the future holds for land-based monasticism in North America.

As North American monasteries have declined and the economy has shifted away from agriculture, many monasteries have had to make adjustments to land tenure arrangements: selling off pieces of land, leasing farmland to neighboring operations or other schemes.[6] Saint Procopius's Abbey was a Benedictine monastic community located in rural Illinois until it became economically unviable in the 1960s. The monks originally managed some 365 acres, housing over 30 monks. The property included the farm—which raised cattle, chickens, turkeys, hogs, beehives, a peach orchard, and a large garden—a boarding school, a small college, and an orphanage (Fletcher 2015).

Theologian Christine Fletcher suggests that while the monks felt a strong agrarian attachment to their land and their vocation as farmers, it was finally agreed that they had reached a threshold. The monastery decided rather than sell the land outright, they would collaborate with a developer to create a "sustainable community" called 'Green Trails', which would devote 40% of total land (135 acres) apart from the monastery proper, to recreation, walking trails, lakes, and park areas. The author sees this compromise as an example of the uniquely Benedictine values being applied to a difficult

---

[6]   Saint Martin's Abbey and Mount Angel Abbey are both Benedictine monasteries who maintained self-sustaining farms until the early 1960s. They have since shifted focus to other apostolates. See (Yocom 1985; Scott 1996).

land-based problem and a solution that uniquely blended the monks' attachment to the land with the pragmatic needs of a changing monastic community and a growing environmental consciousness. Fletcher writes, "The difference Benedictine stewardship makes is clearly visible in Green Trails in the large amount of common areas for people to gather, and in the mix of housing: large and small single-family units, low-rise condominiums, and high-rise apartment buildings" (Fletcher 2015, p. 190). Fletcher argues that this project was "ecologically sustainable" but within the Benedictine frame of human use and occupancy of the land: "Green Trails is an example of Benedictine stewardship of the environment in a situation when the agricultural life envisioned by Benedict could no longer be sustained" (Fletcher 2015, p. 191). In this way the monastery continues its apostolate and its formation of monks and has written its values into the landscape that now surrounds the monastery and its college; a legacy that will continue even if the monastery eventually closes.

Inevitably, some monasteries have been forced to close. However, arrangements with the buyer of the property and the Catholic diocese have ensured that the monks' footprint will survive long after they are gone. The Trappist Abbey of Our Lady of the Holy Trinity in Huntsville, Utah, was founded in 1947. The monks made a living by growing grain, raising cattle, keeping bees, and baking bread. The land, perched in a mountain valley surrounded by the Wasatch Mountains, has a beautiful rural character, boasts hundreds of trees planted by the monks, and harbors a spring that is valuable to the Huntsville water supply. In 2016, the land was officially sold to a private resident of Huntsville, who is working with a local land trust to ensure that the property is preserved through a conservation easement that will restrict development of the site in perpetuity and ensure the sustainable management of the property by future leases. A small footprint near the Abbey church will be gifted to the Roman Catholic Diocese for the construction of a parish church. The process has been facilitated by a team of Utah State University regional planning students to ensure that the land will continue to reflect the monks' contribution to the land. This case, though unfortunate, shows how integral land is to the Benedictine/Trappist lineage and how beloved the monks were in the community, which is largely populated by Mormons (LDS) (Utah State University 2015; Shaw 2017).

The conservation easement is an increasingly popular private conservation tool outside of traditionally designated protected areas. Active monastic communities, such as those discussed in this essay, have used them to gain revenue while improving their land management regimes, and even to restore habitats. Yet, as we have seen, even monasteries who did not implement conservation easements during their tenure as active monasteries have garnered support for their use once they have closed, as is the case in Utah.

7. Conclusions

In this essay, I have shown that Catholic monasticism is deeply intertwined with the land. During the last 50 years or so, monasticism in North America has creatively engaged with environmental discourse in their attempts to improve land and resource management. I have argued that monastics actively bridge their own lineages with environmental discourse. This has resulted in many changes in monastic land management and an increasing awareness of environmental values. These values have, in some cases, been institutionalized through conservation easements, which permanently protect the land, even if the monastery closes in the future, which as we have seen is a very real possibility for some dwindling communities. Thus while the monastic landscape may never reach the extent of influence it once wielded in the middle ages, it is clear that land-based monastic communities will continue their influence on the land and the communities in which they have been founded for many centuries to come.

Funding: This research was funded as part of my dissertation Research at the University of British Columbia, Vancouver. I received a four year International Student Fellowship from the University of British Columbia. The Ethics review of this project was conducted through the UBC Behavioral Research Ethics Board, under the project title "Dwelling in the Wilderness," Certificate Number H14-02005.

Conflicts of Interest: The author declares no conflicts of interest.

References

Alberth, John. 2012. *An Environmental History of the Middle Ages*. New York: Routledge.

Arnold, Ellen F. 2012. *Negotiating the Landscape: Environment and Monastic Identity in the Medieval Ardennes*. Philadelphia: University of Pennsylvania Press.

Bartlett, Robert. 1993. *The Making of Europe: Conquest, Colonization and Cultural Change*. Princeton: Princeton University Press.

Brooke, Christopher. 2003. *The Age of the Cloister: The Story of Monastic Life in the Middle Ages*. Santa Monica: Hidden Spring Press.

Brown, Jason. 2017. Merton, Wildness, and the Sacramental Power of Place. *Merton Annual* 29: 80–89.

Bruno, Debra. 2017. These Monks Saved Their Abbey by Protecting the Earth. *National Geographic*. Available online: http://news.nationalgeographic.com/2017/04/monks-sustainable-holy-cross-abbey/ (accessed on 23 May 2017).

Buckner, Kathryn, Craig Cammarata, Charlotte Coultrap-Bagg, Alexander Linkow, Jessica Neafsey, and Christopher Stratman. 2010. *Holy Cross Abbey: Reinhabiting Place*. Ann Arbor: School of Natural Resources and Environment, University of Michigan.

Cassidy-Welch, Megan. 2001. *Monastic Spaces and their Meanings: Thirteenth-Century English Cistercian Monasteries*. Turnhout: Brepols.

Clements, John M., Chenyang Xiao, and Aaron M. McCright. 2014. An Examination of the "Greening of Christianity" Thesis among Americans, 1993–2010. *Journal for the Scientific Study of Religion* 53: 373–91. [CrossRef]

Ellingson, Stephen. 2016. *To Care for Creation: The emergence of the Religious Environmental Movement*. Chicago: University of Chicago Press.

Fletcher, Christine. 2015. The Border between Wilderness and Garden: Cultivating a Benedictine Spirituality of the Land. In *An Unexpected Wilderness: Christianity and the Natural World*. Edited by Collen Mary Carpenter. Maryknoll: Orbis Books, pp. 182–92.

Graña, Mari. 2006. *Brothers of the Desert: The Story of the Monastery of Christ in the Desert*. Santa Fe: Sunstone Press.

Grim, John, and Mary Evelyn Tucker. 2014. *Ecology and Religion*. New York: Island Press.

Horn, Walter. 1973. On the Origins of the Medieval Cloister. *Gesta* 12: 13–52. [CrossRef]

Kardong, Terrance. 1983. Monks and the Land. *Cistercian Studies* 18: 135–48.

Lane, Belden C. 1998. *The Solace of Fierce Landscapes: Exploring Desert and Mountain Spirituality*. Oxford: Oxford University Press.

Mallarach, Josep-Maria, and Thymio Papayannis, eds. 2007. Protected Areas and Spirituality. Paper presented at the First Workshop of the Delos Initiative, Montserrat, Spain, November 23–26; 2007, Gland: IUCN, Montserrat: Publicacions de l'Abadia de Montserrat.

Mallarach, Josep-Maria, Thymio Papayannis, and Rauno Väisänen, eds. 2012. *The Diversity of Sacred Lands in Europe: Proceedings of the Third Workshop of the Delos Initiative—Inari/Aanaar 2010*. Gland: IUCN, Vantaa: Metsähallitus Natural Heritage Services.

Mallarach, Josep-Maria, Josep Corcó, and Thymio Papayannis. 2014. Christian Monastic Communities Living in Harmony with the Environment: An Overview of Positive Trends and Best Practices. *Studia Monastica* 56: 353–91.

McFarland Taylor, Sara. 2009. *Green Sisters: A Spiritual Ecology*. Cambridge: Harvard University Press.

Merton, Thomas. 1967. Wilderness and Paradise: Two Recent Studies. *Cistercian Studies Quarterly* 2: 83–89.

Mitchell, Donald, and William Skudlarek, eds. 2010. *Green Monasticism: A Buddhist-Catholic Response to an Environmental Calamity*. New York: Lantern Books.

Oram, Richard D. 2008. Holy Frontiersmen? Twelfth-and Early Thirteenth-Century Monastic Colonization and Socio-Economic Change in Poland and Scotland. In *The Northern World: Britain and Poland-Lithuania: Contact and Comparison from the Middle Ages to 1795*. Edited by Richard Unger and Jakub Basista. Leiden: BRILL, pp. 103–22.

Palacios, Santiago Sordo, Thomas P. Gaunt, and Mary L. Gautier. 2015. *Population Trends among Religious Institutes of Men*. Washington: Georgetown University, Center for Applied Research in the Apostolate.

Peters, Greg. 2015. *The Story of Monasticism: Retrieving an Ancient Tradition for Contemporary Spirituality*. Grand Rapids: Baker Publishing.

Pungetti, Gloria, Father Peter Hughes, and Oliver Rackham. 2012. Ecological and Spiritual Values of Landscape: A Reciprocal Heritage and Custody. In *Sacred Species and Sites. Advances in Biocultural Conservation*. Edited by Gloria Pungetti, Gonzalo Oviedo and Della Hooke. New York: Cambridge University Press, pp. 65–82.

Rippinger OSB, Joel. 1990. *The Benedictine Order in the United States: An Interpretive History*. Collegeville: Liturgical Press.

Scott, John C. OSB. 1996. *This Place Called Saint Martin's: 1895–1995: A Centennial History of Saint Martin's College and Abbey Lacey, Washington*. Virginia Beach: The Donning Company Publishers.

Shaw, Mitch. 2017. Huntsville Man on a Mission to Preserve Monastery Open Space. *Standard Examiner*. Available online: http://www.standard.net/Local/2017/04/12/Huntsville-man-on-a-mission-to-preserve-monastery-open-space (accessed on 23 May 2017).

Sponsel, Leslie. 2012. *Spiritual Ecology: A Quiet Revolution*. Santa Barbara: ABC-CLIO.

Taylor, Bron. 2019. Religion and Environmental Behavior (part one): World Religions and the Fate of the Earth. *The Ecological Citizen* 3: 71–79.

Taylor, Bron, Gretel Van Wieren, and Bernard Daley Zaleha. 2016. Lynn White Jr. and the greening-of-religion hypothesis. *Conservation Biology* 30: 1000–9. [CrossRef] [PubMed]

Utah State University. 2015. USU Students Present Options for Huntsville Monastery's Transition. *Utah State Today*. Available online: http://www05.usu.edu/today/?id=54448 (accessed on 23 May 2017).

White, Lynn, Jr. 1967. The Historical Roots of our Ecological Crisis. *Science* 155: 1203–7. [CrossRef] [PubMed]

Vaughan Lee, Llewellyn. 2013. *Spiritual Ecology: The Cry of the Earth*. Point Reyes: The Golden Sufi Center.

Yocom, Neil OSB, ed. 1985. *Mount of Communion: Mount Angel Abbey: 1882–1982*. Mount Angel: Mount Angel Abbey.

MDPI

St. Alban-Anlage 66

4052 Basel

Switzerland

Tel. +41 61 683 77 34

Fax +41 61 302 89 18

www.mdpi.com

Religions Editorial Office

E-mail: religions@mdpi.com

www.mdpi.com/journal/religions

www.ingramcontent.com/pod-product-compliance
Lightning Source LLC
Chambersburg PA
CBHW051316020426
42333CB00028B/3361